Making Development Sustainable

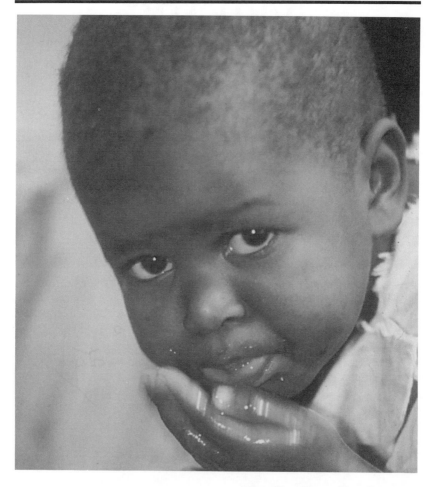

Investing in people, which reduces poverty and population growth, is an urgent moral imperative and is essential for arresting environmental degradation. Providing clean water to the 1 billion people who do not have access to it, while ensuring that the world's use of water resources is sustainable both in terms of quality and quantity, is an enormous challenge.

Making Development Sustainable

THE WORLD BANK GROUP AND THE ENVIRONMENT

FISCAL 1994

THE WORLD BANK
WASHINGTON, D.C.

This report is a study by the World Bank's staff, and the judgments made
herein do not necessarily reflect the views of the Board of Executive
Directors or of the governments they represent.

The text is printed on recycled paper that exceeds the requirements of
the 1988 guidelines of the U.S. Environmental Protection Agency, section
6002 of the Resource Conservation Recovery Act. The paper stock contains at least 50 percent recovered waste paper material as calculated by
fiber content, of which at least 10 percent of the total fiber is postcon-
sumer waste, and 20 to 50 percent of the fiber has been deinked.

Printed on Recycled Paper

ISBN 0-8213-2925-1
ISSN 1014-8132

This report was prepared by the Environment Department of the World
Bank in close collaboration with the regional environment divisions and
country operations departments. The principal authors were Jocelyn
Mason (coordinator), John Dixon, and John Redwood III; the team in-
cluded Jocelyne Albert, Olav Kjorven, Barbara Lausche, Marian Mabel, Jill
Montgomery, Letitia Oliveira, Pushpa Schwartz, Alfredo Sfeir-Younis,
Peter Stephens, Jamison Suter, and Dechen Tsering. The editors were
Nancy Levine, Charlotte Maxey, and Paola Brezny. Andrew Steer and
Mohamed El-Ashry provided guidance.

Contents

Figures

Tables

Foreword

The past few years have seen an important shift in the design of development policies and investment—as the links between the natural environment and economic development have been more deeply understood.

In 1987 the World Bank Group embarked on a major effort to incorporate environmental concerns into all aspects of its work. This report, the fifth major report on progress since that time, focuses primarily on activities in fiscal year 1994. Progress has been substantial in each of the four areas that comprise the Bank's environmental agenda:

- Assisting countries in strengthening their own environmental policies and institutions (chapter 1)
- Assessing and mitigating potential damage from Bank-financed activities (chapter 2)
- Building on the complementarities between sound development and sound environmental policies (chapter 3)
- Addressing global environmental problems (chapter 4).

Good progress has also been made in strengthening the Bank's internal capacity (chapter 5) and the environmental programs of the International Finance Corporation (IFC) and the Multilateral International Guarantee Agency (MIGA) (chapter 6).

While documenting what has been achieving so far, the report also recognizes that there remains a large unfinished agenda and points to what needs to be achieved next.

One key challenge will be to ensure that the rapidly growing portfolio of environmental projects continues to perform well. Over 10 percent of the Bank's new lending is now devoted to projects specifically addressing environmental problems, and over the coming year the portfolio of active environmental projects will rise above $10 billion. This represents a remarkably important contribution to the financing needs identified at the Rio "Earth Summit" in 1992. But helping countries to effectively implement these projects will likely require even more effort than preparing and appraising them. The strong focus on institution building, the need to work across institutional and disciplinary boundaries, and the frequent lack of a powerful constituency for environmental policies and projects will tend to make implementation particularly difficult.

Another key challenge is intellectual. We remain on the steep part of the learning curve, and there are essential lessons that must be distilled from the first generation of environmental policies and projects now under implementation. There are also some tough conceptual and methodological issues in need of further work—including fundamental questions concerning how to measure progress toward environmentally sustainable development.

A third challenge relates to the need to strengthen our focus on the social dimensions of environmental and natural resource management. Resettlement, participation in the preparation of environmental assessments, cultural property, and the social assessment of projects are all areas where more attention will be needed.

A final challenge will be to mainstream global environmental concerns into the Bank Group's regular operations. The Bank will continue to be prominent in this area through its role as a key implementing agency of the Global Environment Facility, but the Bank Group's regular activities potentially have an even bigger role to play.

The Bank Group has a vital role to play in each of these areas. To do so effectively, we must continue to equip ourselves for the task and to deepen our partnerships with others who are also committed to making development more sustainable.

Andrew Steer
Director
Environment Department
The World Bank

Acronyms and Abbreviations

AIDS	Acquired Immunodeficiency Syndrome
ARPP	Annual Review of Portfolio Performance
ASAL	Agriculture Sector Adjustment Loan
BA	Beneficiary Assessment
BP	Bank Procedure
CAS	Country Assistance Strategy
CDB	Caribbean Development Bank
CEM	Country Economic Memoranda
CFC	Chlorofluorocarbon
CGIAR	Consultative Group on International Agricultural Research
DAC	Development Assistance Committee
EA	Environmental Assessment
EBRD	European Bank for Reconstruction and Development
ECA	Europe and Central Asia
EDI	Economic Development Institute
EDS	Environmental Data Sheet
EIA	Environmental Impact Assessment
EIB	European Investment Bank
ESD	Environmentally Sustainable Development
EU	European Union
FAO	Food and Agricultural Organization of the United Nations
FSU	Former Soviet Union
GATT	General Agreement on Tariffs and Trade
GDP	Gross Domestic Product
GEF	Global Environment Facility
GEMS	Global Environment Monitoring System
GET	Global Environment Trust
GIS	Geographic Information System
GP	Good Practice
IAIA	International Association of Impact Assessment
IBRD	International Bank for Reconstruction and Development
ICDP	Integrated Conservation and Development Project

ICZM	Integrated Coastal Zone Management
IDA	International Development Association
IDB	Inter-American Development Bank
IDF	Institutional Development Fund
IFC	International Finance Corporation
IIASA	International Institute for Applied Systems Analysis
IMO	International Maritime Organization
IMS	Investment Market Service
IPPS	Industrial Pollution Projection System
IUCN	World Conservation Union
LPG	Liquefied Petroleum Gas
MARPOL	Marine Pollution
MEDCITIES	Mediterranean Coastal Cities Network
MEIP	Metropolitan Environmental Improvement Programme
METAP	Mediterranean Technical Assistance Program
MFI	Multilateral Financial Institutions
MFMP	Multilateral Fund for the Implementation of the Montreal Protocol
MIGA	Multilateral Investment Guarantee Agency
MP	Montreal Protocol
MSWM	Municipal Solid Waste Management
NEAP	National Environmental Action Plan
NGO	Nongovernmental Organization
NIPA	NGOs for Integrated Protected Areas, Inc.
OD	Operational Directive
ODS	Ozone Depleting Substance
OECD	Organization for Economic Cooperation and Development
OECS	Organization of Eastern Caribbean States
OHS&E	Occupational Health, Safety, and Environment
OP	Operational Policy
PERL	Public Enterprise Reform Loan
PIC	Public Information Center
PID	Project Information Document
PPA	Participatory Poverty Assessment Project Preparation Advance
PPF	Project Preparation Facility
PTI	Program of Targeted Interventions
RAINS/ASIA	Regional Acidification Information and Simulation in Asia
R&D	Research and Development
SAL	Structural Adjustment Loan
SAR	Staff Appraisal Report

SDR	Special Drawing Right
SECAL	Sectoral Adjustment Loan and Credit
T&V	Training and Visit
UIP	Urgent Investment Portfolio
UMP	Urban Management Programme
UNCED	United Nations Conference on Environment and Development
UNCHS	United Nations Center for Human Settlements
UNDP	United Nations Development Programme
UNDRO	United Nations Disaster Relief Organization
UNEP	United Nations Environment Programme
UNESCO	United Nations Educational, Scientific and Cultural Organization
UNIDO	United Nations Industrial Development Organization
UNIFEM	United Nations Development Fund for Women
UNITAR	United Nations Institute for Training and Research
UNSO	United Nations Sudano-Sahelian Office
URBAIR	Urban Air Quality Management Strategy
WCMC	World Conservation Monitoring Centre
WHO	World Health Organization
WID	Women in Development

Overview

The concept of sustainable development implies balancing environmental protection with the generation of increased opportunities for employment and improved livelihoods. In this marine park surrounding the island of Bonaire in the Caribbean, for example, tourism, carefully managed to avoid ecological damage, provides revenue to cover the operations cost of the park and income for the small island community.

World Bank activities to protect and enhance the environment are based on a fourfold agenda:

- Assisting countries in setting priorities, strengthening institutions, and implementing programs for environmentally sustainable development
- Minimizing the potential adverse environmental and social impacts of development projects
- Building on the positive linkages between poverty reduction, economic efficiency, and environmental protection
- Addressing global environmental challenges.

This report is organized around these points. It also describes how the Bank Group has strengthened its internal capacity for dealing with environmental and social issues and summarizes the environment-related activities of the International Finance Corporation (IFC) and the Multilateral Investment Guarantee Agency (MIGA) over the past fiscal year.

From Policy to Practice

Last year's report on the environment signaled a major transition in the Bank's work on the environment, with the emphasis shifting from the design of policies to their implementation in the field. The report highlighted

- The need for governments to strengthen their ministries, agencies, and other institutions to deal more effectively with environmental issues
- Greater integration of environmental concerns into the Bank's economic and sector work
- A growing emphasis on the social aspects of sustainable development.

Over the past year progress has been achieved on all these fronts. Lending for environmental projects, support for national and regional environmental action plans, and assessment and mitigation of environmental and social impacts of project work have assumed more prominence in the Bank's agenda. (See box 1 for highlights of the World Bank Group's environment-related work in fiscal 1994.)[1] Even so, the Bank and its borrowers are continuing to learn important lessons from the implementation of environmental policies, plans, and projects—and to take steps to put those lessons into practice.

Main Themes for the Future

Within the framework of the fourfold agenda, several key themes from this year's review illustrate the emerging direction of the Bank's work in relation to the environment.

Learning from implementation. Environmental initiatives face special implementation challenges, in part because the work cuts across many sectors and in part because of the shortage of good precedents to draw on. Besides requiring strong borrower commitment and adequate institutional capacity, environmental issues are inherently complex, which can, in itself, often cause tensions and problems in member countries. These obstacles are best overcome by the definition of clear priorities, realistic goals, and cost-effective and monitorable actions.

Expanding the scope of environmental assessment. At the project level, environmental assessments are now significantly influencing the design of investment. Beyond this, the Bank is strongly encouraging borrowers to incorporate environmental considerations early in the preparation of sectoral and regional investment programs and major policy reforms. Greater emphasis will also be given to the assessment of social costs and benefits.

Reinforcing the social dimension. Empowering the poor through access to services and credit and a voice in decisionmaking is essential for sound environmental management. Social factors also influence the sustainability of natural resource management and can motivate or discourage needed behavioral change. These concerns will be important for the Bank's future work.

Mainstreaming global concerns. Through many of its regular operations, as well as through the Global Environment Facility (GEF), and in collaboration with individual borrowers and other international agencies, the Bank will seek to integrate global environmental concerns—climate change, ozone depletion, biodiversity conservation, and marine pollution control—into its country assistance strategies and lending programs.

Leveraging private initiative. By means of continual dialogue and growing partnerships with nongovernmental organizations (NGOs) in both industrial and developing countries, and through the activity of the IFC and MIGA, the Bank Group is rapidly expanding its efforts to engage the private sector in environmental management initiatives. This includes activities on the local, national, and even global scale.

Box 1. The World Bank Group and the Environment: Highlights of Fiscal 1994

Finance for environmental improvement continuing to grow

In fiscal 1994 twenty-five new environmental projects were approved, involving total commitments by the World Bank—the International Bank for Reconstruction and Development (IBRD) and the International Development Association (IDA)—of more than $2.4 billion. This represents a 25 percent increase in lending over fiscal 1993, itself a record year, and a fivefold increase over the past five years. More than thirty other new projects had significant environmental components. By July 1994 nearly 120 environmental projects, entailing total commitments on the order of $9 billion, were being implemented. Bank lending for related areas such as population and human resource development also rose, as did support for poverty reduction more generally.

National and regional environmental plans and programs expanding

About twenty-five additional active countries eligible for IDA credits completed national environmental action plans (NEAPs) or equivalent documents during fiscal 1994, and many IBRD countries are also advanced in this process. Many national plans are entering the implementation phase. Regional environmental strategies for Asia and Central and Eastern Europe are presently being implemented. Together with other donors, the Bank continues to support regional environmental action programs for the Mediterranean, Baltic, and Black seas and for the Danube River Basin. New regional programs for the Aral Sea in Central Asia and Lake Victoria in East Africa were developed in fiscal 1994.

First Annual World Bank Conference on Environmentally Sustainable Development (ESD) held

In September 1993 the World Bank hosted the First Annual ESD Conference to assess sustainable development issues, a little more than one year after the United Nations Conference on Environment and Development (the "Earth Summit") in Rio de Janeiro. The Second Annual ESD Conference is planned for September 1994. The theme of this year's conference, which is cosponsored by the Bank and the U.S. National Academy of Sciences, is "The Human Face of the Urban Environment."

Environmental assessment is making a difference

A second review of Bank experience with environmental assessment (EA) recorded significant progress in many areas. Sectoral or "programmatic"

EAs have become more common, and two regional EAs have been completed. Increasingly, EAs are being used to enhance project environmental benefits, as well as to minimize environmental damage.

Bank-wide resettlement review completed and follow-up action initiated

An innovative resettlement review and report on remedial actions, covering nearly 200 projects and relying heavily on evidence gathered in the field, was released simultaneously to the Bank's Board of Executive Directors and the public in April 1994. The review confirmed that, when properly carried out, resettlement and rehabilitation can improve the lives of low-income people, as well as protect them from the economic and social costs of involuntary displacement. Several priority areas for future work were also identified.

Global environmental challenges integrated into Bank work

The Bank is expanding support to key global conventions on biodiversity conservation, climate change, ozone depletion, and desertification. A significant milestone was reached in March 1994 with restructuring of the Global Environment Facility (GEF), which successfully concluded its pilot phase and was replenished with additional donor commitments of $2 billion for the next three years.

Work with the private sector accelerating

Through the International Finance Corporation (IFC) and the Multilateral Investment Guarantee Agency (MIGA), the Bank Group increased financial and technical support to the private sector to strengthen its growing role in environmental management. Bank policy dialogue and operational partnership with nongovernmental organizations (NGOs) also expanded in fiscal 1994.

Disclosure of information broadened, especially for environment

To further enhance the quality and effectiveness of its operations, the Bank adopted a new policy on information disclosure in 1994. Under this policy, many environment-related and other Bank documents are now available through a recently established Public Information Center at the Bank's Headquarters and its various field offices. In addition, to ensure sound management and accountability of all Bank-supported projects, the Bank established an independent Inspection Panel.

Assisting Countries with Environmental Stewardship

Chapter 1 describes the ways in which the Bank helps its borrowers to improve their environmental management. This includes funding for environmental investments, supporting national and regional environmental planning, and enhancing the base of knowledge about environmentally sustainable development. Moreover, the Bank and its borrowers are increasingly learning from the implementation of environmental plans and projects, and what they learn is being fed back into new environmental work.

Lending: To Whom, How Much, and What For

Twenty-five new environmental projects were approved in fiscal 1994, involving total World Bank commitments of more than $2.4 billion.[2] This brings cumulative Bank lending over the past decade to roughly $9 billion in about 120 primarily environmental projects. (See figures 1 and 2 for the evolution of Bank environmental lending over the past decade.)

Figure 1. Cumulative World Bank Environmental Lending, Fiscal 1986–94

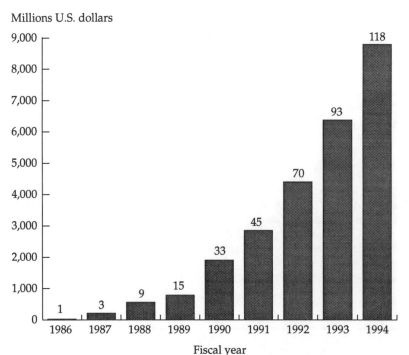

Millions U.S. dollars

Note: Numbers on top of the bars refer to number of projects.

At least that many projects have significant environmental components, including about thirty such operations over the past fiscal year.

As of July 1994 the Bank's largest borrowers for environmental improvement are Brazil, China, India, Indonesia, Mexico, and Turkey, each with five or more environmental projects in the active portfolio. These countries are among the Bank's biggest clients generally.

During fiscal 1994 nine major pollution control, energy conservation, and urban environmental ("brown") projects were approved, amounting to new commitments of more than $1.4 billion. The projects included pollution control initiatives in China, Ecuador, and Estonia; a series of integrated environmental investments along the northern Mexican border; and sanitation and sewerage projects in Algeria, Indonesia, Mexico, and Togo (see box 2).

New lending of almost $900 million was approved for thirteen projects addressing rural environmental problems ("green" projects) involving new environmental borrowers such as Bhutan, Colombia, the Lao People's Democratic Republic (PDR), and Uruguay, as well as older clients such as China, India, Indonesia, Pakistan, Paraguay, Poland, and Tunisia.

Figure 2. Annual World Bank Environmental Lending, Fiscal 1986–94

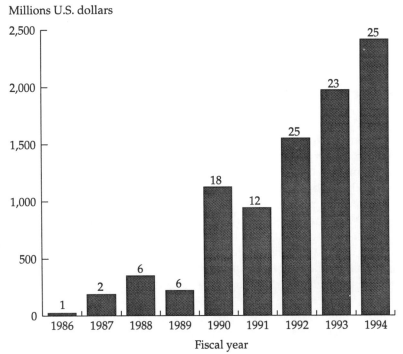

Millions U.S. dollars

Fiscal year

Note: Numbers on top of the bars refer to number of projects.

Box 2. Reducing Pollution

In fiscal 1994, the Bank approved nine projects, involving more than $1.4 billion in new commitments, for urban and industrial pollution control and waste management. This raises total Bank lending for pollution abatement–related activities to roughly $5 billion since the late 1980s, most of which has occurred over the last few years. Three major projects were approved in Mexico during the past fiscal year, including sector loans for urban water and sanitation improvements and solid waste management, and the first phase of a program to address city-specific environmental degradation problems in the highly industrialized northern region on the U.S. border. As in other recent Bank-supported urban environmental operations in Brazil, China, Indonesia, and elsewhere, the Northern Border Environment Project targets both water and air pollution emanating from several sources and is designed to help federal, state, and local authorities strengthen their environmental planning, management, and enforcement capabilities and carry out priority environmental investments.

In addition to institutional-strengthening components in other projects, just under $100 million was approved for three new operations, in the Gambia, the Republic of Korea, and Morocco, to strengthen national institutional capacity for addressing environmental issues. As in several other Sub-Saharan African countries in previous years, the project in the Gambia is the direct result of a national environmental action plan (NEAP).

Problems Encountered, Lessons Learned

The rapid growth of the portfolio of environmental projects makes close monitoring of implementation essential. With this in mind, the Bank's Environment Department has embarked on a careful program of "structured learning" to ensure that lessons from both successes and failures are quickly fed back into project design.

In general, implementation of environmental projects is affected by a set of factors similar to those in other Bank operations, such as the quality of project management, the ability of borrowers to fully comply with loan and credit agreements, the availability of counterpart funding, and the overall efficiency of procurement. However, when examined more closely, environmental projects are distinguishable in several important ways.

Environmental projects can present significant challenges for implementation because they tend to involve many different sectors of the economy, areas of law, and government ministries. The type of environmental project also makes a difference to implementation. For example, pollution control and energy projects are experiencing fewer implementation difficulties than projects that seek to strengthen national environmental institutions or improve management of natural resources, particularly forests.

Experience suggests that projects involving investments in physical infrastructure and equipment are generally easier to implement than those that make great demands on government ministries and agencies or that affect a larger number of potentially conflicting interests. Furthermore, brown, or urban environmental, projects tend to be relatively concentrated in countries with higher incomes, stronger institutions, and better project performance. "Institutional" and, especially, green projects (which address rural environmental problems) tend to be concentrated in poorer countries with weaker institutions.

Experience with the implementation of environmental projects to date indicates a number of factors that tend to promote successful outcomes. These include the need for:

- Strong borrower "ownership" of project objectives, components, and conditionalities
- Genuine local participation in project preparation and implementation, especially in natural resource management projects
- Competent, motivated, and adequately financed executing agencies
- Less complexity and rigidity in project design (bearing in mind the limitations of local capacity)
- Adequate Bank support throughout the project cycle.

Strategies for Environmental Management

Since 1987 the Bank has provided technical assistance to borrowers for the preparation of NEAPs or equivalent documents. By the end of fiscal 1994 most active IDA-9 countries and a number of IBRD borrowers had completed such plans.[3] In addition, over the past year the Bank concluded country environmental strategy papers for Bangladesh, Belize, Bhutan, Ethiopia, Guinea-Bissau, Iran, Lao PDR, Sierra Leone, Uruguay, and Viet Nam. Similarly, Bank country economic memoranda (CEM) for Eritrea, India, Indonesia, the Maldives, Papua New Guinea, and several republics of the former Soviet Union have been given a strong environmental focus.

Preliminary findings from a recent Bank review of country environmental strategies, including NEAPs, suggest that to be effective, such exercises need to establish clear priorities and to be country-driven and participatory, involving the government and as many of the affected segments of society as possible. The most effective strategies also explicitly examine cost-effectiveness in designing solutions and link policy prescriptions to institutional capacity.

Experience over the past few years indicates that economic ministries should be more involved in the national environmental planning process than has typically been the case and that weaknesses in setting priorities, in choosing policies and instruments, and in institutional analysis need to be redressed in the next generation of strategy documents.

At the regional level, strategy papers were completed last year for Central and Eastern Europe and Asia, and programs are now being implemented. The "Environmental Action Programme for Central and Eastern Europe" provides examples of how environmental improvements may be achieved within the context of economic restructuring. The Action Programme has formed the basis for a process that has been adopted by Eastern European countries themselves. They are organizing in-country workshops to implement the Programme's concepts and formulate national policies and investment programs. The principal document is being translated into twenty Eastern European languages, and it is being published together with a series of technical reports.

Another key initiative is the Mediterranean Coastal Cities Network (MEDCITIES), a city-level environmental network associated with the Mediterranean Environment Technical Assistance Program. Supported by the Bank, the United Nations Development Programme (UNDP), the European Investment Bank, and the European Union, MEDCITIES is preparing environmental audits and municipal action plans for five secondary cities in the Mediterranean basin.

The study *Toward an Environmental Strategy for Asia* (Brandon and Ramankutty 1993) describes the serious environmental problems that have accompanied the region's impressive growth but notes that growth has also created opportunities for addressing the problems. Follow-up to the study includes initiatives to improve domestic waste management, promote clean technologies, and assist countries in developing approaches to problems, many of which are common in nature.

Climbing the Learning Curve

While much has been learned about making development sustainable, much remains to be learned. This year the Bank sought to stay at the forefront of policy-oriented research and to support borrower countries in doing the same.

POLLUTION AND THE URBAN ENVIRONMENT. The Urban Management Programme (UMP), funded by the Bank, the UNDP, and the United Nations Center for Human Settlements (UNCHS), continues to promote appropriate policies, tools, best-practice case studies, and related research to strengthen environmental management at the city level. One major UMP output over the past year was the publication of the paper *Toward Environmental Strategies for Cities* (Bartone and others 1994).

In Asia the Metropolitan Environmental Improvement Programme (MEIP) has continued the assistance provided during its first phase (ending in fiscal 1993) to several large urban areas (Beijing, Bombay, Colombo, Jakarta, and Metro Manila) and has expanded its activities to other countries and cities, including the Kathmandu Valley in Nepal. MEIP has contributed directly to the preparation of innovative urban environmental investment projects in China, the Philippines, and Sri Lanka. It has also led to the Urban Air Quality Strategy (URBAIR) project, which focuses on the improvement of air quality in three of Asia's largest cities, Bombay, Jakarta, and Manila.

Over the past twelve months the Bank has undertaken further research into causes of and solutions for industrial pollution; for example, it has developed an Industrial Pollution Projection System (IPPS). It has also achieved substantial progress in revising its guidance materials on industrial pollution control, first issued in the early 1980s.

NATURAL RESOURCES AND THE RURAL ENVIRONMENT. Recent Bank policies on management of forest and water resources are presently being implemented, and the implementation of new forest policy has been submitted to a first review. The assessment concluded that although the principles set forth in the policy paper have proved useful, powerful vested interests in the forestry sector have made introduction of "win-win" policy options difficult. The review found that Bank lending in the sector over the past three years has changed significantly in response to the new forest policy. Greater emphasis is now placed on forest protection and the quality of implementation, and increasing attention is being given to developing projects in close collaboration with direct beneficiaries and other local populations.

The recent policy on water resources is also reflected in changes toward a more integrated approach to national strategies and project design in countries as diverse as Bolivia, Tanzania, and Trinidad and Tobago. The restoration of aquatic ecosystems and pollution reduction in the Aral Sea in Central Asia is also being pursued. The Bank also continues to provide technical assistance to borrowers in support of improved coastal zone management and to carry out studies on management of natural resources—especially forests—in various parts of the world.

NATIONAL POLICIES AND INSTITUTIONS. This year the Bank expanded its program for helping borrowers to improve their legal and institutional frameworks for environmental management. The goal is to overcome obstacles created by inadequate or outdated laws and regulations and to facilitate the introduction of greater public participation and transparency into government environmental decisionmaking (see box 3). Much of this work is geared toward encouraging borrowers to rely increasingly on economic incentives and disincentives, such as pollution charges, and other market-based instruments, such as "ecolabels," in addition to updating or improving more traditional "command and control" measures. Progress was also made in the Bank's analytical work on economic valuation of environmental resources and resource accounting, as well as on environmental indicators and information systems to support the growing volume of country strategy work and environmental investments.

Minimizing Adverse Impacts of Bank-Financed Investments

Chapter 2 discusses experience with environmental assessment (EA) during the past two years and summarizes the main findings of an internal review of performance with respect to involuntary resettlement. In both cases the Bank is working with borrowers to enhance the environmental or socioeconomic benefits of projects, while minimizing any environmental or social costs. Increasingly, the Bank and borrowers use assessments earlier in the preparation phases of projects to improve the environmental quality of project design. In addition, more emphasis is

---

Box 3. Strengthening National Environmental Institutions

Three projects for environmental institution-building at the national level, involving close to $100 million in Bank and IDA funding, were approved in fiscal 1994, increasing total lending for this purpose over the past five years to more than $530 million. One of these operations, the Capacity Building for Environmental Management Technical Assistance Project in the Gambia, will support implementation of the country's environmental action plan. The primary objective of the project is to develop and guide an effective system for environmental planning and management—including an environmental information and monitoring system—in the National Environmental Agency and other relevant institutions. In addition to new institutionally oriented lending operations, over the past fiscal year the Bank has provided direct assistance to borrowers in the development of environment-related laws and regulations in countries as diverse as Cameroon, Chile, Honduras, the Lao PDR, and Moldova.

being placed on reestablishing the social and economic well-being of people resettled during project implementation. The review identified income restoration as a significant shortcoming in the application of Bank policy in recent years.

Environmental Assessment

A review of experience with EA in fiscal 1993–94 confirms that borrowers are making more—and more productive—use of EA in Bank-financed operations. One indication of this is the increasing percentage of recently approved operations requiring full EA; more projects in more sectors and subsectors are being scrutinized through EAs. Altogether, twenty-six projects (in six different sectors) approved over the past year were given full EA, compared with nineteen (in five sectors) in fiscal 1993. Another eighty projects approved over the last twelve months, while not requiring full EA, were submitted to some degree of environmental analysis, including the specification of appropriate mitigation measures.

Related to this growth is the increasing use of sectoral and regional EAs. Sectoral assessments, in particular, are being employed to help launch a programmatic EA process in projects that involve a large number of subprojects (for example, roads, irrigation, and industrial and agricultural credit lines), many of which may not have been identified at the time of appraisal. In other instances, sectoral EA is used as a planning tool early in the preparation of a project without a formal link to subproject EA work.

Fiscal 1994 also witnessed presentation of the first two regional EAs to the Board, one for a natural resources management project in Paraguay and the other for a hydropower project in Nepal.

The Bank is accumulating experience with the use of EA to enhance project design. EA is used in three main ways:

- As part of project identification and early preparation, thus contributing directly to other technical and feasibility studies
- As a criterion for analyzing and recommending alternatives even when EA is not a central part of project preparation
- As a means of identifying additional components and measures for enhancing a project's environmental dimensions.

Examples of good practice in these areas can be drawn from recently approved projects in Brazil (urban transport), Croatia (highways), Estonia (district heating), Indonesia (urban development), Mexico (solid waste management), and Paraguay (natural resources management). Although improvements are still required, marked progress has also been achieved with respect to public consultation in the EA process; but the analysis of project alternatives from an environmental perspective remains a weak area.

The EA review also examined experience with the implementation of EA-related measures in projects in the Bank's active portfolio. Among the principal conclusions were the following:

- Environmental mitigation, management, and monitoring plans need to take country-specific conditions into account in at least three important ways: (a) environmental plans must strike a balance between the desire to address a multitude of complex environmental problems and local institutional capacity; (b) implementation will be improved by supporting autonomous, stable, and competent national implementing units, ensuring adequate counterpart funding, and achieving sustained management support; and (c) contracting out environmental monitoring and management activities should be pursued whenever the responsible agencies do not possess sufficient internal capacity.
- Implementation of EA-related actions benefits when explicit reference is made to them in Bank project documents, especially legal agreements, and when the agencies responsible for carrying them out take part in project negotiations.
- Sufficient allocation of time and resources for environmental supervision in accordance with the specific requirements of each project is essential to EA effectiveness during implementation.

Resettlement

Involuntary resettlement has accompanied development in both industrial and developing countries. Bank-financed programs account for a small (about 3 percent) but significant share of the people displaced by development projects worldwide. Operations currently in the Bank's active portfolio are expected to involve the resettlement of 2 million people over the next eight years. The Bank has the responsibility to help borrowers ensure that every effort is made to restore, and if possible improve, the livelihoods of people resettled in connection with such projects.

The Bank first adopted resettlement guidelines fourteen years ago. Since then, it has increasingly sought to work with governments to promote better domestic policies and legal frameworks for resettlement, both for Bank-supported projects and more broadly.

A Bank-wide resettlement review covering 192 projects, most of which remain active, was completed in April 1994 with the simultaneous release of a major report to the Board of Executive Directors and to the public. This was an innovative exercise that entailed extensive fieldwork, as well as initiation of remedial action. The review found that over the period examined, the Bank had achieved significant progress in three major areas: influencing the resettlement policies of borrower countries; assisting borrowers in avoiding or reducing the scale of displacement; and helping borrowers to improve the ability of resettlers to restore their incomes. The review confirmed that by rebuilding sustainable livelihoods, proper resettlement and rehabilitation can avoid driving people into poverty and can even improve the lives of those subject to involuntary displacement.

However, the review also found that actual performance by borrowing agencies has often not met agreed-on standards. Resettlement is nearly always more difficult, more expensive, and more time-consuming than is generally realized. The inherent difficulty of reestablishing living standards and community services is frequently compounded by the limited technical and institutional resettlement capacity of most executing agencies and by weak commitment on the part of some governments. To address these problems, the Bank's management decided to implement four sets of actions for future resettlement work:

- *Ensure borrower commitment to income restoration.* The Bank will not finance projects involving large resettlement operations unless the government concerned adopts policies and a legal framework that will support resettlement with income restoration. To support this commitment, borrower institutional capacity to manage resettlement will be enhanced. At the same time, project design can be improved by avoiding or reducing the need for displacement, creating clear timetables and linking progress on civil works to that on resettlement, promoting the participation of affected people, internalizing in the project the full costs of resettlement, and providing adequate Bank financing.
- *Take remedial action,* where necessary, to restructure existing projects, provide additional funding, and strengthen resettlement agencies.
- *Improve the analysis of resettlement* at appraisal, the design of development packages for resettlers, the in-house review of projects with resettlement components, and the staffing and organization of operational units.
- *Supervise resettlement components vigorously.* Regular supervision missions for resettlement components will take place at least every twelve months and will make greater use of local specialist consultants.

Progress toward these ambitious but sound actions has already begun in fiscal 1994. These steps will lead to improvement of the actual performance of projects involving resettlement, to the benefit of both the affected people and the national economy.

Building on the Synergies between Development and the Environment

A fundamental concept of environmentally sustainable development is that the environment and development are closely linked and must be addressed together. In consequence, the Bank's specific environmental interventions outlined in chapter 1 are only one part of all Bank activities that contribute to sound environmental management. Increasingly, the links between these activities and environmental protection are being made more explicit, as Bank staff seek to make greater use of the synergies between environment and development earlier in the process of developing strategies and projects.

Chapter 3 is organized around two propositions that are now generally accepted by both environmentalists and development planners: (a) alleviating poverty, reducing population growth, and investing in such life-enhancing activities as better health and nutrition, more-accessible education, and more-advanced farming methods can contribute dramatically to improved natural resource management; and (b) improving the efficiency with which resources are used (through both targeted investments and macroeconomic policy changes) reduces pollution and the exploitation of natural resources. Chapter 3 briefly describes Bank activities during fiscal 1994 that derived from these two propositions.

Poverty Reduction and the Environment

The Program of Targeted Interventions, which tracks Bank-supported projects aimed at directly reducing poverty, included sixty-six operations approved during the last twelve months, of which ten are specifically directed at natural resources management. For example, the Northwest Mountainous Areas Development Project in Tunisia will help restore grazing ranges and develop forest and farming activities, as well as reduce soil erosion and degradation and sedimentation, improving the condition of the environment and the economic well-being of the population. Box 4 further explores these links in a project in China. To help countries focus their poverty reduction strategies better, the Bank also completed twenty-one poverty assessments.

To enhance incomes and provide food security, this year the Bank, in cooperation with other donor agencies, is helping to revitalize the Consultative Group on International Agricultural Research (CGIAR) as it implements the CGIAR strategy for improving the environmental and social sustainability of agricultural development. The Bank is proposing a coordinated strategy for action and restored funding for the sixteen international research centers that make up the CGIAR system.

Box 4. Protecting Natural Resources and Combating Poverty

The Loess Plateau project in China's arid north provides a clear illustration of the link between income levels and environmental management. Poor farmers in the region subsist on low crop yields as the land continues to be heavily eroded by rainwater runoff. Utilizing local ideas and experience, the project seeks to provide 1.2 million people with the facilities to catch some of the runoff, maintaining a reliable water supply and redirecting the silt deposits to fill in eroded channels in an area often described as resembling "the surface of the moon." Earlier localized efforts have been only partially successful because they did not take full account of the need for financial incentives to encourage proper stewardship of the environment. The new IDA-supported project seeks to correct that imbalance and provide strong incentives for farmers to take long-term actions to restore and rehabilitate the area.

Many projects this year continue the Bank's emphasis on assisting women, whose great potential contribution to sound management of natural resources remains largely untapped. To help address this situation, Bank projects increasingly include gender-linked components, such as education and health services for women and girls, family planning services and education, and the inclusion of women in planning and in training for natural resource management. A number of such projects have adopted innovative ways of providing credit to very poor women. This year the Bank endowed the new Grameen Trust with $2 million in seed capital for microcredit schemes, aimed at rural women in several countries, on the model of the Grameen Bank in Bangladesh. As a follow-up to the implementation of chapter 24 of Agenda 21, which promotes an increased role for women in sustainable development, the Bank hosted a three-day International Consultation on Women in Ecosystem Management.[4] The consultation explored ways in which women could be more fully integrated into all levels of society to advance sustainable development.

Within a framework of social assessment, the Bank's Environment Department has led work on developing tools to incorporate stakeholder participation and social analysis into Bank operations. An example is the *Participation Sourcebook*, to be issued in fiscal 1995. In the forestry sector in particular, methodologies for systematically including stakeholder participation into projects are being developed. Participatory poverty assessments have been completed in eight African countries and are under way in a number of Latin American and South Asian countries. Work has increased in beneficiary assessment to ensure that projects meet the expressed needs of those they aim to benefit. Finally, Bank activity on behalf of indigenous people continued, with such initiatives as a conference on Traditional Knowledge and Sustainable Development.

Efficient Resource Use and the Environment

The efficient use of resources, particularly energy, has important beneficial effects on the environment because it reduces both waste and the consumption of natural resources. In Ethiopia, the Calub Gas Development Project will supply liquefied petroleum gas in the remote southeastern region of the country, providing a more efficient source of energy and replacing increasingly scarce supplies of fuelwood.

Economic forces are very powerful. In the energy sector, for example, price reform, an important component of more general structural reform, accounts for about half of all possible energy savings. Successful reformers such as Argentina, Chile, and Malaysia find that energy prices now cover costs, that service has improved, and that funds are being generated for future investments. The Bank increasingly supports projects incorporating renewable energy technology, particularly in cooperation with the GEF.

As with energy, resources such as water, agricultural inputs, and forestry products are often used wastefully. In addition to direct support for reform at the project level, economywide policies that remove major market distortions can have significant beneficial environmental effects. However, such policies may have unintended adverse effects as well. This year the Bank completed the initial draft of a major review, "Economywide Policies and the Environment," based on a comprehensive set of case studies. The analysis argues that attempting to understand such impacts better and to undertake appropriate action would result in significant payoffs for both the Bank and its borrowers. Positive impacts of economywide reforms on the environment can also be used to build constituencies for reform. Potential negative impacts need to be monitored, analyzed, and mitigated. Because both the direction and the extent of the impact of economywide policies can be ambiguous, the review proposes a country-specific approach to assessing the links between policies and the environment.

Addressing Regional and Global Environmental Challenges

Over the past year, the Bank's attention to regional and global environmental concerns has expanded. The Bank's work in protecting the regional commons focuses primarily on programs for regional seas and river basins. A variety of channels are used for the work on global issues, but the largest is the GEF. As one of GEF's three implementing agencies, together with UNDP and United Nations Environment Programme (UNEP), the Bank administered and chaired the GEF during its pilot phase. It is also a trustee for GEF funds and is responsible for managing the facility's portfolio of investment projects, many of which are cofinanced by regular Bank loans and credits. These diverse activities are described in chapter 4.

Regional Environmental Initiatives

Implementation of existing environmental action programs for the Mediterranean, Black, and Baltic seas and the Danube River Basin has accelerated over the past twelve months. The Bank also launched new regional initiatives for the Aral Sea in Central Asia and Lake Victoria in East Africa. The Aral Sea Environment Assistance Program was approved by the governments of Kazakhstan, the Kyrgyz Republic, Tajikistan, Turkmenistan, and Uzbekistan in January 1994. Jointly administered by the Bank, the UNDP, and the UNEP, it will seek to restore part of the Aral Sea to its previous state, revitalize some of the adjacent wetlands, and mitigate much of the ecological damage caused by development-related desiccation and salinization over the past several decades. With the participation of Tanzania, Uganda, and Kenya, the Lake Victoria Pollution Project is a concrete application of the Bank's water resources management policy, approved in 1993. In addition to these programs, the Bank has dedicated increasing effort to issues of soil degradation and desertification at the regional level, as illustrated by its active role in the drafting of the Desertification Convention.[5]

Global Environmental Programs

The Bank continued to strongly support key global environmental initiatives during fiscal 1994. As an implementing agency of the Multilateral Fund for the Implementation of the Montreal Protocol (MFMP), the goal of which is to reduce substances that contribute to depletion of the ozone layer, the Bank and its clients presently have investment operations in about twenty countries involving close to $100 million. The Bank has also helped the GEF to emerge as an important catalyst for the integration of global environmental concerns into national development goals. Through grants and concessional funding, the GEF enables developing country governments and private companies to address global environmental issues that they would otherwise be unable or unwilling to undertake, in the process demonstrating a new approach to global cooperation. During the pilot phase, the GEF helped countries to deal with four global environmental problems that have been recognized as high priorities in recent international treaties and conventions: (a) global warming, particularly the effects of greenhouse gas emissions from the use of fossil fuels and the destruction of carbon-sequestering forests; (b) loss of biological diversity through the degradation of natural habitats and the overuse of natural resources; (c) pollution of international waters through oil spills and the accumulation of wastes in oceans and international river systems; and (d) depletion of stratospheric ozone due to emissions of chlorofluorocarbons (CFCs), halons, and other gases (for countries not eligible for support under the Montreal Protocol).

In March 1994 representatives from more than seventy countries agreed to restructure and replenish the GEF, concluding negotiations carried out over a fifteen-month period. Under this agreement, the Facility will continue to address the problems indicated above, but land degradation—primarily desertification and deforestation—will also be eligible insofar as it relates to one of the four main focal areas. Decisions will generally be reached on the basis of consensus. The new arrangements will include (a) a universal assembly that will meet every three years to review GEF policies; (b) a council of thirty-two developing and industrial countries, with roughly equal representation, which will constitute the main governing body and will meet at least twice a year; and (c) a functionally independent secretariat that will be administratively supported by the Bank but will report directly to the council. Donors agreed to contribute more than $2 billion to the GEF's Core Fund over a three-year period. These funds will be over and above resources channeled to regular official development assistance.

Building Capacity for the Task

Last year's report highlighted two institutional milestones that had significant implications for Bank environmental work:

- The creation of a new vice presidency for Environmentally Sustainable Development (ESD), as part of a broader reorganization that also included strengthening environmental capabilities in the departments directly responsible for project preparation and supervision
- The launching of an action plan to move the management of projects under implementation to center stage and increase the involvement of borrowers and beneficiaries so as to enhance project "ownership" and improve results.

The ESD vice presidency, in particular, was charged with providing policy guidance, giving technical support to projects under preparation and implementation, and disseminating best practices for the Bank's overall environmental work. The past twelve months have seen the consolidation and implementation of the first full-year environmental work program of the ESD vice presidency, a continued strengthening and diversification of the Bank's internal technical capacity, and an increased openness to and expanded cooperation with bilateral and multilateral agencies, NGOs, and other interest groups. Chapter 5 details institutional progress in these three areas.

Equipping the Bank

The past year has provided an opportunity to strengthen the Bank's mix of skills in line with its growing commitments. The complement of technical environmental staff rose by around 30 and now stands at almost 300. Most of the increase this year was in country departments, in line with the policy of mainstreaming environmental concerns into the Bank's work.

Training of Bank staff in environmental issues also expanded. A major new course, "Fundamentals in Environmental Management," was introduced and is being taught six times a year. Twenty-one other environmental courses have been taught, many of them more than once, over the past year, with almost 600 staff participating.

Building Partnerships for Change

This year the Bank was an active partner within the United Nations system, through the Commission on Sustainable Development, in several environment-related activities: working to bring the Biodiversity and Climate Change conventions closer to implementation, participating in the negotiations of the Desertification Convention, and mobilizing funding for environmental programs at the country and regional levels.

The Bank's interaction with NGOs—both operational collaboration and substantive dialogue on policy issues—has deepened. Expanding Bank-NGO discussions over the past year have been fruitful for all concerned and have addressed a broad range of often controversial issues such as the links between adjustment and macroeconomic policies and the environment, the preparation of NEAPs, resettlement, and public access to information.

Improving Openness and Accountability

The Bank firmly believes that openness about its activities fosters accountability and transparency in the development process, facilitates coordination of interested parties, stimulates useful debate among and between policymakers and affected populations, and broadens understanding of development challenges—all of which ultimately enhance the quality of Bank-supported operations. To this end, the Bank adopted a new policy on information disclosure in January 1994. Under this policy, environment-related documents—including project environmental data sheets, EAs, and NEAPs—are now among a broad range of Bank (or Bank-supported) documents that are publicly available, many for the first time, through a new Public Information Center in Washington and the Bank's field offices.

Strengthening the Private Sector Role: The IFC and MIGA

Awareness is growing in the private as well as in the public sector regarding the high cost and potential liabilities of environmental cleanup. Businesses are increasingly taking environmental factors into account in decisions about production, investment, and trade. Chapter 6 describes the recent activities of the IFC and MIGA in support of the private sector's expanding role in improved environmental management. By encouraging businesses to become more energy efficient, minimize resource use, waste, and pollution, improve the workplace environment, and identify new environmentally friendly products, the IFC is helping firms to pursue environmentally sound operations as they plan for expansion, new ventures, or the privatization of government services and enterprises. To meet these multiple challenges, the IFC has developed an environmental program that addresses not only the physical impact of economic development—the use of land, minerals, water, and air—but also socioeconomic and cultural aspects.

The IFC's environmental activities include (a) ensuring that the projects it finances are environmentally sustainable; (b) strengthening the environmental capability of project sponsors and financial intermediaries through training and technical assistance; (c) helping project sponsors adopt efficient, clean technologies and taking measures to enhance environmental and socioeconomic benefits; (d) promoting investments in the environmental business sector; (e) assisting in the revision of the Bank's guidance materials on control of industrial pollution; and (f) addressing global environmental challenges by participating in the GEF and the Montreal Protocol Fund. Over the past year IFC's environment-related work has expanded most significantly in relation to environmental risk management, the environmental business sector, and global environmental activities. During fiscal 1994 the Environment Division in the IFC's Technical and Environment Department increased its staff to accommodate growth in all these areas.

MIGA, established in April 1988, promotes foreign direct investment for economic and social development in borrowing member countries by guaranteeing investments against political risks, helping countries to create an attractive investment climate, and providing promotional and advisory services. Under a mutually agreed arrangement with MIGA, the IFC acts as environmental adviser for all MIGA projects and ensures that MIGA operations comply with all relevant environmental guidelines.

Notes

1. The "World Bank Group," as used in this report, refers to the International Bank for Reconstruction and Development (IBRD) and its affiliates the International Development Association (IDA), the International Finance Corporation (IFC), and the Multilateral Investment Guarantee Agency (MIGA). IBRD and IDA together are commonly referred to as the World Bank.

2. All dollar amounts are current U.S. dollars except where noted. A billion is 1,000 million.

3. IDA-9 countries are those covered by the terms of the ninth agreement to replenish IDA's resources.

4. Agenda 21 is the primary policy document agreed on by countries at the Earth Summit.

5. The Desertification Convention is the United Nations Convention to Combat Desertification in Those Countries Experiencing Serious Drought and/or Desertification Particularly in Africa.

PART 1

The Fourfold Agenda

Part 1 of this report consists of four chapters corresponding to the Bank's fourfold agenda:

- To help member countries set priorities, build institutions, and implement programs for sound environmental stewardship
- To ensure that potential adverse environmental impacts from Bank-financed projects are addressed
- To help member countries build on the connections among poverty reduction, economic efficiency, and environmental protection
- To address global environmental challenges through participation in the Global Environment Facility.

1. Assisting Countries in Environmental Stewardship

Among the difficulties caused by the dramatic growth of the cities along the U.S.-Mexico border is that of providing environmentally safe disposal of municipal waste. This year a Bank-supported project to improve environmental management includes a program to retrain and educate open-dump scavengers such as this woman.

Within just a few years, World Bank support for borrower environmental stewardship has increased substantially. Lending specifically targeted to the environment has risen by a factor of five over six years. Twenty-five new primarily environmental operations with commitments exceeding $2.4 billion were approved in fiscal 1994, raising the Bank's total active environmental portfolio to about $9 billion in loans and credits for 118 projects. More than thirty other projects approved last year had significant environmental components. A majority of developing countries have now completed NEAPs or equivalent documents and are beginning to implement them—in many cases with Bank assistance. Clearer definition of national environmental goals has led to greater cooperation among countries as they recognize common priorities and seek to address them through regional strategies. Within the Bank, new policies for managing forests and water resources are being put into practice. Technical assistance and analytical work have expanded to meet increased demand from member countries for support to improve their policy and project design and implementation.

This chapter summarizes the Bank's principal activities in support of environmental stewardship—lending, definition of strategies, and research and technical assistance—during fiscal 1994. It begins with a discussion of lessons emerging from project implementation and then reviews recent experience in relation to pollution and the urban environment, natural resource management and the rural environment, and environmental planning and institution building at the national level. These sections also give special attention to implementation experience to date.

Managing the Environmental Portfolio

The Bank assists its borrowers through a variety of lending instruments including loans for specific investments, sector investment and maintenance, financial intermediation, technical assistance, and structural and sectoral adjustment. Environmental projects under implementation at the end of fiscal 1994 use many of these instruments, particularly specific investment loans. Environmental projects and components are included in a variety of traditional investment sectors and incorporate a range of approaches and instruments, including credit lines for industrial pollution control and soil and forest conservation. Nearly all give considerable emphasis to institution building through training, studies, and technical assistance. Box 1.1 provides additional information on environmental projects and components.

At the beginning of fiscal 1995 close to 120 active environmental projects, entailing Bank commitments of nearly $9 billion, were under

---

Box 1.1. Environmental Projects and Components

The growth in World Bank lending for environmental management over the past six years is reflected both in the increasing number of projects having primarily environmental objectives and in the equally expanding number of projects having environmental components. Roughly half of all active environmental projects—and over a third of total lending for such projects—are concerned mainly with management of natural resources (forestry, fisheries, land and watershed management, and so forth). One-third of all active environmental projects and more than half of total commitments in such operations involve abatement of urban and industrial pollution, waste management, or energy conservation. One-sixth of environmental projects support environmental institution building at the national level.

Environmental projects are defined as those that are undertaken largely for purposes of environmental protection, conservation, rehabilitation, planning, management, education, or institutional strengthening. Many environmental components are undertaken for the same purposes but form only part of total project costs or benefits—as, for example, an energy sector development project that contains an energy efficiency component or an agricultural production project that contains a soil conservation component. Projects may also have specific environmental components to mitigate or compensate for potential adverse environmental impacts of nonenvironmental investments such as hydropower plants, irrigation schemes, or major new transport infrastructure (see annex E).

Projects with primarily environmental objectives may be found in a range of traditional investment sectors such as energy, industry, transport, urban development, and, especially, agriculture, water supply, and sani-

---

implementation. These operations were approved between fiscal 1986 and fiscal 1994. However, most went to the Bank's Board of Executive Directors for approval after fiscal 1990 and thus have been under implementation for less than four years. (Environmental projects under implementation at the beginning of fiscal 1994 are listed in annex D; those approved during the past fiscal year are briefly described in annex C.)

Environmental projects are widespread geographically, in more than fifty countries and all six Bank operational regions. The largest individual portfolios are in Brazil, China, India, Indonesia, Mexico, and Turkey, which together had forty-four active environmental projects at the end of fiscal 1994. In Sub-Saharan Africa, South Asia, and the Middle East and North Africa environmental portfolios are dominated by natural resource management projects; in Europe and Central Asia pollution and

tation. The specific criteria used to identify environmental projects and components within each sector are indicated in annex B. In the transport sector, for instance, environmental projects or components include those primarily concerned with traffic management (to reduce congestion and air pollution), vehicle fuel efficiency and modification (such as the elimination of lead), reduced vehicle emissions, reduction of ship waste, spills, and other forms of marine pollution, environmental safety and cleanup in ports, and so on. Primarily environmental energy projects and components include those aimed at supply-side efficiency, improved demand-side management and conservation, reduced emissions, and alternative and renewable energy development.

Projects approved in fiscal 1994 that have environmental components are listed in annex C. Typical examples are:

- The National Agricultural Research Project in Mali, which supports research programs and extension on natural resource management and other appropriate agricultural practices
- The Leyte-Cebu and Leyte-Luzon geothermal projects in the Philippines, which replace coal burning plants with geothermal energy plants, thereby reducing carbon dioxide emissions, and also strengthen environmental management within the power sector
- The Water Companies Restructuring and Modernization Project in Bulgaria, which provides technical assistance to build capacity for management of water resources and sewerage investment to reduce pollution in sensitive watercourses
- The Belize City Infrastructure Project, which provides for traffic management to reduce congestion and improve sidewalks and bicycle lanes and also includes a coastal zone management component.

energy-related projects predominate; and in East Asia and Latin America and the Caribbean the numbers of brown, green, and institutional projects are roughly equal.

According to the Bank's standard supervision ratings, environmental projects as a whole were performing slightly better than the average for the entire portfolio of active Bank projects at the beginning of fiscal 1994. This holds for all regions except Latin America and the Caribbean, where environmental projects were performing below the Bank-wide average. There, a large number of environmental operations were experiencing moderate implementation problems, and four projects—including a forestry and environment operation in Haiti that was subsequently canceled because of the uncertain political situation in that country— were suffering from more significant difficulties with implementation.

The main problems identified in these operations, leaving aside the one in Haiti, included design complexity, which hampered interagency coordination, institutional weaknesses, shortages of counterpart funding (often related to broader macroeconomic management problems), procurement difficulties, and insufficient borrower ownership of some project goals and components. In general, however, regional differences in performance were similar for environmental and nonenvironmental projects.

Considering the environmental portfolio as a whole, the main problems encountered during project supervision—as is the case with other types of Bank operations—involve the quality of project management, the extent of borrower compliance with legal agreements, and difficulties with counterpart funding and procurement (including the hiring of consultants). In some cases these problems appear to be associated as much with project design factors—for example, unrealistic covenants and objectives or implementation requirements too ambitious for the borrower's institutional capacity—as with implementation as such. In regional terms, environmental projects in Sub-Saharan Africa appear to be the ones most affected by management shortcomings and incomplete compliance with loan and credit covenants. These problems suggest the presence of comparatively weak institutions and possibly less-than-full borrower commitment to project objectives. Counterpart funding problems appear to be as serious in South Asia, Europe and Central Asia, and Latin America and the Caribbean as in Africa, reflecting country macroeconomic difficulties and the policy responses to them, such as necessary cuts in public expenditures. Significant problems with training, studies, and technical assistance have been experienced mainly in Africa.

Part of the explanation for the seemingly above-average performance of environmental projects at present is that many environmental projects are rather new and have not been under implementation as long as the average for all Bank projects. Bank experience shows that implementation problems increase with age—a trend also evident for environmental projects. This suggests that as the environmental portfolio matures, average performance ratings may decline somewhat. Controlling for time under implementation, it is probably more accurate to conclude that environmental projects are performing about the same as the Bank's active portfolio as a whole.

There are also significant differences in performance among the various types of environmental projects. Pollution control and energy conservation projects are presently performing considerably better, on average, than those primarily concerned with natural resource management and environmental institution building at the national level. Projects involving forest management are the most problematic, particularly older operations in Sub-Saharan Africa and South Asia. Pollution-related projects in East Asia and Europe and Central Asia are among the better performers to date.

These variations in performance can be explained in two ways. First, projects that primarily involve physical investments (infrastructure or pollution-control devices), as is the case with most pollution-related operations, are generally easier to implement than those having comparatively larger "software" (including institutional) components, as is the case with many green and all institutional projects. Second, pollution-related projects tend to be relatively more concentrated in countries with higher average incomes—and thus higher average levels of development—stronger institutions, and a record of better project performance generally, while natural resource management projects are situated to a greater extent in lower-income countries with weaker institutions and poorer overall project performance. Many pollution-related projects also involve fewer executing agencies than natural resource management or institution-building projects, which simplifies implementation. Other relevant aspects, such as the relative complexity of institutional projects and the above-average political sensitivity of many natural resource management operations, are discussed below.

Beyond these factors, the cross-sectoral, cross-media, and cross-jurisdictional nature of many environmental issues, as well as the relative newness of many borrower initiatives in this area, make implementing environmental projects especially challenging. Together, these characteristics add up to relatively new—and often weak—policies, legal and regulatory frameworks, and institutions for environmental management in many developing countries, which may hamper project implementation. In addition, because the Bank and its borrowers are still at a comparatively early stage of the learning curve with respect to the most effective ways of achieving environmental improvement goals, systematic monitoring and assessment of the progress of environmental operations are essential. More generally, however, many of the elements influencing the implementation of environmental projects are the same as those that affect the performance of other types of Bank operations. They include both country and sector factors—such as political and macroeconomic conditions and borrower financial capacity—and the quality and consistency of Bank (and other donor) support throughout the project cycle.

Several clear lessons emerge from the Bank's implementation experience with Bank environmental projects to date.

Institutional capacity and commitment. Capable institutions and strong borrower ownership of project objectives, components, and conditionalities appear to be especially important for satisfactory implementation of environmental projects. Recent environmental operations in the large Chinese cities of Beijing and Tianjin bear this out. The highly motivated and competent staff and strong local political commitment to project objectives have sustained the generally smooth implementation of these operations to date (see box 1.5, p. 40).

Design complexity. Avoiding unnecessary complexity in project design, in light of borrower administrative and technical capacity, and maintaining adequate flexibility during implementation are important. The perhaps excessive comprehensiveness of many of the first generation of environmental institution-building projects has made implementation a continuous challenge. Obstacles to efficient implementation include institutional conflicts, inadequate interagency cooperation, and, particularly in Africa, occasional difficulties in external donor coordination (see box 1.10, p. 58). These obstacles also increase the burden on Bank supervision. However, the need for simpler projects has to be balanced with the intersectoral and multidisciplinary nature of many environmental interventions, as described above. Box 1.2 describes the experience with maintaining this balance in Mexico, which is relevant worldwide.

Participation. Substantial local participation is likely to improve the chances for success of environmental projects, especially those dealing with natural resource management. This is illustrated by a series of projects for improving land management and soil conservation at the watershed level in south-central Brazil (see box 1.6, p. 42). Among the key features of these operations are decentralized decisionmaking and intensive farmer and private sector involvement in subproject planning and implementation, which have also been central elements in a number of recent forest and natural resource management projects in Africa and South Asia.

Pollution and the Urban Environment

The most critical environmental challenges facing cities in the developing world—such as urban waste management and control of industrial pollution—have been collectively labeled the brown agenda. This section summarizes Bank activity in support of borrower efforts to address this agenda during the past year. Following a brief overview of the principal elements of the Bank's approach to reduction of urban and industrial pollution, the next section surveys experience with pollution reduction and urban environmental projects that are presently under implementation, describes lending operations in this field approved in fiscal 1994, and examines recent support to borrowers through the definition of urban environmental strategies, the provision of technical assistance, and research.

Box 1.2. Mexico: Learning from the Bank's Expanding Portfolio

The government of Mexico has been eager to begin implementation of environmental projects. Its national strategy takes two mutually reinforcing approaches: (a) actions on particular *regions* using an integrated multisectoral approach, and (b) national or multiregional actions on particular *sectors*. Bank support for such efforts includes projects in all the critical sectors, including the Northern Border Environment Project, the Second Water Supply and Sanitation Sector Project, and the Second Solid Waste Project, all of them approved this year.

Early experience with implementation indicates that Mexico is not immune from the kinds of problem that affect other environment projects around the world. For example, start-up problems, including the reorganization of and frequent staff changes in the new environmental agencies, delayed the early implementation of the National Environment Project. In addition, the multisectoral nature of environmental programs imposes demands on coordination between implementing agencies that exceed those under other Bank operations. The effectiveness of the Transport Air Quality Project was delayed a year mainly because of conflict between different levels of government on how to finance the project.

Despite a slow start, rapid progress has been recorded in developing a legal and regulatory framework, building up a monitoring infrastructure and database, shifting toward cleaner fuels and vehicles, and protecting important ecological resources. Learning from the implementation experience so far, the lending program for Mexico will include more pilot projects to test what works best. To the extent possible, projects will be tailored for implementation by a single agency or fewer agencies than in the past. Institutional strengthening, especially at the subnational level, will remain a key element, to be phased in gradually as the capacity of environmental agencies increases. For example, the proposed Environmental Enforcement Capacity Technical Assistance Project will be a pilot program for agencies in only three states, whose experience will help design programs in other states. The government's continuing commitment to improving Mexico's environmental performance will reinforce these effects.

There are two strands in the evolution of the Bank's approach to the brown agenda in recent years. First, more and more city-specific strategies and investment projects are addressing environmental issues in a cross-sectoral and cross-media way. Second, pollution prevention—as well as pollution abatement—has become a growing focus of Bank environmental policy dialogue and lending.

The Bank's urban development projects initially concentrated on slum upgrading and sites-and-services programs. Over time, however, the focus has shifted to infrastructure, urban transport, municipal development, and urban management in general. Accompanying this shift has been an increasing emphasis on improving the urban environment through investments in water supply, basic sanitation, solid waste management (further described in box 1.3), and control of industrial pollution.

In recent years efforts to integrate sectoral interventions and to link them to broader sustainable development initiatives have expanded following the Bank's adoption in 1991 of a new urban policy paper (World Bank 1991b). This paper provides a framework for guiding investments in cities by highlighting the links between urban economic activities and macroeconomic performance, on the one hand, and between growth, poverty, and degradation of the urban environment, on the other. Partly as a result, Bank lending for urban environmental

---

Box 1.3. Evolution of World Bank Lending for Municipal Solid Waste Management

Despite heavy municipal spending on solid waste management, most cities fail to provide efficient and universal collection services or environmentally safe disposal. This failure exacts a high cost from public health and the environment. A recent Bank review of seventy-one projects with municipal solid waste management (MSWM) components for fiscal 1974–88 concluded that many fell short of environmental expectations because of insufficient attention to building institutional capacity, lack of strategic planning, and failure to provide for safe disposal facilities. The exceptions were a few large, focused MSWM projects (in Mexico, Nigeria, and Singapore) or successive municipal development projects that steadily built up local MSWM capacity, as in India and Indonesia. Current Bank-supported efforts have built on these lessons to produce a new generation of MSWM projects, components, or sector studies. These emphasize one or more of four key issues:

- *Strategic service planning.* Strategic MSWM plans are included both in metropolitan area projects, as in Colombo, Tehran, Belo Horizonte, Curitiba, and São Paulo, and in national strategies, as in Turkey and Mexico. In the latter case, on-lending through a national solid waste fund requires target cities to prepare their own strategic plans.
- *Better institutional arrangements.* Several projects deal explicitly with the common and critical problem of interjurisdictional conflicts through the creation of a metropolitan authority for solid waste transfer and disposal (in Metro Manila, Colombo, Antalya, and

management and pollution control has grown rapidly over the past several years. The increasing awareness of the importance of the urban environment is reflected in the selection of this issue as the theme for the Bank's second Environmentally Sustainable Development (ESD) Conference, in September 1994.

As concerns the second strand, pollution prevention and abatement, over the past five years research into sources of and means of combating industrial pollution has shown that clean technologies and other forms of pollution prevention are generally more cost-effective than end-of-pipe solutions. This is recognized both in the ongoing revision of the Bank's guidance materials on industrial pollution control (discussed in more detail below) and in several new investment operations, especially in East and South Asia, currently under preparation.

Curitiba, for example) or the creation of a regulatory body at the municipal level and the contracting out of solid waste management operations to the private sector (as in Bursa, Turkey). In most cases, public participation is an important contribution to finding effective solutions.

- *More efficient management and finance.* To gain efficiency, most of the new generation of Bank-supported MSWM projects introduce competition and greater involvement of the private sector in service delivery. Some examples are contracting for garbage collection and street-sweeping services (in Colombo, Shanghai, Antalya, and Bogota) and awarding concessions for financing, building, and operating transfer stations, sanitary landfills, and resource recovery facilities (in Colombo, Lahore, and Antalya). All forms of privatization require strengthening of the management capacity of municipal authorities for preparing performance specifications and tender documents, management of the tender process, and monitoring and supervision. Finally, introducing service cost accounting and financial management is an essential feature of all projects.

- *Environmental protection.* Closing existing dumps and opening new sanitary landfills are key elements in existing loans or projects under preparation in the metropolitan areas of Manila, Colombo, Shanghai, Lahore, Antalya, Belo Horizonte, Curitiba, San Salvador, and São Paulo. Each of these projects paid special attention to environmental impacts and mitigation. Several of the landfills (in San Salvador, Belo Horizonte, and Lahore) have incorporated innovative bioreactor features for accelerated biostabilization with leachate recycling and the recovery and use of methane (an important greenhouse gas produced by landfills).

*Implementing Projects in Pollution Control and the Urban
Environment*

By the end of fiscal 1994 forty projects addressing pollution and the urban
environment, involving total Bank commitments of more than $5 billion,
were under implementation. Table 1.1 shows the regional distribution of
these projects and identifies countries having three or more such operations in the active environmental portfolio at the beginning of fiscal 1995.
These projects include a broad range of investments: basic urban environmental sanitation (especially sewage collection and treatment), control of industrial pollution, district heating (or domestic fuel conversion),
energy conservation, development of renewable energy sources, solid
waste management, control of vehicle-related air pollution, and disposal
of ship wastes. (See box 1.4 for a review of current urban transport
projects.) Virtually all include institutional-strengthening measures.

Implementation of most of these projects is proceeding well. Two
operations—a water supply and sewage treatment project in Istanbul,
Turkey, and an energy conservation project in Niger—are currently
experiencing significant implementation problems. On average, projects
in this sector are performing better than the Bank's environmental portfolio as a whole, with operations in China, Cyprus, the Czech Republic,
India, the Republic of Korea, Mauritania, Poland, and Turkey performing
particularly well (see box 1.5).

**Table 1.1. Portfolio of Pollution Control and Urban Environmental
Projects, by Region, End of Fiscal 1994**

Region or country	Number of projects	Total commitments (millions of dollars)
Sub-Saharan Africa	5	114
East Asia and the Pacific	8	975
China	5	650
South Asia	2	346
Europe and Central Asia	10	1,636
Turkey	4	705
Latin America and the Caribbean	11	1,708
Brazil	4	481
Mexico	5	1,163
Middle East and North Africa	4	290
Total	40	5,069

Note: The four countries with the largest portfolios are shown separately but are
included in the portfolios of their respective regions.
Source: World Bank data.

New Lending for the Brown Agenda in Fiscal 1994

Fiscal 1994 lending for control of urban and industrial pollution is presented in table 1.2. A sample of these projects indicates how the work has been designed to meet the specific needs of each area.

The Northern Border Environment Project in Mexico ($368 million) covers the highly industrialized area along the 3,300-kilometer boundary between Mexico and the United States. A large part of the region is arid or semiarid, although there are some forested areas and irrigated farmlands. Dramatic growth of the major cities along the border, spurred by rapid industrial expansion, has caused pressing environmental problems in several sectors. Air and water pollution and industrial and hazardous waste are serious problems. Urban services are overstretched: water supply and sanitation services are inadequate, facilities for managing municipal solid waste are scarce, and traffic (on unpaved roads) has caused severe urban pollution. The natural environment is under pressure both from expansion of built-up areas and from increasing agricultural activity—each threatening rich endemic biodiversity. The project will assist municipal, state, and federal authorities in strengthening their environmental planning, management, and enforcement capabilities and in designing and carrying out priority investments effectively. Other operations—the Second Solid Waste Project Management ($200 million) and the Second Water Supply and Sanitation Project ($340 million)—will apply to the whole country. The first project includes an innovative retraining and education program for open-dump scavengers to provide them with alternative employment options as the dumps are closed.

The Lomé Urban Development Project in Togo ($26 million) includes a citywide program to upgrade transport and traffic conditions and measures to improve the environmental and sanitary conditions of the Bè Lagoon and its surrounding neighborhoods. It also promotes institutional capacity building in urban environmental management. The project will involve the active participation of local residents, community groups, and NGOs in neighborhood environmental improvement activities and will promote the use of small contractors in the construction sector, thus having a significant effect on the employment and incomes of the urban poor.

The principal objective of the District Heating Rehabilitation Project in Estonia ($38 million) is to foster energy efficiency and economy. This will benefit the environment because energy production and consumption practices are responsible for most of the air pollution in the country. District heating systems, primarily for urban homes and for hot water and steam for industry, provide about 46 percent of the total heat

---

Box 1.4. Urban Transport Projects

The negative environmental impacts of motor vehicles in urban areas of developing countries are even more serious than in industrial countries—mainly because of the poor condition of most of the vehicles, the low quality of fuels, and the usually high concentration of motor vehicles in a few large cities. The large proportion of the population thus exposed to pollutants is in urgent need of alternative means of urban transport.

Recent studies and projects show growing attention to the transport needs of the urban poor, especially through nonmotorized transport (NMT), defined as any form of transport in which the primary source of energy is nonmechanical or is natural propulsion (for example, sailboats). Bicycles are not only the predominant mode of NMT but are also the world's leading vehicle for personal transport. If bicycles are adequately integrated into the transport system, they can improve the efficiency of mass transit substantially—for example, by enlarging the area served. Two examples of projects with NMT components are described here.

- The Peru Transport Rehabilitation Project will increase bicycle use in the Lima metropolitan area. An NMT pilot component will provide (a) separate, safe, and convenient bicycle paths, (b) promotional campaigns demonstrating the bicycle's relative cheapness, (c) access to credit for the poor to enable them to purchase bicycles, and (d) educational campaigns to improve traffic safety. The project will reduce the growth in demand for motorized transport, which in turn will help reduce the steady increase in air pollution, vehicle-generated noise, and traffic accidents.

---

production in Estonia. These systems generate heat in combined heat-and-power plants in the main cities and in about 5,000 boiler houses, most of which employ outdated technology and burn heavy fuel oil, shale, or coal. The project will improve the efficiency of fuel use through provision of meters and spare parts for boilers, improvements to distribution systems, conversion of boilers from heavy fuel oil to peat and wood (to be harvested and used sustainably), and reduction of water wastage. District heating institutions will also be strengthened and restructured. The project will significantly reduce emissions of sulfur dioxide and nitrogen oxides.

Technical Assistance for the Urban Environment

The environmental management component of the Urban Management Programme (UMP), sponsored by the Bank, the UNDP, Habitat, and sev-

- The Ghana Urban Transport Project will provide for better traffic management, resulting in less traffic congestion and vehicle emissions. It should also mean safer conditions for NMT, particularly for the poor, by providing footways and separate lanes for non-motorized vehicles.

Part of the answer to the substantial economic and welfare losses from congestion, traffic accidents, and noise and air pollution lies in new transport infrastructure. Bank involvement in the past has favored additions to existing bus services through exclusive busways and better road access, instead of building underground railways or elevated highways. In some megacities, however, capital-intensive investments such as rapid rail systems may be best, especially if the more flexible busway alternatives have already reached maximum capacity. Another consideration is that bus transport has in many cases had a severe impact on the urban environment (as is the case with the Avenida 9 de Julho busway in São Paulo). Accordingly, Bank-supported urban transport projects are now giving increasing consideration to intermodal options, including rail-based transit or metros.

The Integrated Urban Transport Project in São Paulo contains an infrastructure and equipment investment component for building and operating a rail connection between the suburban train systems and a rapid-transit connection between the suburban train systems and the metro. The environment-related objectives of the project will be achieved through an air quality and traffic safety component, with an inspection and maintenance program for vehicles emissions and noise, a traffic management and safety program, and provision of a vehicle emissions and noise laboratory and equipment for monitoring and sampling emissions.

eral bilateral agencies (German, Swedish, Dutch, and others) in association with the World Health Organization (WHO), focuses on demand-oriented approaches to urban pollution reduction and waste management. The environmental component of the UMP is housed in the Bank's central vice presidency for Environmentally Sustainable Development (ESD) but is closely linked to the regional vice presidencies. During the past fiscal year this component continued to promote appropriate policies, strategies, tools, best-practice case studies, and related research to strengthen environmental management at the city level and respond to the problems of the brown agenda. In particular, the UMP issued a new policy paper, *Toward Environmental Strategies for Cities* (described in box 1.6).

In Asia, Phase I of the Metropolitan Environmental Improvement Programme (MEIP), which is funded by the UNDP and implemented by the Bank, has assisted five large cities—Beijing, Bombay, Colombo,

Box 1.5. Improving the Urban Environment in China

Since late 1991 the Bank has approved four projects focusing on management of the urban environment in China. The first such operation, approved in November 1991, involves the municipality of Beijing, with a total
resident population of about 10 million. The second, approved in June
1992, was for Tianjin, the country's third largest city, with about 5 million
inhabitants. The third, in February 1993, concentrates on four large urban
areas (Changzhou, Suzhou, Wuxi, and Zhenjiang) in southern Jiangsu
province, near Shanghai. And the fourth, approved in March 1994, is for
the municipality of Shanghai, with a total population of 14 million. The
first three operations are under implementation.

The Beijing, Tianjin, and southern Jiangsu projects have similar objectives and components. All three seek to improve environmental
planning and management capabilities and help to finance priority
urban environmental infrastructure and pollution control investments
at the municipal level. Pollution control funds have been established in
all three cases. The Jiangsu project also includes a pilot subcomponent
for township and village industrial enterprises (TVIEs) in rural areas.
The Beijing and Tianjin projects address solid waste management; the
Beijing and Jiangsu operations include hazardous and toxic waste
management. The Beijing project has an additional district heating
component to reduce the burning of coal and associated air pollution,
and the Tianjin project has urban transport and resettlement components. Institution-building measures in all three projects include a
variety of studies, such as the preparation of an environmental master
plan for Beijing. All three provide technical assistance and training for
local environmental and other municipal staff.

Despite their ambitious objectives and the scale of the investments
involved—the total costs of the Beijing and Jiangsu operations, for
example, are estimated at $304.5 million and $588 million, respec-
tively—implementation of all three projects is generally proceeding
well. Experience with the Beijing project has been especially positive.
Among the key factors associated with successful implementation of
the Beijing operation are the highly motivated and competent staff of
the project executing agencies and their strong commitment to project
objectives. Counterpart funding has also been available on a timely
basis. Those delays that have occurred mainly involve procurement—
especially of sophisticated pollution control and monitoring systems
that required external assistance—and the assembly of databases and
associated analysis for the environmental master plan. Some costs have
been higher than expected, particularly those related to land acquisition and resettlement that required the realignment, and thus redesign,
of a planned sewerage line. Other project components are proceeding
more rapidly than anticipated.

**Table 1.2. Projects for Urban Environmental Management
and Pollution Control, Fiscal 1994**
(millions of dollars)

Country	Project	Loan/credit (L/C)	World Bank financing	Total project cost
Algeria	Water Supply and Sewerage Rehabilitation	L	110	170
China	Shanghai Environment	L	160	457
Ecuador	Mining Development and Environmental Control Technical Assistance	L	14	24
Estonia	District Heating Rehabilitation	L	38	65
Indonesia	Surabaya Urban Development	L	175	618
Mexico	Northern Border Environment	L	368	762
Mexico	Solid Waste Management II	L	200	416
Mexico	Water and Sanitation Sector II	L	350	770
Togo	Lomé Urban Development	C	26	29
Total new lending			1,441	3,311

Source: World Bank data.

Jakarta, and Metro Manila—in tackling their rapidly growing environmental problems. In Phase II, which began in early 1993, MEIP follows up on and implements the activities outlined in city-specific strategies developed earlier, expands the MEIP approach to other cities in those countries, and extends the program to the Kathmandu Valley in Nepal. Two projects currently under preparation, the Industrial Efficiency and Pollution Control Project in the Philippines and the Colombo Environmental Project in Sri Lanka, are based on MEIP's pioneering work in these countries.

Under MEIP, the URBAIR project focuses on the improvement of air quality in three of Asia's largest cities: Bombay, Jakarta, and Manila. Kathmandu, a smaller city but one with severe air quality problems, was added to the URBAIR study during the year. The URBAIR project emphasizes both improved modeling and measurement of ambient pollution levels and economic analysis of impacts, largely in terms of health effects. Supported in part by the UNDP and by trust funds, the project produced city reports in fiscal 1994 for Bombay, Jakarta, and Metro Manila. The report on Kathmandu will follow in fiscal 1995.

A new joint UMP/MEIP initiative on the economic valuation of environmental degradation involves studies in Bombay, Colombo, and Metro Manila that examine the economic dimension of selected urban environmental problems. The first-phase reports are due in early fiscal 1995. The

---

Box 1.6. Toward Environmental Strategies for Cities

Cities are the engine of economic growth, but the environmental implications of such growth need to be assessed and managed better. The critical and most immediate problems facing developing country cities are the health impacts of urban pollution that derive from inadequate water, sanitation, drainage, and solid waste services; poor urban and industrial waste management; and indoor and outdoor air pollution—the brown agenda. This set of problems disproportionately affects the urban poor and takes a heavy toll on urban health and productivity.

Individual cities may also face many of the green issues, such as the depletion of water and forest resources, inefficient transport systems and energy use, the degradation of environmentally fragile lands, and the occupation of areas prone to natural hazards. With such a multiplicity of problems, it is important for each city to identify specific priorities, policies, and actions needed to address the most immediate issues.

A key recommendation from the 1992 "Earth Summit" in Rio de Janeiro was that each major city prepare its own "local Agenda 21" for environmental improvement and sustainable development. As part of the Bank's efforts—which also include an increasing number of environmentally oriented lending operations—to support urban leaders in this task, the UMP has prepared a paper (Bartone and others 1994) that provides a process for setting local priorities and agreeing on a local Agenda 21. Such an agenda is based on mobilizing public support and participation; choosing policy instruments that will change behavior, relieve conflicts, and encourage cooperative arrangements; building local institutional capacity; strengthening urban service delivery; and increasing local knowledge about the urban environment.

The strategic planning process described in the paper has been successfully applied in many cities. Case studies are presented to show how institutional, informational, political, and technical problems related to urban environmental management can be addressed in a strategic manner.

Regional Acidification Information and Simulation in Asia (RAINS/ASIA), a project to evaluate the extent and seriousness of acid rain, focused on regionwide environmental impacts, using a PC-based software tool to assess the consequences of emission-reducing strategies. It is based on a model that is already being used in Europe to help identify feasible goals for reduction of sulfur dioxide emissions. RAINS/ASIA was funded by $1.2 million from multinational trust funds; work was completed in mid-1994.

Another important brown agenda activity is MEDCITIES, a city-level urban environmental network that is part of the Mediterranean Technical Assistance Program (METAP). Supported by the Bank, the UNDP, the

European Investment Bank, and the European Union, MEDCITIES is preparing environmental audits and municipal action plans for five secondary cities in the Mediterranean Basin. Regional programs for the Black and Baltic seas, including a Baltic Cities Network similar to MEDCITIES, also have important pollution control components.

Regional Strategies for Pollution Prevention

The Bank continues to support borrowers' environmental work through analytical studies. Two regional strategy papers emphasizing the urban environment were completed last year and entered the implementation stage in fiscal 1994. Other programs and studies provided forums for discussion as well as practical models of and guidance for environmental issues.

The premise of the "Environmental Action Programme for Central and Eastern Europe" is that because of the scarcity of financial resources, human health impacts must be regarded as the primary criterion in setting environmental priorities. The strategy focuses mainly on pollution problems that affect both cities and the surrounding countryside and are common to the countries in the former Soviet bloc. The program encourages consensus among Central and Eastern European countries and donor agencies on environmental priorities. It endorses a mix of policy, investment, and institutional actions such as cutting air emissions from specific types of industrial plants, reducing particulate and sulfur dioxide emissions in urban areas (especially emissions linked to the use of coal in the household and service sectors), launching low-cost, high-gain programs such as energy efficiency and environmental audits in the industrial sectors responsible for the most pollution, protecting groundwater from wastewater discharges and hazardous wastes, and undertaking municipal wastewater investments for improving ambient water quality at low cost.

During the past twelve months numerous activities to implement the program have started:

- The Kyrgyz Republic is preparing a national environmental strategy organized around the themes of the Regional Action Plan.
- The Bank is reviewing a number of the strategy studies prepared jointly with borrowing countries, starting with Bulgaria, and is providing inputs.
- An Environmental Performance Review for Poland, led by the Organization for Economic Cooperation and Development (OECD) will draw on the Bank's 1992 Environmental Strategy Study for that country.

- An ambitious training plan has included a two-week seminar (organized jointly with the Japanese government) in Varna, Bulgaria, that brought together thirty-eight officials from, among others, the ministries of Finance and Economy, Health and Environment, and Industry in the Czech Republic, Hungary, Poland, Romania, and the Slovak Republic, as well as nine officials from the Japanese government. The "Environmental Action Programme for Central and Eastern Europe" is being translated into nineteen Eastern European languages, and a shorter version is being published this year.
- Two experts supported by the Swiss and U.S. governments are being placed in the Bank to work with the relevant country departments on the program.

The study *Toward an Environmental Strategy for Asia* (Brandon and Ramankutty 1993) describes the serious environmental problems that have accompanied Asia's impressive economic growth. The report notes that even though green issues such as deforestation and soil fertility loss continue to be serious, industrial and urban pollution are the rapidly emerging environmental challenge in the region. The study points out that conditions for addressing these problems are more favorable in Asia than in other parts of the world. Asia's advantages include high rates of domestic savings that provide public and private capital for investment in infrastructure and technology, rapid gains in poverty alleviation, wide application of sound macroeconomic principles that lays the groundwork for good environmental management, and increasing willingness by governments to deal with environmental problems.

Several areas of activity have been developed as a follow-up to the Asia strategy report. A clean-technology program begun under the MEIP and other environmental project work in China and India have been expanded into a free-standing effort. Regional workshops and country training oriented toward common pollution problems and analytical techniques for environmental agencies are being planned in South Asia. These efforts are supported by country analysis, priority setting, and improved coordination of activities both in country discussions and in Bank work on improving the policy dialogue that must underpin the environmental lending program.

Research on Pollution Control

Over the past year the Bank has undertaken numerous studies on the causes of and remedies for pollution. For example, a series of studies undertaken by the Bank's Policy Research Department (PRD) has reviewed data sources in OECD countries that could yield valuable insights for decisionmaking in the developing world. Useful data came from examining the costs of the U.S. Superfund program for cleaning up toxic wastes. These data reinforce the importance of setting standards carefully and examining both the benefits and the associated costs of proposed measures. The Industrial Pollution Projection System (IPPS) developed by the Bank has been used in a study to predict industrial pollution loads and costs of pollution abatement in several developing countries from data on the volume and composition of industrial activity. The IPPS has been applied in recent sector work in Indonesia, Mexico, and elsewhere.

Following up on earlier pollution-related work by PRD in Indonesia and Mexico, two major studies on pollution in Santiago were jointly undertaken by staff from the Latin America regional vice presidency, PRD, and ESD in collaboration with Chilean researchers. Applying the principles of environmental economics to air and water pollution, these studies assessed the benefits and costs of reducing transport-related air pollution and water pollution from domestic sewage. Using innovative approaches, the studies traced the links between sources of pollution and health impacts. They then compared the expected health benefits (in both physical and monetary terms) from pollution reduction with the costs of actions to reduce the pollution.

Progress has been made in updating and revising the Bank's existing guidelines on pollution control, originally issued in 1984 and 1988 (see box 1.7). A looseleaf binder on prevention and abatement of industrial pollution is being developed to provide guidance for use in projects financed by the Bank. The new documents will contain important information on major pollutants, commonly used pollution abatement technologies, and emerging concepts regarding pollution prevention, waste minimization, and cleaner production. This material is being developed in collaboration with the United Nations Industrial Development Organization (UNIDO) and the UNEP.

Natural Resource Management and the Rural Environment

Most poor people in the world still live in rural areas. Hence sound management of natural resources is fundamental to both national economic development and the well-being of billions of people. Bank lending that supports borrower efforts to promote sustainable natural resource management has increased, guided where appropriate by the policy papers on the forest sector (World Bank 1991a) and water resources management (World Bank 1993b), the latter issued in fiscal 1994.

Box 1.7. From Pollution Abatement to Pollution Prevention: The World Bank's Guidelines

In the last six to ten years, since the Bank first issued its Environmental Guidelines, many borrowing countries have developed their own environmental laws and regulations. In some cases, these are as strict as or stricter than corresponding regulations in OECD countries, but enforcement of environmental standards is often weak and compliance falls short of desired targets. Increasingly, both donor and borrower countries are looking to the Bank not so much for setting new environmental standards, as for providing guidance on how to make the best decisions in the face of scarce resources and competing claims.

The Bank and the IFC have joined forces to produce revised guidelines. By the end of fiscal 1995, more than thirty new guidelines are expected to be available, covering sectors from coal mining to leather tanning, from petroleum refining to dairy production. The guidelines will focus initially on investments in new plant. Instructions on how to deal with the complex issues associated with rehabilitation of existing plant will be added later in 1995. Simultaneously, an operations policy and associated Bank procedures are being prepared.

Some industrial projects inevitably require difficult decisions. For example, should a coal-fired power plant be required to meet strict standards for emissions of certain kinds of gases if these are emitted over the ocean or the desert and cause no harm to humans or ecosystems? Or, where a project provides financing to dozens of small industries, and enforcement of environmental practices is difficult or impossible, what are the potential

---

The Bank also continues to study the links between policy measures and the rate of use of natural resources.

Implementing New Policies for Forests and Water Resources

Forestry projects, especially those involving tropical moist forests, have recently received a great deal of attention because of increasing concern both inside and outside the Bank about global trends in deforestation, loss of biodiversity, and unsustainable patterns of natural resource use. This year a major review is being carried out to assess the lessons learned in implementing the policy paper on the forest sector. Since 1991 the World Bank has approved more than $2 billion in loans for twenty new forestry projects. These loans formed the basis for the implementation review.

The review has found that although the principles set forth in the policy paper have proved useful, the existence of powerful vested inter-

hazards that must be addressed because of the serious harm they could cause? However, in many cases, sound environmental practices make good business sense. As some of the IFC's work demonstrates (see box 6.3 in chapter 6), it has also become clear that a cleaner environment does not necessarily demand big investments. Instead, it requires a real commitment of managerial effort combined with simple investments in continually improving processes, installing controls, and monitoring performance. In many cases, these measures generate substantial economic benefits so that the environmental improvements involve no cost penalty. An important aspect of the Bank's economic and sector work is to recommend changes in prices, taxes, and other instruments to reinforce the link between economic efficiency and good environmental performance.

When the Bank issues its new operational policy directive, and the revised Environmental Guidelines become available for discussion with borrowing countries later in fiscal 1995 and 1996, these documents will emphasize a wider concern with pollution prevention and the adoption of cleaner production technologies that use fewer resources, are more energy efficient, and generate less waste, emissions, and effluents. The new guidelines will stress the human and organizational dimensions of environmental management. For example, they will make explicit the Bank's requirement that pollution control equipment be operated to design standards which, in turn, should permit the achievement of emission targets. The work on the guidelines is being undertaken in close collaboration with the Industry and Environment Programme of the UNEP, and UNIDO studies on clean technology.

ests in the forestry sector has made introduction of new approaches difficult. Often, officials of the very agencies responsible for reform have strong personal motives for resisting change. One solution is to broaden the circle of stakeholders for forest policy reform to include such groups as planning and finance agencies and NGOs.

The review has also found a significant transformation in Bank lending in the sector over the past three years, with forest protection and the quality of implementation receiving more emphasis in the technical content of projects. An equally important change is the style of project development. Increasingly, attention is being given to developing and implementing projects in close collaboration with both project beneficiaries and local populations. Project design has also evolved from focusing on a single output (for example, on fuelwood) to an approach that addresses policies and resource constraints across the forest sector. A project in India, for example, considered forest subsectors as diverse as energy, industrial wood, parks and protected areas, and agriculture and soil conservation. Such changes should help improve development impacts by promoting the efficient allocation of resources across the entire sector. Comprehensive sectorwide projects are being implemented in Bangladesh, China, Colombia, Indonesia, Lao PDR, and Tanzania, as well as in India.

Implementation of the Bank's policy on water resources management began in 1993, after Operational Policy 4.07, "Water Resources Management," was issued. The recommended first step is for countries to conduct a cross-sectoral water resources assessment for each river basin. That assessment of problems, needs, and opportunities then forms the basis for a water resources management strategy. The priority actions under that strategy are to be highlighted in the Bank country assistance strategy that will guide the lending program for different sectors. In Tanzania, one of the first countries to choose this approach, the stand-alone water resources management project was funded by the UNDP, the Danish government, and the Bank (see box 1.8). A comprehensive approach to developing a water resources management strategy was also begun as part of sectoral projects for strengthening water resources institutions in Trinidad and Tobago and for controlling industrial and mining pollution in Bolivia during fiscal 1994. Such strategies have also been included in a GEF-supported initiative to restore aquatic ecosystems and prevent pollution discharges in the Aral Sea Basin of Central Asia.

Implementing Natural Resource Management Projects

By the end of fiscal 1994 sixty-two natural resource management projects were under implementation, with total Bank commitments of nearly $3.2 billion. These operations include forest conservation and biodiversity protection, fisheries management, agricultural development (including integrated pest management), soil rehabilitation and land management, watershed management and rehabilitation, management of parks and protected areas, and natural resource management generally (see table 1.3). IDA credits are particularly important for natural resource management projects. The IDA donors have indicated that environmentally sustainable development should continue to be one of IDA's overriding objectives. "First IDA-10 Implementation Report: Review of the FY94 Program," to be distributed to the executive directors in September 1994, describes environmental activities in IDA borrowing countries in the past year.

The percentage of natural resource management projects experiencing implementation difficulties was roughly twice as high as for brown and institutional projects during fiscal 1994. The majority are experiencing at least some implementation delays or other problems, suggesting that

Box 1.8. Tanzania: Preparation of a Water Resources Management Strategy

In 1993 discussions among Tanzanian officials, the UNDP, and the World Bank resulted in the expansion of a planned water sector review into a development of a more comprehensive water resources management strategy, as recommended by the Bank's new water resources management policy. An interministerial steering committee was established to oversee the process, and workshops were held with ministry officials, external support agencies, and major stakeholders to develop coordination. A nine-person technical team was seconded from various Tanzanian ministries to prepare an assessment of water resource problems, needs, and priorities in each river basin of Tanzania. The assessment included water supply and sanitation needs, industrial water pollution, water-related health issues, groundwater contamination, overfishing, coastal zone protection, irrigation issues, land use topics, data needs, and regulatory and institutional issues.

This approach of supporting the Tanzanian team in conducting the interdisciplinary assessment provides a broader understanding of the conflicts in water and land use and encourages cooperation between team members representing different sectoral interests and their government ministries. Following this multidisciplinary assessment, priorities can be determined, potential complementarities between different sectoral actions and protection of the water environment can be identified, and actions for achieving these complementary benefits can be initiated as part of a strategy. For example, such an analysis may result in a recommendation that less water be diverted for irrigation so that downstream aquatic ecosystems can be sustained or that agricultural programs for erosion or pollution control be targeted only to certain priority basins. It may mean that funding for the needs of coastal zone management take precedence over certain sectoral programs so that fragile resources valuable for tourism can be protected. The priorities in different basins will be different and must be determined in a participatory manner with affected stakeholders. During fiscal 1994 the water resource assessment phase was completed in Tanzania, and the formulation of strategies has begun.

green projects are generally more difficult to execute than pollution reduction projects. The eight projects having the most serious problems are located in Africa, South Asia, and Latin America and the Caribbean. Five—including one in Haiti that was subsequently canceled—involve forest resource management; the other three involve fisheries, land use rationalization, and agricultural development and natural resource management. According to recent Bank supervision missions, two or more

Table 1.3. Portfolio of Natural Resource Management Projects, by Region, End of Fiscal 1994

Region or country	Number of projects	Total commitments (millions of dollars)
Sub-Saharan Africa	18	438
East Asia and the Pacific	9	820
Indonesia	5	155
South Asia	14	657
India	6	433
Pakistan	4	118
Europe and Central Asia	3	272
Latin America and the Caribbean	13	851
Brazil	5	517
Middle East and North Africa	4	144
Total	61	3,182

Note: The four countries with the largest portfolios are shown separately but are included in the portfolios of their respective regions.
Source: World Bank data.

of these operations have experienced significant problems with project management, legal agreements, counterpart funding, or procurement.

Despite these difficulties, implementation seems to be proceeding smoothly in a number of projects, including natural resource management operations in Egypt, Pakistan, and the Philippines; forestry and watershed management projects in Algeria and Tunisia; and a rural land management operation in Pakistan. Projects that, while experiencing some implementation problems, seem to be well on the way to achieving positive outcomes include a series of land management and watershed protection projects in southern Brazil (see box 1.9 for details). Strong beneficiary, local community, and private sector involvement, together with capable and experienced public sector institutions, appear to be critical factors in the comparative success of these operations.

New Lending for the Green Agenda in Fiscal 1994

During fiscal 1994 just under $900 million was committed for thirteen projects addressing rural environmental problems, seven of which were IDA credits. These operations encompass forest management and biodiversity conservation, water resource and watershed management, marine and coastal zone management, and improvement in the ecology of agricultural practices. Examples include the following (see table 1.4 for a complete list).

The Third Forestry Development Project in Bhutan ($5 million) supports the government's efforts to develop and implement a sustain-

Box 1.9. Managing Rural Land and Watersheds in Brazil

Over the past several years the Bank has been supporting a series of innovative land management projects in south-central Brazil. The first two were approved in 1989 and 1990 for the states of Paraná and Santa Catarina, and two more for São Paulo state and Mato Grosso do Sul are due next year. All four operations seek to increase agricultural production and rural incomes by encouraging farmers at the microcatchment level to adopt sustainable forms of land management and soil and water conservation. To that end, the projects provide support for reducing soil loss, erosion, and the associated siltation and pollution of rivers and other watercourses. Technical improvements on the farms and the realignment of rural roads to correct poor drainage round out the plans.

In addition, the projects promote agricultural practices such as crop rotation, green manuring, alternative cultivation practices, small-scale mechanization, and weed and pest control. Support for these changes is provided by rural extension, land use monitoring and control, farm-level incentives for improved land management, soil conservation and pollution abatement, erosion control works along rural roads, forestry development, and natural resource protection. To help improve land management at the farm and watershed levels, each project establishes a soil conservation fund. The forestry development and natural resource protection components include strengthening of state forestry institutions, production of seedlings for reforestation for both commercial and conservation purposes, and improved management of state parks and biological reserves. The projects also emphasize training public and private sector technicians and farmers in modern land management and soil conservation practices.

The two projects currently under implementation are proceeding well, with the Paraná operation, two years short of completion, having already surpassed key project targets. Both are expected to produce significant positive and sustainable results.

A key feature of these projects is extensive local community and farmer participation in the planning and implementation of watershed management activities. The experience thus far in Paraná also demonstrates the importance of taking a decentralized approach to the selection of microcatchments and the definition of interventions in each one. Another important feature is the choice of interventions that generate both economic (that is, increased productivity and farm incomes) and environmental (reduced soil erosion) benefits. The project has received several boosts toward its success. There is effective coordination and private sector involvement at the municipal level, including on-farm technical assistance by private extension services. The project grew out of an existing state initiative, PMISA (the Integrated Water and Management Program). "Pilot" watersheds are monitored to demonstrate the benefits of coordinated farm-level soil conservation and microcatchment management to farmers and government officials throughout the state and elsewhere in Brazil.

Table 1.4. Projects for Natural Resource Management, Fiscal 1994
(millions of dollars)

Country	Project	Loan/credit (L/C)	World Bank financing	Total project cost
Bhutan	Third Forestry Development	C	5	9
China	Forest Resource Development and Protection	C	200	356
	Loess Plateau Watershed Rehabilitation	C	150	249
Colombia	Natural Resource Management Program	L	39	65
India	Andhra Pradesh Forestry	C	77	89
	Forestry Research Education and Extension	C	47	56
Indonesia	National Watershed Management and Conservation	L	57	488
Lao PDR	Forest Management and Conservation	C	9	20
Pakistan	Balochistan Natural Resource Management	C	15	18
Paraguay	Natural Resources Management	L	50	79
Poland	Forest Development Support	L	146	335
Tunisia	Northwest Mountainous Areas Development	L	28	51
Uruguay	Natural Resources Management and Irrigation Development	L	41	74
Total new lending			864	1,889

Source: World Bank data.

able way of protecting, managing, and using its forest resources in line with its national development priorities. The project will (a) adopt multiple-use management of forest lands; (b) involve local people in managing the forest to meet their basic requirements, as well as increase the level of economic activity through social forestry practices; (c) rehabilitate degraded forests to maintain their economic and environmental benefits; and (d) improve the planning and implementation capacity of government organizations. A social forestry plan, following the government's Community Forestry Rules, will involve local people in forest resource management through a system of shared benefits and responsibilities.

The National Watershed Management and Conservation Project in Indonesia ($57 million) seeks to raise the living standards of poor upland farmers by improving and restoring the productive potential of their resource base. At the same time, it will enhance watershed environmental quality and protect downstream watershed resources. In addition to conservation, regreening, and reforestation activities, the project includes a significant training and extension component. Because large numbers of male farm laborers migrate seasonally to urban centers, women currently do most of the work in the upland farming areas. The project will therefore provide women with the same training as men and will give them greater representation in village participatory land use planning. A concerted effort will also be made to remove gender-specific barriers to participation in, for example, extension activities.

The overall objective of the Forest Development Support Project in Poland ($146 million) is to assist the government in executing its Program for the Development of Selected Forestry Branches and Protection of Ecosystems in National Parks for 1993–97, thereby protecting Poland's forest ecological capital and providing social benefits. A forest management component seeks to reverse the effects of past damage and misuse; to increase the vitality of forest stands, particularly to help with air pollution; to restore pollution-damaged forests to protect watersheds and prevent soil erosion; to afforest land previously converted to agriculture; and to conserve genetic resources. A conservation component is planned for Poland's national parks. An institutional-development component will provide technical support and equipment, help develop a strategy for environmentally sound forest use, and support the creation of an information system, including a geographic information system (GIS) integrated into the planning system.

The Natural Resources Management Project in Paraguay ($50 million) has four main objectives: (a) to establish the institutional framework necessary for dealing with the major agricultural and natural resource problems of the project area; (b) to generate information through research and implement a system of natural resource protection; (c) to assist small farmers in establishing sustainable agricultural production systems and conservation measures; and (d) to encourage the direct participation of the local population in project implementation. The project would increase the productivity and incomes of small farmers, enabling them to accumulate capital.

Technical Assistance and Research on Natural Resource Management

A REGIONAL STRATEGY FOR AFRICA. A majority of the Bank's borrowing countries in Sub-Saharan Africa have now completed NEAPs or equivalent documents, and some countries—Ghana, the Gambia, Mauritius, Madagascar, and the Seychelles—have already begun implementing them. Following closely on these completed strategies, the Bank has begun a two-year process of defining a regional strategy for environmentally sustainable development in Sub-Saharan Africa. The strategy will build on and continue to generate consensus behind national environmental plans. To help the countries address common problems more effectively, the Bank has begun compiling common lessons from environmental experience over the past thirty years. From this starting point a broader process has been launched with the participation of prominent African and non-African institutions, universities, NGOs, and bilateral and multilateral agencies.

The African ESD strategy incorporates the main features of Agenda 21 but gives special focus to a number of key issues, the links between them, and their geographic dimension. To define the strategy, a scenario for Africa in 2025 has been projected as a goal, taking stock of the current situation and identifying the best transition course for minimizing environmental, social, and economic costs while maximizing benefits. Teams inside and outside the Bank have been organized to examine population dynamics in relation to the environment; knowledge, information, and dissemination; natural resource management; and the urban environment. Special attention is paid to planning, policies, capacity building, institutional development, and communication. Thematic and cross-cutting papers are being prepared for workshops throughout Sub-Saharan Africa (see the discussion on coastal management below).

COASTAL ZONE MANAGEMENT. As more and more people crowd into the coastal zones of all countries, the wise management of coastal resources becomes increasingly important. Technical assistance on coastal and marine issues is therefore featured in Bank work in several regions supported by GEF projects, as well as in regular Bank lending and sector work. In Latin America, for example, support is under way for operations in the coastal regions of Colombia and Ecuador. Extensive work has also been devoted to helping prepare NEAPs for countries in Central America and the Caribbean. Some of these initiatives have been problematic, as the interaction of a large number of resource users in the coastal zone often complicates implementation. In several cases, Bank studies have examined the difficulties, such as the tradeoffs between ecological and economic goals in the management of marine parks in the Caribbean.

A major challenge is to manage the natural capital of coastal resources so that a society can live on the annual "interest" and not consume its "principal." The Bank is preparing technical guidelines for integrated coastal zone management (ICZM) and has this year issued an "Environmental Assessment Sourcebook Update" (no. 7) on coastal zone management. ICZM attempts to balance the physical requirements for the continued health of coastal zones with the competing pressures from current and future economic development of these fragile areas.

The Bank is supporting improved management of the extensive coast-lines of several countries in Asia. An ICZM plan is being developed in Indonesia, for example, and Viet Nam is planning the use and management of its coastal area, especially its rich fisheries and extensive mangrove forests. Coastal and marine issues are also important in countries such as India, the Republic of Korea, and Thailand.

Africa's long coastline and heavily populated coastal areas make it increasingly the focus of much coastal and marine work. Coastal resources are used for recreation and tourism as well as for production of fish and other products, making coastal zone management a prime issue for the regional strategy for Africa discussed above. Mozambique is an example of a country where coastal issues, especially ICZM, are prominent.

FOREST AND LAND MANAGEMENT IN LATIN AMERICA. A number of sector studies and research programs have focused on natural resources this year. In Chile a study was carried out on the options for managing native forests in the southern part of the country, where there is strong pressure to convert the remaining native forests to plantations of fast-growing imported species. The study examined management options for the native forests, comparing the returns from plantation, mixed-species, and introduced-species forests. The protection of endangered species as part of the national park system and the returns from other uses, including benefits from recreational and tourism development, were also assessed. The study found ways of meeting legitimate needs for biodiversity protection while allowing commercial development of certain native forestlands.

Many rural environmental issues in Latin America stem from the uncontrolled development of the frontier. A Bank report to be presented to the Board in fiscal 1995, "Brazil: The Management of Agriculture, Rural Development and Natural Resources," examines the reasons for the loss of important natural capital. The report forms the basis for discussions with the government, as well as for regional workshops involving NGOs, farmers' groups, and other stakeholders on the problems of unsustainable agricultural practices, the environmental consequences of insecure land titles, and perverse legislation. During fiscal 1994 environmentally related economic and sector work was completed for Costa Rica, El Salvador, Mexico, and other countries. Broader examinations of the sources, nature, and impact of deforestation and of the factors affecting the management of biodiversity in Latin America and elsewhere are being carried out by the Policy Research Department.

Initial results from one study identified a "Kuznets curve" for deforestation whereby the rate of deforestation increases up to a certain income level (about $5,000 per capita) and then declines.

Supporting National Environmental Management

In addition to supporting reduction of urban and industrial pollution and management of rural natural resources, the Bank supports borrower efforts to improve environmental management through new and continuing lending operations for environmental institution building and in the preparation of national environmental strategies. The Bank also increasingly incorporates environmental concerns into its country economic studies and associated policy dialogue, provides assistance for the improvement of national legal and institutional frameworks, and seeks to improve environmental information, natural resource accounting, and the valuation of environmental costs and benefits.

Implementing Institution-Building Projects

At the end of fiscal 1994 sixteen environmental institution-building projects were under implementation, involving total commitments of over $530 million (table 1.5 indicates their regional distribution). All of these projects were approved after 1989. The five African projects were the direct results of NEAPs (the Gambia, Ghana, Madagascar, and Mauritius) or Bank country environmental sector work (Nigeria). All sixteen operations include significant training, studies, and technical assistance components.

As in the case of active natural resource management projects, most of these projects are facing tough implementation challenges because of the difficulties inherent in strengthening institutions charged with influenc-

Table 1.5. Portfolio of Environmental Institution-Building Projects, by Region, End of Fiscal 1994

Region	Number of projects	Total commitments (millions of dollars)
Sub-Saharan Africa	5	84
East Asia and the Pacific	4	212
South Asia	1	29
Europe and Central Asia	1	18
Latin America and the Caribbean	4	184
Middle East and North Africa	1	6
Total	16	533

Source: World Bank data.

ing behavior across several sectors or jurisdictions (as box 1.10 illustrates for Africa). Only three such projects were found to be largely problem free by recent supervision missions. Competent executing agencies, an enabling macroeconomic environment (and thus reliable counterpart funding), and strong borrower commitment to project goals help to explain the comparatively smooth implementation of these three projects to date.

Various projects illustrate the challenges encountered by this segment of the Bank's environmental portfolio. The National Environment Project in Brazil, approved in February 1990, suffered delays in implementation from the beginning and, like similar first-generation institution-building operations in Madagascar, Mauritius, and Poland, required partial restructuring after a midterm review. Two other projects, in Mexico and Nigeria, each required a full year to become effective (the average for the active environmental portfolio is slightly over eight months). Projects in Bolivia, Chile, Madagascar, Mexico, and Nigeria were affected by significant political or institutional changes soon after approval by the Bank's Board.

Because the principal executing agencies of environmental institution-building projects are often new or relatively weak, a range of problems— inadequate staffing, internal conflicts, unclear interagency division of labor, unfamiliarity with Bank policies and procedures, difficulties with procurement and with hiring of consultants, shortages of counterpart funding, and less-than-full borrower ownership of project objectives— has made the early years of implementation difficult. In some cases these difficulties have been exacerbated by country macroeconomic problems, complex project designs, and the need to coordinate multiple donors. More recent environmental institution-building operations have sought to avoid many of these problems by simplifying project design, strengthening borrower commitment, and increasing support to borrowers during project preparation and implementation.

New Lending for Environmental Institution Building in Fiscal 1994

Three projects, representing loans of $99 million for improving country institutional capacity for both the brown and the green agendas, were approved in fiscal 1994 (see table 1.6).

The primary objective of the Capacity Building for Environmental Management Technical Assistance Project in the Gambia ($3 million) is to strengthen the country's National Environment Agency (NEA) and other relevant entities. These agencies will develop a system for environmental planning and management to ensure the full integration of environmental concerns into the social and economic development process. The program, which includes technical assistance and training of

---

Box 1.10. Strengthening Environmental Institutions in Africa: The Challenges of Implementation

Environmental institution-building projects tend to focus on a few common objectives: (a) to strengthen institutional capability for policymaking, planning and design, implementation, and monitoring and evaluation; (b) to develop management capacity for more sustainable use of the country's environmental resources; (c) to support environmental research and studies and develop environmental information systems or networks; and (d) to provide technical assistance and training. In Ghana, Madagascar, Mauritius, and Nigeria these operations cover a broad spectrum of agencies and institutions.

Implementation experience with these projects reflects the factors that typically make environmental institution building difficult. The need for new institutions tends to arise alongside the need for new technical skills—in areas such as environmental information or ecosystem management. Moreover, experience in Africa suggests that work programs for environmental institutions should be limited to a few essential functions. Otherwise, inexperienced agencies may take on more than they can manage.

In both Madagascar and Nigeria the key public sector institutions under the projects were new, with little operational experience and, consequently, little influence on the civil service structure. Their mandates were untested, their staff not well trained, and their role in national development policy planning not yet clearly established. Partly as a result, both projects have suffered slow implementation. In contrast, the implementing agency for the Ghana project was established in 1972 and is a semiautonomous institution long familiar with Bank policies and procedures.

The tendency toward complex design and highly ambitious objectives is common in institution-building projects. These projects usually require communication and collaboration among multiple donors and implementing agencies. As a result, simplicity of organizational design and management for project implementation is often difficult to realize. The Madagascar project, for example, has six components and thirty-two subcomponents and required the creation of a multidonor secretariat to coordinate plans among the project's nine cofinancers.

The challenges of design complexity can be compounded by insufficient government commitment, changes in management, or poor administration. In Madagascar, for instance, the key implementing agency was moved from a central point in the government to a sectoral ministry shortly after project approval, thereby reducing its capacity to mobilize other public sector institutions. Similarly, in Nigeria the central government agency has experienced significant turnover in senior management since the project was approved, and political instability in the country has further frustrated effective performance. The Madagascar project has an advantage, however, in having a more fully articulated NEAP that was worked out through a broad participatory process and is associated with a private sector and national NGOs that are making good progress.

**Table 1.6. Free-standing Projects for Environmental Institution
Building, Fiscal 1994**
(millions of dollars)

Country	Project	Loan/credit (L/C)	World Bank financing	Total project cost
The Gambia	Capacity Building for Environmental Management Technical Assistance	C	3	5
Korea	Environmental Technical Development	L	90	156
Morocco	Environmental Management	L	6	11
Total new lending			99	172

Source: World Bank data.

local staff in the NEA and its collaborating agencies, is designed to
provide continuous technical guidance and gradual development of
capacity without the sustained presence of international advisers. The
program will also help the NEA develop ties with the technical and
sectoral ministries involved in national development so that they can
integrate environmental issues into their operations and work together
on issues of overlapping responsibility. The NEA will also be encouraged
to work closely with NGOs and community organizations.

In recent years the Republic of Korea has developed environmental
policies and created the institutional and legal frameworks needed
to implement them. There is urgent need now for research and development to improve the technical understanding of environmental
problems and to develop the technology for solving them. The research institutes are well staffed with highly qualified researchers,
but shortages of up-to-date equipment inhibit the development of
advanced research capability. The Environment Technology Development Project ($90 million) will provide equipment and overseas training,
visiting experts, and library materials. The project will help the Ministry
of Environment take a stronger lead in coordinating and monitoring
environmental planning activities by improving its monitoring capability and its ability to assess the economic impact of environmental
activities.

The Environmental Management Project in Morocco ($6 million) will
help the government establish environmental institutions and promul-
gate environmental laws. Morocco is experiencing serious degradation
of its natural resources (groundwater, soil, and forests) and loss of flora
and fauna. (Of 100 mammal species that have been identified, 40 have
disappeared.) An additional burden on the country is the rapidly increasing urban, agricultural, and industrial pollution. The program will

develop a combination of command-and-control and market-driven mechanisms to enable Morocco to meet European standards, with an eye to a free trade agreement with the European Union (EU). The program also includes an environmental education and awareness program outside the formal education system.

National Environmental Strategies

National development policies need to take into account activities that depend on the natural resource base. In addition, there are often important links between the brown and green environmental agendas—for instance, the potential impacts of improved rural watershed management and conservation on urban water supply and quality—that require a broader, cross-sectoral analytical, and policy framework. The Bank has been actively encouraging its borrowers to develop national policies that include appropriate environmental strategies and objectives. Where such strategies and objectives become an integral part of the development planning and decisionmaking process, policymakers are better able to take issues of environmental sustainability into account in the country's overall development agenda.

Since the late 1980s the Bank has been actively assisting borrower governments to prepare national environmental strategies. These strategies are commonly built on environmental profiles, national conservation strategies, and sectoral and economic analyses undertaken by the countries themselves, sometimes with the help of international and bilateral organizations. Since 1990 the Bank has sought to strengthen the environmental sustainability of development programs. As part of this strategy, it has formalized its commitment to encourage and support countries in their efforts to develop NEAPs or equivalent documents.[1]

NATIONAL ENVIRONMENTAL ACTION PLANS. The NEAP has become an increasingly important tool for developing a country's environmental strategy. The Bank has supported NEAPs through policy dialogue, sector work (including Bank-prepared country environmental strategy papers), technical assistance, and project lending. Even though borrowers are responsible for preparing NEAPs, Bank staff have been involved in launching the process, monitoring progress, arranging for technical support, and, in many cases, preparing investment projects identified as part of the NEAP process. Once a plan is completed, its findings are factored into country priorities and into the plans of the Bank and other donors for projects, sector studies, and the policy dialogue.

The NEAP process is a continuing rather than a one-time effort. To strengthen its effectiveness, the process requires public participation in the formulation and implementation of the plan. Completed plans are updated periodically as new information emerges and priorities change.

Most active IDA borrowers (not counting new members) completed their plans during fiscal 1993 and fiscal 1994. During fiscal 1994 about twenty-five additional NEAPs or equivalent documents were completed by active IDA-eligible countries (twenty-two had been completed previously). New IDA members (for example, the Kyrgyz Republic) are initiating NEAP processes with Bank encouragement. IBRD borrowers continue to prepare and complete NEAPs, which will provide the foundation for future IDA and IBRD lending. This year also saw the initiation of more issue-specific plans (for example, on desertification, climate change, and biodiversity), which are being integrated into the overall NEAPs. It is anticipated that, as agreed by IDA donors, over the next two years countries will prepare national sustainable development strategies, of which the NEAPs and sector-specific plans will form a part.

REVIEW OF COUNTRY STRATEGIES. The World Bank is currently conducting a study, to be completed in fiscal 1995, on country environmental strategies, including NEAPs. The study identifies lessons from the preparation of country strategies and suggests methods that can be used to formulate more effective strategies in the future. It will offer practical suggestions to governments and agencies charged with the development of environmental policies and investment strategies at the national level. Case studies from both developing and industrial countries will be used to identify best practice and workable solutions that set priorities, strengthen institutional capacity, and improve the integration of environmental concerns into national economic decisionmaking.

Experience with the preparation of country environmental strategies has varied considerably from country to country. Such plans need to be country driven and participatory, involving the government and as many affected segments of society as possible. It is also true that national plans are more feasible to implement where priorities are clear. Achieving both objectives simultaneously has sometimes proved difficult. Other important factors contributing to the success of national strategies include identifying major underlying causes and problems, prioritizing them and finding ways to solve them, and improving institutional performance. Experience also suggests that planning and economic ministries should be closely involved and shows that there have been weaknesses in priority setting, policy and instrument selection, and institutional analysis.

Part of the country environmental strategy review concerns how well NEAPs address urban environmental issues. While almost all NEAPs deal with urban environmental issues to some extent, the treatment is frequently partial and ad hoc. One reason may be that most NEAPs have been prepared for IDA countries, where urban pollution problems are generally of lower priority than natural resource management issues. The most commonly identified urban environmental problems are inadequate solid waste management, water supply, and sanitation. A number of NEAPs have identified water pollution and air pollution from cars and buses, settlements in hazard-prone areas, and loss of cultural assets. Industrial pollution and disposal of hazardous waste were also mentioned in several cases.

A general criticism of NEAPs and equivalent documents is that they rarely address the links between economic policies and the environment. This crucial step in making environmental concerns an integral part of countrywide economic policymaking is discussed more fully in chapter 3.

Integrating the Environment into Bank Country Economic Work

COUNTRY ECONOMIC STUDIES. The trend toward including environmental issues in Bank CEM and other country economic studies continues. CEM are analyses of overall country economic conditions on the basis of which strategies for improvement can be derived. The environment is increasingly seen to play a critical role in economic performance and is featured in CEM. Bank country assistance strategies (CASs) are also devoting greater attention to environmental concerns, and this tendency is expected to intensify in the future as more borrowers complete their environmental action plans. CEM with a major environmental focus that were completed in fiscal 1994 include the following:

Eritrea. The first CEM for Eritrea was prepared in connection with that country's imminent entry into the World Bank's membership. It highlights environmental rehabilitation and protection as an important issue, reflecting the government's concern that environmental issues be incorporated. The CEM includes a comprehensive analysis of land degradation and water resource management and highlights the broad actions needed to guide future growth in environmentally sustainable directions.

India. The CEM observes that over a relatively short time the government of India has developed the legal framework, institutions, and programs for dealing with environmental issues. However, the analysis reveals that in order to consolidate the progress achieved thus far, the amount of resources dedicated to the environment should be increased. Given tight budgets, it is even more important to establish clear priorities, develop more efficient and effective strategies, and encourage better implementation by the institutions responsible. The NEAP that was adopted this year is a vital first step toward these goals.

Indonesia. The CEM for Indonesia, completed this year, drew on the Bank's environment report for that country, which focused specifically on the links between environmental issues and economic development (see box 1.11).

Maldives. An Updating Economic Memorandum identifies the environment as one of the priority areas of concern. The memorandum

---

Box 1.11. Linking the Environment and Development in Indonesia

A recent Bank report on environment and development challenges in Indonesia reviewed natural resource management and pollution control issues in eight sectors and subsectors, taking into account political, social, economic, and environmental issues and trends. The main conclusions of the report are that growth and development over the medium term will depend increasingly on Indonesia's key natural resources and ecosystems and that urban and industrial pollution threaten prospects both for future growth and for improvements in health and human welfare. Meeting these challenges will require making environmental issues and concerns central to the development process. The report has already been used as an input for preparation of Indonesia's Second 25-Year and Sixth 5-Year Development Plans.

The report observes that because financial and administrative resources in Indonesia—as in developing countries generally—are limited, the government will not be able to address every environmental issue with the same degree of urgency. It therefore stresses that the establishment of priorities should be based on a careful assessment of the costs and benefits involved. On the basis of "order of magnitude" estimates of such benefits and costs, the report identifies several areas that merit special attention: water supply and sanitation, solid waste management, and vehicle emissions in the country's main urban centers; industrial pollution control, especially on Java; and the management of forest concessions in the outer islands. Other important issues include the protection of regional and local watersheds and coastal and marine ecosystems and the sustainable management of nature forests, areas that are significant from both a national and global—particularly for biodiversity conservation—standpoint.

The report also highlights the challenges of implementation. While concluding that institutional shortcomings are a serious impediment to sound environmental management, it recognizes that centralized government planning is increasingly ill suited for dealing with many environmental problems, and it emphasizes the need to enhance participation in the definition of environmental priorities and to adopt "creative interim solutions" to overcome existing institutional constraints.

concludes that the future prospects of two important sectors of the economy, fisheries and tourism, are dependent on improved environmental management and the protection of coral habitats.

Other countries. CEMs with an environmental emphasis were also concluded this year for Kazakhstan, the Kyrgyz Republic, Papua New Guinea, and Tajikistan.

National Legal and Institutional Assistance

One of the most important instruments for translating environmental policies into action is the *law*—not only as a means of command and control but also as a framework for economic planning and market mechanisms.[2] Yet the legal process, which ought to facilitate progress toward sustainable patterns of development, is often ill adapted to the scale and pace of economic and social change—and the degree of public participation and transparency of decisionmaking—required for this purpose. To overcome the obstacles created by inadequate or outdated laws and to make full use of the opportunities available through innovative legal techniques, legal reform can be essential, and the Bank is assisting several of its borrowers with this task.

Environmental law covers a wide spectrum ranging from broad cross-sectoral elements (such as those associated with evaluation of environmental risk) to distinct sectoral rules and standards for pollutant emissions, product quality, resource use quotas, and so on. While interdisciplinary legal principles for environmental management are usually to be preferred over sector-specific regulations, laws become effective only to the extent that they succeed in changing administrative and technical behavior on the ground. It thus may be necessary, for example, to coordinate the application of environmental provisions with that of legal regimes dealing with property rights, land tenure, taxation, local government, and customary institutions and practices. Furthermore, there is an increasing emphasis on the use of economic incentives and disincentives (such as effluent charges) and other market-oriented mechanisms (such as "ecolabels") to bring about environmental change. All these measures need a legal basis to become fully operational.

Even though innovative legal techniques—such as environmental impact assessments (EIAs), first developed in the United States in the late 1960s—tend to spread rapidly around the globe, there is no universal "model law" suitable for all locations. For instance, when the GEF needed local legal institutions to ensure the long-term continuity of projects for protected areas, these bodies had to be set up through a national fiduciary fund in one jurisdiction, a civil law foundation in another, and an offshore charitable trust in yet another country. The technical assistance in environmental law provided by the World Bank therefore does not promote one-way North-South transfers of legal concepts but makes use of local expertise, including the South-South exchange of lessons learned in adaptation to change.

Legal technical assistance can contribute to gradually harmonizing environmental standards between countries and can facilitate efforts for implementing existing international standards. For example, the GEF-financed Wider Caribbean Initiative for Ship-Generated Waste is assisting fourteen Caribbean countries in bringing their waste management laws up to the requirements of the International Convention for the Prevention of Pollution from Ships. It has long been recognized that the effective operation of international environmental agreements is crucially dependent on an appropriate legal and institutional framework at the national level.

Over the past twenty years the World Bank has provided assistance to more than sixty countries in the field of environment-related law and regulations, usually in one of three ways:

- In the context of specific loan or credit agreements, where the enactment, revision, or implementation of environmental laws in the borrowing country is considered an essential project component. These actions are sometimes mandated by Bank environment-related operational policies and are often sanctioned by explicit provisions and covenants in the project documents—for example, regarding the legal status of protected forest areas in Uganda, in connection with an IDA development credit agreement for forestry rehabilitation.
- In free-standing projects designed primarily to strengthen national and local institutions for environmental management and pollution control. For example, the current Environmental Institutional Development Project in Chile includes legal technical assistance for the preparation of a new environmental law (formally promulgated this year), the establishment of an information system for environmental laws and regulations, and the provision of training in environmental law.
- As part of the preparation and implementation of national environmental plans and strategies, which frequently involve taking an inventory of existing environmental legislation to identify gaps and shortcomings with an eye to improvement and reform. The environmental action plan for Mauritius called for such an inventory, which in turn provided the basis for a project financed jointly by the UNDP and the World Bank to develop the legal and institutional framework for environmental and natural resource manage-

ment. The environment strategy paper for Romania included specific proposals for draft legislation, which were subsequently taken into account by the government in new laws and regulations.

The following are recent examples of environment-related laws and regulations promulgated with Bank assistance.

Chile's Basic Environmental Law (Ley de Bases del Medio Ambiente), approved in March 1994, provides measures for environmental protection, including environmental education and environmental impact assessment, and a chapter on public participation. Other interesting features include a mandatory environmental management plan for natural resources and special provisions on the right of inspection. An Environmental Protection Fund was created to finance the protection of the environment.

In *Gabon*, Law No. 16/93 (August 1993) on the Protection and Enhancement of the Environment provides a general framework aimed at preserving nature and using natural resources sustainably, controlling pollution, improving living conditions, and harmonizing development and environmental protection. The ministry in charge of the environment is to promote and implement a policy of rational management and exploitation, supported by planning, training, and institutional measures for classifying and zoning polluting industries, listing toxic chemicals, conducting EIAs, and granting permits and licenses.

The Gambia's National Environmental Management Act, enacted in April 1994, is the product of a broadly participatory effort under the country's Environmental Action Plan. The act creates a general institutional framework for subsequent, more specific, environmental laws and regulations. It provides for a National Environmental Agency under the political leadership of a National Environmental Management Council made up of the president (as chair) and key ministers. The agency receives technical support from advisory committees, planners, and an environmental inspector. Offenses are to be referred to courts, which can order forfeiture of goods, cancellation of permits, and performance of community service as penalties.

In June 1993 *Honduras* enacted a comprehensive General Environmental Law (Ley General del Ambiente) that provides the country's legal and institutional framework. The main features of the new law are (a) the creation of the offices of Environmental Secretariat and attorney general of the environment; (b) the requirement of EIAs for public or private-sponsored projects; (c) the requirement to preserve historical, cultural, and artistic values; (d) the identification of environmental violations; and (e) a requirement for public participation. The law also contains provisions for the protection of specific environmental resources such as air, water, and flora and fauna.

In the *Lao PDR*, Decree No. 169/PM (November 1993) on the management and use of forests and forestland provides an interim legal framework for institutional reform in the forestry sector and establishes a centrally unified structure and national jurisdiction over a resource that formerly was a provincial responsibility. The law emphasizes sustainable management and use, with incentives for reforestation. Implementing decrees still need to spell out participatory mechanisms for protecting traditional access rights and the procedures for registering operations, maximizing forestry revenues, and controlling illegal timber trade.

In June 1993 *Moldova* enacted its first comprehensive law on the environment. The Law on Environmental Protection identifies the rights and responsibilities of government agencies, businesses, and citizens toward the environment and natural resources. Some of its features are the establishment of an ecological fund, definition of methods for conducting environmental assessments, legal coverage of all surface and ground waters (including aquatic ecosystem management), and express reference to certain international environmental obligations.

A significant factor in the World Bank's program in environmental law—and one way of ensuring the sustainability of new legislation—is professional training. In addition to providing the legal training called for in specific projects, Bank staff have contributed to several specialized training programs in environmental management for lawyers and civil servants from developing countries. These include courses and seminars organized by the UNEP, the United Nations Institute for Training and Research (UNITAR), the International Development Law Institute, the International Law Institute, and the Hague Academy of International Law.

Measuring Environmental Progress

Environmental data and indicators of sustainability are needed to make sound policy and operational decisions about environmental and natural resource management. Yet even in industrial countries data are often incomplete or site-specific, making accurate application to the country as a whole difficult. To overcome such deficiencies, several Bank efforts are under way in close collaboration with national governments, other international agencies, academia, and NGOs.

INDICATORS OF ENVIRONMENTALLY SUSTAINABLE DEVELOPMENT. The Bank is adapting the OECD core set of environmental performance indicators for its own use. An initial proposal, "Towards Environmentally Sustainable Development," was presented to the General Assembly of the World Conservation Union (IUCN) in January 1994 and was circulated extensively in the international community. An amended version of the framework is currently being finalized on the basis of comments received. Like the OECD, the Bank is using its framework both to compile best-available indicators in the short term and to build consensus about priorities for further work. The Bank's framework is designed with rapid assessments in mind. It is considered a complement to ongoing efforts by the Bank and others to promote environmental satellite accounts in conformity with the new United Nations System of National Accounts and more rigorous approaches to valuation.

RAPID ASSESSMENTS. For many environmental issues, rapid assessment techniques and short-cut methods have been used to compile an initial set of indicators at the national level. It is expected that rough baseline figures can be compiled for most Bank borrowers during the next fiscal year. Although the results will be too crude for many purposes, they should flag key problem areas, including major deficiencies in basic data collection. New indicators are in preparation for natural capital (with commercial and noncommercial aspects treated separately), deforestation, air and water quality, "green" per capita income, and an adjustment to measures of saving that includes environmental loss or gain. Where possible the Bank is relying on recent work by others, such as the index of natural disasters compiled by the United Nations Disaster Relief Organization (UNDRO).

ECOSYSTEM-BASED INDICATORS. Frameworks and rapid assessments are useful for identifying problems, but policy formulation and implementation normally require an additional "bottom-up" approach to data and indicators. These indicators depend on monitoring each ecosystem, which may be subnational or may cross national boundaries. For example, Bank work on land quality indicators will first develop indicators relevant for moist-tropical savannahs, intensively irrigated areas, and overgrazed pastoral zones. For successful project design and implementation, such subnational and regional efforts must be linked to national indicators. The Bank is exploring ways in which technical targets and policy-oriented goals can provide the links, building on techniques pioneered by the Netherlands Ministry for Public Health, Spatial Planning, and the Environment.

COLLABORATION AND CAPACITY BUILDING. Initiatives are under way throughout the international community to help developing economies improve environmental data and indicators. The Bank assigns high priority to ensuring that its work on indicators supports that of others, including multilateral, bilateral, and research institutions, in order to assist Bank borrowers in planning a balanced approach to environmental monitoring and evaluation.

DISSEMINATION. There are risks in early publication of tentative indicators that may prove inaccurate. However, dissemination of preliminary findings is required because feedback is necessary for improving indicators quickly. The Bank is therefore preparing to publish a set of "optimally inaccurate indicators" in fiscal 1995 to show that available information can shed light on some key policy issues. Besides being produced in the usual Bank paper and PC diskette versions, this set of indicators is expected to be made available over Internet, with procedures for reader response. Electronic versions will include extensive documentation and the detailed data underlying the indicators.

Economic Valuation and Resource Accounting

As the Bank works to put into operation the concept of sustainable development, policymakers are increasingly asking for help in placing monetary values on environmental impacts. Valuation is a systematic means of incorporating environmental externalities into development decisionmaking. The Bank has three priorities in its economic valuation work: (a) to apply the technique more widely at the project, sectoral, and national levels; (b) to further refine the methodology; and (c) to incorporate a broader range of biological, ecological, and sociological expertise into its methods and results.

The "state of the art" of valuation methodology is still somewhat primitive. Nevertheless, much can be done, and valuation techniques are increasingly being used as part of project development. These efforts are supported by a training program on valuation methodology for Bank staff and by the production and dissemination of case studies as environmental economics is applied to more and more lending operations. Valuation was also a major theme of the first Environmentally Sustainable Development Conference, held in Washington, D.C., in September 1993.

During the past year applied work in this area has ranged from three economic studies of environmental issues in Chile to work in Eastern Europe on estimating the benefits of reducing sulfur emissions in heavily forested areas. In Chile two studies applied the principles of environmental economics to evaluating the costs of urban pollution in Santiago and examined the benefits and costs of reducing transport-related air pollution (largely suspended particulates) and water pollution (from domestic sewage). The sources of pollution were then linked with likely health effects, such as sickness and premature death. The costs of reducing the sources of pollution were compared with the physical and monetary benefits of health. The resulting calculations can be evaluated in proposed policy changes and urban infrastructure investments. Plans are being made to use innovative approaches in certain cases—for example, using contingent valuation studies to estimate demand for improved water and sanitation services or the travel cost approach to estimate consumer surplus from safari tourism in East Africa. The measurement and economic valuation of the health impacts of pollution control investments are also receiving increased attention. In the past year work in these areas was carried out in Chile, Indonesia, and Mexico.

Notes

1. See OD 4.02, *Environmental Action Plans,* to be reissued as OP/BP/GP 4.02.

2. See chapter 8.B, "Providing an Efficient Legal and Regulatory Framework," in *Agenda 21, Report of the United Nations Conference on Environment and Development,* A/CONF.151/26/Rev. 1, Vol. I, p. 100 (1992).

2. Minimizing Adverse Impacts of Bank-Financed Investments

OLAV KJORVEN

Environmental assessments (EAs) are increasingly being used to enhance project design, and new approaches continue to be developed. For example, an EA of the mining sector in Bolivia was undertaken to help design a Bank-supported project that will reverse serious environmental damage and strengthen environmental management at mines such as this one.

The World Bank funds between 230 and 250 development projects in some 85 countries every year. In earlier years, the role of development projects was largely thought of as removing strategic bottlenecks in the economy, such as the lack of basic infrastructure, and creating the under-pinnings for economic growth. As the negative environmental and social impacts associated with some of these projects became better known, however, ways to identify and minimize these negative effects were sought. EA is one of the most effective of these measures and has been a formal requirement for Bank-funded projects since 1989, as defined in Operational Directive (OD) 4.00, Annex A, *Environmental Assessment*.[1]

Under this policy, full environmental assessment and detailed mitiga-tion plans are required for all investment projects proposed for Bank financing that are expected to have significant adverse environmental effects (category A projects). Less-extensive environmental analysis, in-cluding definition of appropriate mitigation measures where necessary, is required for projects having less-severe impacts (category B projects). As a result of its experience with project-specific EA, the Bank is increas-ingly encouraging its borrowers to undertake environmental assessment or analysis earlier in project preparation, not only to avoid negative impacts but also to enhance the environmental and social quality of investment projects and programs. For this chapter, the Bank has re-viewed the effectiveness of its EA procedures, and the findings are summarized in the first part.

In addition to possibly causing environmental damage, projects can also have direct adverse social effects. Of particular importance are those development projects that must be located in populated areas. Although most projects are specifically designed to improve people's everyday lives—by providing them with electricity, clean water, or adequate roads, for example—the consequent relocation of some people may lead to a worsening of their condition. The Bank's resettlement policy, effective since 1982, seeks not only to minimize the suffering of these people by ensuring that their new surroundings provide them with at least the same opportunities they had before relocating but also to use the process as a means of improving their lot. However, despite these objectives, implementing the Bank's policy has often proved extremely difficult. This year the Bank undertook a special review of its resettlement per-formance, and the conclusions will be discussed in the second part of this chapter.

Overview of the Portfolio

The recent EA review, covering fiscal 1993–94, confirms that borrower EA experience in Bank-financed projects is rapidly deepening and broadening. One indication of this is the increasing number of projects requiring full EA (that is, category A projects) over the last few years. Category A projects grew from 7 percent of the total approved by the Board in fiscal 1991–92 to 9 percent in 1993–94. More significantly, they accounted for nearly 25 percent of all new Bank/IDA commitments in nonadjustment lending in fiscal 1994, compared with less than 19 percent in fiscal 1992–93 and 11 percent in 1991. This increase indicates the growing acceptance—both in the Bank and among borrowers—of the usefulness of EAs in a wide range of sectors, as there is no indication that projects with potentially significant environmental impacts are becoming more common.

Category A projects were present in six sectors in fiscal 1994, as compared with four sectors in 1991 (see table 2.1). The sectors with the largest numbers of such projects, however, continue to be energy and power, agriculture, and transport. In geographic terms, the largest number of category A projects continues to be in East Asia—particularly China, on account of the significant number of major infrastructure and energy projects—followed by Latin America and the Caribbean.

Another noteworthy trend is the increasing variety of EA approaches to meet different project circumstances. Sectoral EA, in particular, is increasingly being used to launch a "programmatic" EA process in cases where sector investment projects and loans through financial intermediaries involve numerous subprojects. In some instances sectoral EA is also used as a planning tool to assess sectoral environmental management

Table 2.1. Distribution of Category A Projects by Sector, Fiscal 1991–94

Sector	*Number of projects*			
	1991	*1992*	*1993*	*1994*
Energy and power	6	14	10	9
Agriculture	2	1	3	7
Transport	2	2	3	5
Urban	0	0	0	3
Mining	0	0	0	1
Solid waste management	0	0	0	1
Industry	2	1	0	0
Water	0	2	2	0
Tourism	0	0	1	0
Total projects	12	20	19	26
Commitments (millions of dollars)	2,206	3,438	3,683	4,796
Percentage of Bank and IDA total[a]	11.1	18.8	18.3	24.7

a. Excluding adjustment loans.

capacity in the early stages of project preparation without a formal link to subproject EA work. Experience with regional EA is also growing. In fiscal 1994 the first project with a full regional EA—the Natural Resources Management Project in Paraguay—was submitted to the Board. A regional EA and an associated Regional Action Program to address induced impacts were also presented for the proposed Arun Hydroelectric Project in Nepal, which is under consideration by the Bank.

More conventional project-specific EAs have also improved. Quality has been enhanced considerably in such key areas as impact identification and analysis, public consultation, and mitigation, monitoring, and management planning. In addition, and perhaps even more important, the Bank has seen a diversification of EA into new types of lending operations such as privatization, technical assistance, and on-lending. In several of these cases the Bank has promoted new and innovative approaches.

The Bank may be generating even greater cumulative EA experience through the preparation of category B projects. Between 80 and 100 category B projects have been approved over each of the last four fiscal years, covering virtually all sectors and lending instruments in all of the Bank's operational regions. All of these projects were subject to some degree of environmental analysis involving a range of methods and approaches, some of which were similar in scale and scope to full EAs. The variety of approaches to environmental analysis of category B projects reflects the diversity of project designs as well as the differing degrees of environmental concern associated with these operations. Bank regional environmental staff help ensure that the appropriate level and type of analysis are applied.

EAs in Project Preparation

Bank experience with EA is showing that, in general, borrowers have made significant progress over the last two years in making EA a more effective tool in project planning. This is particularly true with respect to the preventive dimension of EA—that is, assessing a project's adverse environmental impacts. However, significant progress has also been made in using EAs to improve project and broader investment program design so as to increase their contribution to environmental quality.

Avoiding and Minimizing Negative Impacts

Using EAs in the planning of development projects and programs helps to avoid or minimize undesirable impacts by (a) identifying potential adverse impacts and assessing their significance; (b) recommending modifications in project design to avoid or minimize these impacts; and

(c) designing mitigation, management, and monitoring plans to reduce or manage adverse impacts or compensate for those that are unavoidable. A review of Bank EA experience has found that most EAs for category A projects have successfully identified and assessed impacts and that mitigation, management, and monitoring plans are now generally of higher quality than they were just two or three years ago. Two examples of high-quality work are described below.

The Safir-Hadramout Road Project in Yemen. The most important environmental issue was the project's potential impact on possible archaeological and prehistoric remains located along the planned road alignment. The EA identified eighty-five sites through an extensive survey of the affected area, and the EA consultants were able to prioritize the sites according to their aesthetic, historic, scientific, and social value. The government was then advised on appropriate measures to protect the most important sites as the road was built. The mitigation plan also thoroughly addressed environmental impacts—including indirect impacts such as land clearing—and potential social effects. A $2-million component has been designed to implement the environmental management plan. This plan includes provision of services and enhancement of the environment for affected tribal nomadic and seminomadic communities.

The Calub Energy Development Project in Ethiopia. The EA for this project is of high quality, and the impact assessment and mitigation, monitoring, and management plans more than meet the requirements of the Bank's EA Operational Directive. The mitigation plan, for example, includes a comprehensive environmental monitoring system for the project impact zone. This system has both natural resources and socioeconomic components. The first component will monitor changes in the local biophysical environment, including vegetation (range condition), water quality and availability, livestock movements and numbers, and roadside erosion. The second component will monitor changes in the human environment, including population density and distribution, availability of grains and other goods in local markets, the terms of trade for livestock and grain, health and education, and local attitudes toward the project. Given the fragility of the environment, the EA strongly recommended that monitoring be carried out continuously throughout the life of the project, not just at fixed intervals.

The main reasons for improved EA quality on the preventive side over the past several years are that local capacity has continued to improve as experience and training have grown and that Bank environmental staff are devoting greater effort to EA review and support, particularly with respect to mitigation, monitoring, and management plans. Analysis of indirect, induced, and cumulative environmental impacts remains a challenge not only in the assessment of Bank-financed projects but more generally. The above-mentioned EA for the Safir-Hadramout Road Project (Yemen) is an example of pioneering work in this respect, and there is reason to expect further progress in the future as EA techniques evolve and EA capacity continues to improve in developing countries.

To date few EAs submitted to the Bank have included an economic analysis of environmental costs and benefits. However, the Yacyreta II Hydroelectric Project in Argentina (fiscal 1993) and the Minas Gerais Water Quality and Pollution Control Project in Brazil (also fiscal 1993) are exceptions. The Brazil project is also one of the few cases where EA results were incorporated into the Bank's financial cost-benefit analysis at appraisal.

Some EAs propose the elimination or downsizing of certain project components to avoid negative impacts. In fact, proposed project components that might have significant adverse environmental consequences are often eliminated or significantly reduced in scale at the time of environmental screening, allowing for a reclassification of the project (typically to category B). The need for the Bank to remain vigilant persists, however, as some borrowers may seek funding for these components from other sources and proceed without adequate EA. Encouraging the use of sectoral and regional EAs as upstream planning tools and linking them with the Bank's economic and sector work can help reduce this risk.

Enhancing Project Design

Bank experience is growing in the use of EAs to improve the design of investment projects and programs from the start. The main ways EA can actively influence a project are by (a) being part of the project identification and design process and thus contributing directly to other feasibility and technical studies; (b) being used to analyze and recommend alternatives (for example, in design, technology, or siting) even if EA is not a central part of project preparation; and (c) recommending additional measures or components to enhance the project's environmental dimensions. Along these lines, box 2.1 describes how EA in urban projects has changed since introduction of the Bank's first EA Operational Directive in 1989.

EA AS PART OF PROJECT DESIGN PROCESS. Most EAs are still not an integral part of the project identification process but are relatively independent assessments that feed into the final stages of project design. Some sectoral EAs, however, have been intimately linked to project identification and early preparation, as in the following examples:

Estonia District Heating Rehabilitation Project. The project supports the improvement of district heating systems in Estonia's three largest cities—Tallin, Tartu, and Parnu—and in smaller towns and villages throughout the country that use indigenous fuels, peat, and wood. A seminar on Bank and Estonian EA procedures was held in the early stage of project identification, and a series of site visits was made by Ministry of Environment and Bank staff to review potential environmental impacts. A sectoral EA was prepared by a joint international and local team during the design phase of the project to evaluate the potential short-, medium-, and long-term environmental impacts of harvesting, processing, and using peat and wood as fuels. The sectoral EA also analyzed possible alternative programs for the sector as a whole, including the following: (a) continuing to rely on heavy fuel oil; (b) introducing more modern boilers and heat distribution networks using imported fuel and modern air pollution control equipment; and (c) relying solely on peat or wood fuel. Environmental reviews were likewise undertaken for a number of subprojects. Considering economic, social, and environmental factors, the proposed program was selected as the best option for the sector subject to adoption of a well-defined mitigation plan that includes measures to protect biodiversity. The EA process helped shape the project through both a series of policy recommendations for the sector and concrete measures for subprojects. Regular reviews, for example, will be held to assess user fees for public and private harvesting of peat and wood, including management and site rehabilitation costs. Peat harvesting is to be conducted at currently drained sites, and woodfuel harvesting should occur in the context of forest management plans.

Mexico Second Solid Waste Management Project. This project is designed to improve environmental quality on a broad scale in Mexico by financing a modern system of municipal solid waste management throughout the country. The Bank suggested to the Mexican government that a sectoral EA coupled with project-specific EAs for individual landfills would be an appropriate and cost-effective approach. This plan would provide a full overview of the regulatory and institutional framework of the sector, as well as impact assessments at particular sites. The approach was adopted and has so far proven successful. The sectoral EA also covered the Northern Border Environment Project, which includes a solid waste management component. To a large degree, project design grew out of the sectoral EA that was fully integrated into project identification and preparation. The EA identified specific gaps and overlaps in the regulatory and institutional frameworks. It further clarified sectoral needs in terms of environmental norms and regulations and institutional strengthening. The sectoral EA was aided by integrated solid waste management plans already developed for seven cities and is currently

---

Box 2.1. Environmental Assessment in Urban Projects

Urban environmental issues are a growing concern for the Bank and its borrower clients. Rapid urbanization coupled with increasing industrialization and energy consumption put high pressure on urban ecosystems. In time these pressures can result in deteriorating environments, health hazards, and losses in productivity. Already five out of the six cities with the world's worst air pollution are in developing countries. Bangkok, to cite a specific case, loses one-third of its potential gross city product because of congestion-induced travel delays.

Fortunately, an increasing number of examples show that deteriorating environments are not inevitable results of urban development and that sensible management can harness economic development for the improvement of urban environment. Examples include the successful experiences with land-use management in Singapore and public transport development in Curitiba.

Stringent EA requirements enforced by the Bank since 1989 have allowed both borrowers and Bank staff to better identify potential environmental impacts early in the project cycle. Before 1989, 60 percent of Bank-financed urban water supply projects made no mention of how the increased water supply would be drained from the city. Similarly, half the solid waste projects were limited to upgrading collection without regard to final disposal, while environmental considerations in urban transport projects were limited and vague. Now water supply projects routinely consider related sanitation and water pollution problems and look for innovative ways to address them. For instance, the Brazil Water Quality and Pollution Control Project (fiscal 1992) was one of the first to propose a watershed approach in an urban water project. With a watershed approach upstream *and* downstream, environmental impacts are fully integrated into project design and management.

---

feeding the experience in Mexico into plans being developed for other municipalities.

ANALYSIS OF ALTERNATIVES. The Bank's EA Operational Directive 4.01, Annex B, requires that EAs undertake "systematic comparison of the proposed investment design, site, technology, and operational alternatives in terms of their potential environmental impacts" (p. 1). To date, Bank experience in this area has been mixed. Too many EAs still contain only short sections on alternatives and do not demonstrate a serious attempt to analyze them from an environmental standpoint. A growing number of EAs do, however, look at technical and operating alternatives within a given basic design—for instance, heights of a dam, pollution

Careful consideration of landfill siting and disposal technologies are also common today, as illustrated by the Organization of Eastern Caribbean States Waste Management Project (fiscal 1995) and the Colombo Environmental Improvement Project (fiscal 1995). Similarly, pollution prevention and control are increasingly factored into energy, industrial, and transport projects, as demonstrated in the Liaoning Environmental Project (fiscal 1994).

Building on these improvements, an ongoing review of EAs in urban-related projects suggests further areas of concern:

- The scope of urban EAs should be broadened. Current EA efforts—particularly in sectoral projects affecting urban areas—tend to concentrate on direct pollution impacts while limiting consideration of other urban environmental issues such as land use, resource consumption, impacts on fragile ecosystems, and so-called induced impacts.

- Country and technical departments could benefit from more developed guidelines and increased dissemination of best practices. Project reviews and interviews conducted with task managers suggest that there are wide differences in the scope and depth of EAs among regions and projects.

- Training and guidelines for borrowers and consultants could help develop institutional capacity among borrowers and disseminate the best approaches and practices among consulting firms involved in EAs.

- Finally, because of the recent introduction of detailed EA requirements into Bank projects, a follow-up of the environmental action plans proposed in the EAs is needed to assess whether their recommendations are being fully taken into account in project implementation and operation.

control technologies, or timing of discharges. Some EAs now also examine alternative locations or designs. Highlights from fiscal 1994 include the following projects:

Indonesia Semarang-Surakarta Urban Development Project. This project, which is one of a series of urban development projects in Indonesia, encompasses a broad spectrum of activities. Four EA reports were prepared on the drainage and solid waste components, which were identified as those having the highest potential for significant environmental impacts. Alternative sites were considered for some of the wastewater treatment plants, and siting changes were subsequently approved. The solid waste disposal strategy for Semarang was also altered as a result of the EA process. Factors that contributed to these successful results include (a) the extended preparation period, which provided time for issues to be identified and addressed; (b) the analytical effort, which was highly focused on issues of substance; (c) the continuity of the environmental consultants within the government's project preparation team over the preparation period and their integration into the design team, which allowed for productive interaction with the design engineers; (d) similar continuity on the Bank's side, which ensured that its position was consistent over time; and (e) the active role taken by the Bank in the identification and resolution of issues.

Croatia Highway Project. The EA considered six alternative road alignments on the basis of their impact on agricultural land, forests, watercourses, and settlements, as well as the pollution impacts on air, water, and soil and from noise. A system was developed to rank the variants, and the findings were presented at public meetings. The final choice was modified by the addition of two tunnels to further reduce the impact on the landscape.

Brazil São Paulo Integrated Urban Transport Project. The EA process for this category B project resulted in the redesign of a maintenance area at the end of the metro line—significantly reducing the number of families needing relocation from 200 to 27. The redesign was a result of an analysis of alternatives and of consultation with the affected people. Sites affected by project impacts in the Vila Sonia neighborhood were reduced to seventy-nine (40 percent of the original number), only half of which are residential.

Using EA to weigh the environmental merits of various alternatives to guide project design is difficult in practice because of many reasons; the following illustrate the complexity of the process:

- Timing may be a serious constraint as the Bank's project preparation process may not be synchronized with the borrower's planning process; the principal design decisions, for instance, may already have been taken before the Bank became involved. The only major alternative remaining for the Bank may be not to finance the project. It is partly because of this problem that sectoral and regional EAs are increasingly being used to address environmental concerns closer to the beginning of the project planning process. The findings of sectoral or regional EAs may also more readily find an audience among senior officials than those of project-specific EAs, which tend to address site-specific issues of less general relevance to policymakers.
- There is more at stake for the institutions involved during project and program design discussions, and EA consultants and the Bank

may have less leverage at this stage. To address this, the Bank seeks to ensure that EA terms of reference explicitly call for analysis of major alternatives, support the EA process, and review its results.

- Contributing to design and overall planning is more challenging and requires greater skill—and, often, more innovative analytical approaches—from EA practitioners. Many countries do not yet fully possess this capacity. Specialized external consultants may therefore be required. Over the long run, this deficiency can best be addressed through in-country training and capacity building.

ADDING COMPONENTS. EAs also recommend additional measures for improving project environmental quality. This may occur once local EA consultants and the general public are informed of potential project impacts and are able to identify additional—or better—measures for addressing a particular problem. The Natural Resources Management Project in Paraguay, for example, incorporated all but one of a dozen or so specific EA recommendations proposed by local EA consultants. These suggestions were recognized as clearly improving the project.

Progress in Public Consultation

Bank policy requires consultation with affected groups and local NGOs during at least two stages of the EA process, shortly after the EA category has been assigned and after a draft EA has been prepared. Consultation throughout preparation is also encouraged, particularly for projects that are community based from the start. In projects with major social components, such as those requiring involuntary resettlement or affecting indigenous people, the consultation process should be more extensive (see the discussion in the last section of this chapter).

Public consultation in the EA process is important both to identify potential adverse impacts and to influence project design. It reveals how significant or acceptable impacts are likely to be to the people affected by them. It provides a way for the affected people to add their perspective to the proposed project design and potential alternatives. It helps identify and design suitable mitigation, monitoring, and management measures and provides a way for consulted groups to take an active part in monitoring the project's implementation—as has been seen in a number of Bank projects. Box 2.2 describes a project where a significant environmental impact, not identified by the EA consultants, was discovered through public consultation.

The Bank has seen encouraging progress with respect to public consultation over the past year. Increasingly, meetings are being held for

---

Box 2.2. Identifying Impacts through Public Consultation: The Caribbean Waste Management Project

The Organization of Eastern Caribbean States (OECS) plans to embark upon a Solid Waste Management Project, which will be presented to the Bank's Board of Directors in early fiscal 1995. The project aims to develop port reception facilities for wastes from ships and to upgrade waste management systems and facilities in its member states (Antigua and Barbuda, Dominica, Grenada, St. Kitts and Nevis, St. Lucia, and St. Vincent and the Grenadines). Project preparation focused on both ship-generated and shore-generated waste management systems and the links between the two.

Preparation of the project included separate EAs for all the countries involved. As part of these EA processes, extensive consultations were held with local NGOs and affected communities in each of the six island countries. The consultation process included public meetings, most of which were televised—some had call-in participation. One meeting in Grenada resulted in the identification of an important impact overlooked by the EA consultants: that a landfill could infringe on the habitat of a critically endangered bird species, the Grenada dove (*Leptotila wellsi*). The world population of this species is only about seventy birds, occurring in two populations of fifty and twenty. The landfill is proposed for a part of Perseverance Estates, where the population of twenty lives. At least two of these birds feed and nest exactly where the landfill would have been located. As a result of the consultation, the government of Grenada and the Bank have agreed to study the area further to find ways to protect the dove while still providing solid waste disposal at an appropriate site.

---

active discussion with affected communities rather than relying on passive communication techniques or opinion surveys. This trend needs to grow in several ways. For instance, progress appears to have been stronger in consultations with local NGOs than with affected community representatives, and in consultations about resettlement than about other social and environmental effects. Furthermore, special groups such as women and the poor are still not reached in too many cases. Finally, documentation of the process can be improved; some EAs still do not record lists of meetings, participants, and agreements and conclusions reached.

Several recent projects have approached public consultation innovatively:

Indonesia Semarang-Surakarta Urban Development Project (see above). Extensive multistage meetings with the affected neighborhoods and local NGOs were held in relation to the Semarang drainage component of this project. A local NGO was also commissioned to investigate further issues that arose from the EA study.

Hungary Energy and Environment Project. Preparation of this project included an innovative EA consultation process that consisted in part of an "electronic" public meeting through a closed-circuit TV program that could be viewed by residents in the area. A thirteen-minute film was shown about the project, viewers called in with questions, and explanations were given by a panel of sector and local officials. The major concerns expressed by the viewers were about the existing air pollution in the area (caused chiefly by a major local refinery) and the noise levels and water effluent from the proposed power plant. The explanations about how these problems related to the plant and how they would be reduced under the project had two important outcomes: (a) the openness about the objectives and nature of the project reduced unwarranted fears and suspicions; and (b) the meeting helped form a political consensus, thereby expediting the process of obtaining the necessary local permits and licenses. Following the EA work, the project incorporated measures to minimize impacts, including soundproofing and planting of trees and bushes around the facility.

Public consultation, however, remains a challenge because many governments lack appropriate policies and experience at the national level. Many project preparation and EA consultant teams also lack the necessary expertise to carry out effective public consultation and to increase the participation of affected communities more generally. Inadequate national legislation and insufficient guidance for undertaking consultation are also persistent problems.

The Bank has recently taken steps to improve the quality of consultation in the EA process. In the fall of 1993, an EA Sourcebook Update (no. 5) was issued, providing specific guidance on the topic. Internal and external EA training courses are also focusing increasingly on this subject. The new Operational Policy on Disclosure of Bank Documents (OP 17.50) is helping to ensure greater transparency in EA and project preparation by ensuring affected groups and NGOs access to EA and project documents (see chapter 5 for discussion of the Bank's new disclosure policy). The Bank is also preparing a Participation Sourcebook.

The evolving Bank EA experience reviewed for this chapter leads to the following recommendations for further improving public consultation:

- The Bank should work more with borrower governments and implementing agencies to ensure that stakeholders are consulted at the required stages of project preparation. In particular, greater effort should be devoted to ensuring appropriate consultation at the scoping stage—*before* EA terms of reference are written and while the project is still being planned conceptually.

- The Bank should give greater attention to the need to strengthen borrower capacity to plan and carry out consultation with stakeholders. An important indicator of such capacity is the number of qualified professionals in social and communication sciences among executing agency staff.
- The Bank should encourage the borrower or the EA team to conduct a social assessment (an analysis of the social context of the project) to answer three vital questions: (a) who are the relevant stakeholders? (b) what are the customary institutional forms of decisionmaking in the country? and (c) what are the customary forms of communication preceding decisionmaking?
- The Bank should encourage the borrower to identify the appropriate arenas for, and participants in, consultation. Not all social groups can or should be consulted on every detail. For example, some decisions are purely technical and do not require public input. However, for those decisions that intimately affect the living conditions of communities, the members of these communities should take part in decisionmaking directly.
- Sufficient funds should be allocated to undertake the consultation process, and the burden should not fall on the affected groups. The implementing agency, not the stakeholders, for instance, should pay for the necessary equipment, transport, and per diem. The Bank should support the borrower in identifying sources of funding if needed.

New EA Approaches

PROGRAMMATIC EA. The increased use of sectoral EAs as an early planning tool is largely a reflection of the growing number of programmatic sector and financial intermediary lending operations. These projects generally involve large numbers of subprojects, most of which have not been developed—or in some cases even identified—at the time of appraisal. In addition to designing the mechanisms for subproject EAs downstream, this type of assessment focuses attention on the major impacts of concern in the sector and prescribes standard approaches (through environmental manuals, standards, or guidelines) to project design and mitigation. Bank efforts to strengthen borrower EA capacity are thus multiplied through management of the environmental impacts of a large number of investment activities.

The programmatic approach has been followed for both category A and category B projects. Recent examples include four Water Consolidation Projects in India, the Kabupaten (district) Roads Projects in Indonesia, the Natural Resource Management Project in Paraguay, and the District Heating Rehabilitation Project in Estonia. The Bank's regional environment division for Asia, ASTEN, has developed standard EA procedures for such projects (box 2.3).

A recent internal review found that applying programmatic EA to a series of sector investment projects in Indonesia had gradually increased the effectiveness of all EA work in relation to such projects. In the urban sector, for example, full EAs were gradually limited to investment components expected to have major environmental impacts (such as landfills or dredging operations), while smaller components were subject to standard operational guidelines and monitoring. As a result, the amount of paperwork was reduced while EA effectiveness was improved.

A programmatic approach is also quite common in financial intermediary lending (typically category B projects), where banks within the borrowing countries on-lend funds provided by the World Bank to

---

Box 2.3. Sectoral EA for Programmatic Projects in the Asia Region

Extensive experience with programmatic lending has spurred development of a standard EA approach in the Bank's Asia Region for ensuring cost-effective consideration of all possible impacts on the environment. The first step is a sectoral EA that should help establish

- A screening process to identify subprojects having potentially significant issues to be addressed in a subproject EA
- A general assessment of the kinds of impacts that might be associated with the different types of subprojects
- A sectoral environmental action plan to eliminate, minimize, or mitigate the impacts identified in the sectoral EA and to provide general guidelines for long-term management and monitoring

Environmental screening of the subprojects is included in the sectoral EA, in two categories:

- Subprojects that might create a few minor and easily recognizable environmental problems but no significant ones.
- Subprojects with potentially adverse impacts that warrant project-specific EA work.

The first category of subprojects is addressed primarily through the sectoral EA itself plus standard guidelines or codes of practice for different types of subprojects. These guidelines or codes cover areas such as construction practices, site selection, resettlement and compensation, and consultation and participation.

the private sector. An example is the dual approach taken for the EnvironmentalManagementandEnterpriseRestructuringprojectsinRussia. A complete system for environmental screening and review (including EA and environmental auditing) has been developed, with detailed procedures that cover participating banks, private enterprises, and government agencies. This approach, which was developed in close coordination with the European Bank for Reconstruction and Development (EBRD), is being replicated with some adjustments in several other countries.

The Bank is currently examining the effectiveness of EA in relation to financial intermediary operations. Early findings suggest that EA procedures involving commercial banks and other financial intermediaries are most effective when these institutions perceive a self-interest in environmental screening and review of investment proposals. The degree of self-interest depends on the capacity of the authorities to enforce environmental regulations and the associated degree of risk when investment proposals do not comply with environmental regulations. The Bank and other financing agencies can play a role by offering technical assistance and training to government agencies and participating banks and by helping to establish clear procedures and requirements.

EA ISSUES IN PRIVATIZATION. Over the last couple of years the Bank has developed an increasingly systematic approach to addressing the environmental issues related to privatization. Examples of activities from recent projects include

- Adjustment operations such as in the Second Public Enterprise Restructuring Adjustment Loan (PERAL II) in Argentina, the Private Sector Development Adjustment Loan in Jamaica, and the Economic Recovery Loan for Slovakia
- Technical assistance operations such as the privatization projects in Russia and Peru
- Sector investment operations such as in the Mining Sector Rehabilitation Project and the follow-up Environment, Industry and Mining Project in Bolivia
- Hybrid investment operations such as in the Energy Sector Deregulation and Privatization Project in Jamaica
- Financial intermediary operations such as the Enterprise Restructuring Project in Russia.

Most of the privatization loans that are not adjustment operations are classified in category B because they generally do not support investment activities as such but only the divestiture process by helping prepare enterprises for private takeover. When such operations do support direct investment for construction and expansion, as in the case of the Jamaica EDP project, they are more likely to be placed in category A. Interestingly, both category C technical assistance projects and adjustment operations supporting privatization have increasingly become subject to environmental analysis and requirements and have included environmental components. Box 2.4 describes the EA approach recommended in the recent EA Sourcebook Update (no. 6) on privatization. The Bank has also issued a full report on privatization and environmental liability in Central and Eastern Europe. The report discusses the weak institutional capacity in the region for effectively dealing with the complex liability issues in the privatization process. Because of the political requirement not to delay privatization, various shortcuts for smaller enterprises may be needed without compromising environmental concerns. These formed the basis for a special training program with the Bank's Economic Development Institute (EDI) for policymakers in the region.

ADJUSTMENT OPERATIONS. Adjustment loans and credits currently do not fall under the Bank's policy on EA. However, in a number of cases, important environmental analytical work is taking place. A recent example is the Agriculture Sector Adjustment Loan (ASAL) to Jordan, where Bank consultants analyzed the environmental issues in the sector and the potential impacts of the proposed macroeconomic and policy interventions. The study concluded that the loan would most likely have positive effects on natural resource use in the sector and would contribute to environmental protection. However, it proposed several measures to further enhance the environmental benefits of the loan. For example, the study recommended that the national water policy address the water allocation needed to maintain the biodiversity of natural ecosystems. The study also recommended that producer subsidies for cereals and producer supports for vegetables be removed.

Cost of EA

The normal cost range for EAs of category A projects is between $60,000 and $200,000, or from about 1 to 10 percent of project preparation costs. The full range of EA costs in the Bank's experience to date is from as little as $7,000 to as much as $500,000.

The following are the factors that largely determine the cost of EA work: (a) the extent to which international consultants are used; (b) the complexity of the project and its potential impacts; (c) the depth, scope, and duration of data collection and analysis; and (d) whether—and how

---

Box 2.4. Recommended EA Approach in Privatization Operations

In Environmental Sourcebook Update No. 6, the Bank recommends the following major steps during project preparation:

- Screen enterprises scheduled for privatization for pre-existing environmental impacts and potential hazards from such impacts and for impacts associated with ongoing operations and new investments (if any)
- Conduct environmental audits of enterprises that have had real or potentially significant adverse environmental impacts related to past or ongoing operations and environmental assessments of expanding enterprises
- Prior to the sale of an enterprise, ensure that the state and new private investors agree on the allocation of responsibility for carrying out and funding the mitigation measures identified through the audit or assessment process
- Put in place mechanisms, including financial resources, for monitoring and enforcing the agreed actions.

The Bank generally recommends that the state as prior owner take on most or all of the financial and legal responsibility for environmental problems associated with past operations, while new investors should be obliged to bring the enterprises into compliance with newly applicable environmental standards (perhaps over a certain amount of time). A clear legal statement underpinning such a policy—as opposed to relying on contracts for individual privatizations—generally increases investor confidence and may thus contribute positively to the overall privatization process.

An interesting and new lesson on the government role can be learned from the Jamaica Energy Deregulation and Privatization Project. Supported by the Bank through the privatization process, the government was able to clarify previous conflicting interests and to take on a much more effective regulatory role in monitoring compliance with the environmental standards set out in the EA process.

---

many—separate EAs for different subprojects need to be prepared. In projects where there are likely to be significant and complex impacts and where important environmental data are still lacking, there will normally be a need for data collection over a period of one year and, in many cases, for the use of international consultants for particular tasks. Costs may then exceed $250,000. If many subproject EAs are needed, the absolute resource requirements will naturally increase but not necessarily as a share of the total preparation costs of subprojects.

EA work is increasingly cost-effective as it continues to improve in quality, to affect project design, and to have a relatively low overall cost. However, the real test of effectiveness comes with project implementation.

The Emerging Implementation Experience

Bank experience with implementing projects subject to EA is still relatively limited. The first category A projects (under the Bank's current EA Operational Directive) were approved in 1991, and many are still in the early phases of implementation. The most in-depth reports on implementation experience are mid-term reviews, and these are available for only one operation previously subject to full EA so far—the Thailand Pak Mun Hydropower project. For the other projects listed below, Bank supervision reports are the main source of information.

Thailand Pak Mun Hydropower Project. This project is an example of a very large and complex EA, including resettlement. The vast EA documentation, which was reflected in detailed provisions in the staff appraisal report (SAR) and the legal agreements, provides a good yardstick for gauging implementation performance. The midterm review found that the core environmental issues—identified through the EA process—were largely being addressed adequately, with some exceptions. The resettlement plan was being implemented in compliance with conditionalities, although some corrective measures were needed. The fisheries mitigation plan was being implemented on schedule, but the review team identified weaknesses in the proposed design of the fish ladder and recommended ways to improve it. The work under the health impacts mitigation plan was found to be less effective. Implementation of the five main work plans to mitigate potential health problems was lagging behind schedule, with less than 30 percent implemented. The midterm review gave concrete recommendations to rectify these weaknesses, and the main implementing agency agreed to comply and keep the Bank informed of the progress. Supervision of environmental mitigation measures and resettlement will continue beyond project completion.

China Guangdong and Henan Provincial Highway Projects. These projects include construction of a new divided four-lane, controlled-access highway in Guangdong and a two-lane, controlled-access highway in Henan; improvement programs for about 2,300 kilometers of roads; institutional strengthening and training for the highway agencies; and equipment for a number of purposes, including environmental protection. Full EAs were prepared for the highways. A programmatic EA approach was taken for the road improvement programs, which are being implemented over several years. The EAs were fully reflected in the implementation plan and budget in the SARs as well as in the legal agreements and bidding documents. The Bank also agreed with the borrower that each of the local project supervision teams will have at least one environmental specialist. A Bank supervision mission in 1993 found that mitigation was generally on track but that the monitoring of noise and dust for the expressways required improvement and that additional training and better communication between monitoring staff in different locations was needed. A supervision mission in 1994 found that significant progress had been made in implementing the monitoring measures. One of the interesting aspects of this EA process was that a representative of the Archaeology Department was stationed in Henan, in the important archaeological area of Luoyang, during earthwork operations to ensure adequate treatment of archeological remains.

India Cement Industry Restructuring Project. The project finances modernization and expansion in the private sector cement industry in India through a line of credit. It has also established mechanisms for EA, for review and enforcement of strict environmental design standards prior to approval of subprojects, and for environmental and pollution control monitoring and reporting during implementation. A recent supervision mission found that most of the cement plants were implementing their investment plans in accordance with the environmental requirements. Several plants had made significant progress in efficient use of waste materials, water management, and reforestation in the quarries and around the plants. At one plant, the company had created an environmental management unit equipped with advanced monitoring equipment and laboratory facilities. Major reasons for the successful implementation experience are that (a) environmental regulations are increasingly being implemented and enforced in India, especially at the state level; (b) the cement industry has become more responsive and competitive in the area of environmental management and has accepted environmental standards that exceed current Indian standards; and (c) the EA work was well done and was followed up in final project design and Bank supervision.

Preconditions for Effective Implementation

The recent EA review has identified several key preconditions for successful implementation of EA recommendations and plans. Three of the major circumstances needed are discussed below.

First, EA recommendations and mitigation, management, and monitoring plans need to take into account country-specific circumstances and constraints. While this may seem obvious, it means that the three following points require special consideration:

- The objectives of environmental plans must strike a balance between the desire to redress a multitude of complex environmental problems and the limitations in local absorptive capacity. For example, high-priority objectives may be to build local institutional capacity, redress key policy failures, and develop practical solutions for high-risk problems.
- Implementation will be improved by various actions taken in advance, including (a) establishing an autonomous, stable and qualified implementation unit; (b) ensuring adequate counterpart financing and sufficient logistical capacity; and (c) providing assurance of sustained management support.
- If the project implementing agency lacks sufficient commitment or capacity for carrying out environmental measures, it may be best to contract out operational responsibility for these measures to other organizations. Some activities—such as monitoring, data analysis, or protected area management—may benefit from being contracted out to NGOs, universities, or consulting firms.

Second, implementation of EA-related actions benefits from having explicit reference made to them in Bank project documents (including legal agreements) and from ensuring that the agencies responsible for implementing them take part in their negotiation. The EA review encourages environmental and legal staff to work closely in the drafting of appropriate legal language.

Third, sufficient allocation of time and resources for environmental supervision, according to the needs of each project, is essential to EA effectiveness during implementation.

Significant progress has been achieved in these areas over the last couple of years as greater attention has been given to translating EA recommendations into explicit actions and responsibilities. All category A projects in fiscal 1994 made reference in the legal documents to EA recommendations or plans, although with varying degrees of specificity. Most of the SARs for these projects also included environmental actions in the implementation plan and budget.

Supervision of Implementation

Strong Bank supervision of EA-related aspects is essential throughout the project cycle because the institutional and policy setting as well as the project itself can change over time, and because Bank expertise and leverage may help resolve critical implementation bottlenecks. The recent EA review recommends that the Bank be more flexible in the frequency and timing of supervision missions in accordance with the relative seriousness of the problems observed during implementation. It also strongly recommends that the Bank make extra efforts to maintain contact with local implementation offices between missions.

An increase in the amount of time and resources devoted to environmental supervision of category A projects is reported since 1992. This increase has come about in large part because task managers voluntarily seek support from environmental staff and consultants and because the Regional Environment Divisions, as well as the central Environment Department, are putting greater effort into environmental supervision. For instance, the regional environment division for Latin America and the Caribbean, LATEN, invested twenty staff-weeks (for one environmental engineer, one ecologist, and two social scientists) in the supervision of the Yacyreta II Hydropower Project in Argentina, in which a new dam will affect two cities and a large delta area. Since the environment divisions have no formal role in project implementation, however, the total supervision effort depends on the resources available to task managers and their priorities. A central message of the recent EA review is that greater resources should be allocated to environmental supervision to ensure satisfactory implementation of EA recommendations.

Building Capacity in Borrowing Countries

As was recommended by the first EA review completed in fiscal 1993, the Bank has significantly expanded its support to building and strengthening EA capacity in borrowing countries. This work occurs in various ways, but the main clusters of activities are the following: (a) environmental institution-building projects and related objectives (for example, training, financing of international consultants, information management development, and so forth); (b) technical assistance components of regular investment projects for developing EA capacity; (c) in-country training, spearheaded by the EDI and the Regional Environment Divisions; and (d) advice on EA legislation and procedures. A sampling of fiscal 1994 projects that focused on capacity building would include many of the programmatic category A sector investment operations such as the Haryana Water Consolidation Project in India and the Natural Resources Management and Irrigation Project in Uruguay, technical assistance projects such as the Environmental Management Project in Russia and the Environmental Management Capacity Building Project in the Gambia and the Mining Technical Assistance Project in Ecuador, and regular investment projects such as the Natural Resources Management Project in Colombia.

External training targets both government agencies (central, provincial, and local) and, increasingly, the nongovernmental sector (consultant industry, banks, universities, and local NGOs). In several financial intermediary projects, commercial bank staff are being trained to do environmental screening and review of private investment proposals in industry and agriculture. The EDI and regional environmental staff are also involved in ongoing training for an agriculture sector investment project in Venezuela.

Some regional environment divisions have an EA training strategy for borrowing countries. In the environment division for LATEN, for example, every category A project is screened for the EA training needs of the implementing and regulatory agencies. Whenever the LATEN EA reviewer sees a need for training, assistance is offered to the task manager, with funding allocated from LATEN's own divisional resources. The environment division for Sub-Saharan Africa (AFTES) has also sponsored and provided intensive EA training for African borrowers. As a result of this training and the Bank's insistence that local consultants take part in the EA work, EA capacity has improved significantly in many African countries.

Creating and strengthening environmental assessment units is crucial to ensuring the success of institutional reform in environmental management. To date, the Mediterranean Technical Assistance Program (METAP) has provided support for EA units in Algeria, Morocco, Syria, and two governates in Egypt. Follow-on phases have been developed for the Algeria and Morocco units as well as further strengthening of the regional Egyptian managerial units and establishment of regional Environmental Directorates in two provinces in Syria.

The Bank has likewise taken the lead in developing advanced but user-friendly tools to support EA work in borrowing countries. One example is the geographic information systems (GIS) that have been developed for several countries. Computer software has been developed for environmental screening and impact assessment in the power sector and will soon be made available at no charge to interested borrowers that are preparing power projects for Bank consideration.

The lack of full compatibility between the EA requirements and procedures of borrowing countries and of the Bank is sometimes a challenge. When national EA procedures vary considerably from those of the Bank and neither party is familiar with the other's requirements, problems and delays may occur during project preparation, as, for example, when the Bank began to work in the formerly centrally planned economies of Central and Eastern Europe and the former Soviet Union. However, the Bank's vice presidency for Europe and Central Asia (ECA), in consultation with several countries in the region, including the Russian Federation, has taken practical steps to close information gaps and move toward a more closely coordinated EA process.

In this connection, the Bank and many of these countries have agreed that the Bank's Environmental Data Sheet (EDS), which is issued at the earliest stage in the project cycle, will be made available to the national environmental agency. This agency subsequently shares the EDS with the implementing agency for the project. This is expected to facilitate understanding of the Bank's screening process and the involvement of the relevant agencies in the process. Similar steps have been taken with respect to subsequent stages in the project cycle.

Building Capacity in the Bank

The first EA review called for a strengthening of Bank staff EA capacity. Since that time, not only has the number of environmental staff increased significantly, but a large number of nonenvironmental staff—particularly project task managers—have taken in-house EA and other types of environmental training. An EA training manual is expected to be available in late 1994 to support trainers delivering courses across several sectors, both inside and outside the Bank.

The Environmental Assessment Sourcebook, issued in mid-1991, continues to be a major source of EA information for Bank staff and is in high demand both externally and internally. A diskette version of the Sourcebook has also recently become available. In addition, the Sourcebook is being expanded in the form of EA Sourcebook Updates. Seven Updates have been produced to date:

- "The World Bank and Environmental Assessment: An Overview"
- "Environmental Screening"
- "Geographic Information Systems for Environmental Assessment and Review"
- "Sectoral Environmental Assessment"
- "Public Involvement in Environmental Assessment: Requirements, Opportunities and Issues"
- "Privatization and Environmental Assessment: Issues and Approaches"
- "Coastal Zone Management and Environmental Assessment."

The Updates are in high demand both inside (some 700 staff members are on the mailing list) and outside the Bank (1,000 institutions, firms, and individuals in 170 countries). Forthcoming Updates will provide guidance on topics such as regional EA, economic analysis in EA, forestry, analysis of alternatives, urban environmental audits, and indigenous people. To promote better analysis of alternatives, two Updates will also be produced on this topic in fiscal 1995. One will provide guidance on the types of alternatives that might be appropriate for various projects, and the other will describe economic analysis in EA to help in the assessment and selection of alternatives.

Emerging lessons on specific aspects of EA preparation and implementation are being collected and discussed in many parts of the Bank in the form of internal papers and seminars. Even a small sampling of regional publications reveals the breadth of coverage, from papers on public consultation and participation in Africa and Latin America to EA experience in water supply, wastewater, and sanitation projects in Asia to experience with municipal environmental audits in Europe and the Middle East and North Africa. The central Environment Department has sponsored papers on such issues as EA in urban projects and EA experience in financial intermediary lending. Seminars have covered an equally wide variety of topics, including computer support systems for EA work, strategic EAs for policies and programs, country-specific EA experience, and EA and forestry.

External Interactions and Relations

The Bank has expanded the level of collaboration on EA matters with external parties—especially other multilateral financial institutions (MFIs)—with which it cofinances a number of projects. The Bank also works on EA issues with OECD members in the Development Assistance Committee (DAC), and the Bank's environmental assessment adviser is currently chairman of the International Association of Impact Assessment (IAIA), the leading professional body in the EA field.

In September 1993 the Bank hosted the first annual Environmental Technical Workshop for MFIs. This meeting focused on ways to collaborate on and ensure consistency in EA. The workshop revealed that policies and procedures of major MFIs are largely similar and that most of the organizations face similar challenges in EA work. In September 1994 the Bank will host the second MFI workshop on EA, in which the main items on the agenda will be environmental screening, financial intermediary lending, natural resources management, and public disclosure and consultation.

Involuntary Resettlement

Involuntary resettlement has accompanied development throughout history, in industrial as well as developing countries. Bringing essential services to large numbers of poor people by installing major hydropower dams or irrigation systems or by extending transport networks has also entailed displacement, hardship, and deprivation for some. In developing countries, the scale of development-related population displacement has grown rapidly in the past few decades due to the accelerated provision of infrastructure and growing population densities. The displacement toll of an average of 300 large dams on which construction begins each year is estimated to be more than 4 million people. The urban infrastructure programs started each year are estimated to displace an additional 6 million.

Bank-financed programs account for only a small share of this displacement. Projects currently in the Bank's active portfolio are expected to involve the resettlement of 2 million people over an eight-year period. Nevertheless, while limited in relative terms (Bank-assisted projects account for less than 3 percent of all resettlement worldwide), the Bank's involvement in resettlement is of great importance. For those people resettled in connection with the projects it finances, the Bank has a responsibility to help borrowers ensure that every effort is made to restore, and if possible improve, their livelihoods. The Bank's involvement also has a broader significance. Since the Bank established resettlement guidelines fourteen years ago, it has increasingly sought to work with governments to promote better policies and legal frameworks for resettlement, thereby improving the situation of displaced people in both Bank-assisted and other projects.

As a result of concern about the status of the Bank's portfolio, a Bank-wide Resettlement Review began in 1992. This review covered 192 projects in the Bank's portfolio between 1986 and 1993 in which resettlement occurred, 146 of which were still active during the review itself. To assess the consistency between Bank policy and operations, the review had three main objectives:

- To ascertain the scale of involuntary resettlement in the Bank's portfolio, and determine regional and sectoral trends and composition
- To analyze ongoing resettlement programs for their quality, consistency with policy, and outcomes
- To identify recurrent problems affecting performance, initiate midstream remedial actions, and prepare a follow-up strategy for addressing resettlement more effectively.

The review entailed a broad process of analysis in the field, carried out jointly by the Bank's relevant regional and central units and the borrowers. During 1993 alone the Bank sent 160 resettlement supervision missions, three times as many as any previous year, to projects under implementation, and numerous other missions to projects in preparation that were anticipated to involve resettlement. Of these missions, about two-thirds were conducted by resettlement specialists, twice the average percentage prior to the review. The main product of this review was not just the final report but the process that it generated across the Bank and on the ground. This process consisted of (a) intensified field supervision; (b) analysis of project preparation, appraisal, supervision, and implementation; (c) on-site consultations with NGOs; (d) sectoral resettlement studies; (e) development of new technical tools for resettlement planning; and (f) a considerable number of joint remedial actions begun by the Bank and the borrowers for projects failing to meet the set objectives.

The review confirmed that the Bank had made significant progress between 1986 and 1993 in three major areas:

- Influencing the resettlement policies of borrowing countries
- Assisting borrowers in avoiding or reducing the scale of displacement
- Assisting borrowers in improving the ability of resettlers to restore their incomes.

The review looked beyond Bank-assisted projects and considered the Bank's potential role in influencing policy and legal frameworks for resettlement in borrower countries. Bank policy dialogue with governments has contributed to new or improved legal and policy frameworks at the national, state, or sectoral level in Brazil, China, Colombia, India, the Philippines, and Turkey. The critical significance of success in the first category is that benefits extend to the 97 percent of resettlement that occurs outside of Bank-assisted projects. Furthermore, policies, as well as institutional capacity, can be applied to future projects, not just those currently under implementation. This upstream emphasis on policy is central to the Bank's strategy for improving resettlement performance.

The single most important message of the review is that by rebuilding sustainable livelihoods, proper resettlement and rehabilitation can avoid driving people into poverty and improve the lot of those already impoverished. However, the review has shown that resettlement nearly always proves to be more difficult, more expensive, and more time consuming than generally anticipated. The largest resettlement operations move tens of thousands of people—often very poor people—long distances in a very short time, and reestablishing their standard of living is a hard task. The inherent difficulty in reestablishing standards of living and community services is compounded by the limited technical and institutional resettlement capacity of most borrowers and by weak commitment from some executing governments.

Field research, project evaluations, and sectoral and legal studies confirm that:

- The Bank's policy toward involuntary resettlement, while ambitious, is sound and its goals reasonable.
- Projects that follow Bank policy have demonstrably better resettlement outcomes than projects that do not. Resettlement operations under projects guided by the Bank's policy are usually superior to those outside Bank-assisted projects.
- Resettlement performance is directly associated with the presence of a domestic policy and organizational frameworks on resettlement. Countries, states, or sectors with an adequate resettlement policy, therefore, generally achieve better outcomes in preventing impoverishment and restoring livelihoods than do those that lack them.
- The Bank's resettlement portfolio is much more sound than in 1986, the year the previous resettlement review was completed—and radically different from the state of the portfolio at the time the resettlement policy was issued. However, in a number of projects resettlement operations and outcomes are not consistent with the standards defined and demanded by the Bank's policy.
- The planning processes and criteria established through the Bank's policy have significantly improved the practices of some borrowing governments, other international donors, technical agencies implementing large projects, and the Bank itself. However, progress in this respect has been insufficient and uneven. Much more needs to be done to ensure consistency of planning, outcomes, and impact monitoring with policy goals.

Despite the vast differences among countries, much more is now understood about the major common factors that explain—by their presence or absence—why resettlement has worked in some cases and has failed in others:

- Political commitment by the borrower, expressed in law, official policies, and resource allocations
- Systematic implementation of established guidelines and procedures by the borrower and the Bank
- Sound social analysis, reliable demographic assessments, and widely available technical expertise in planning for development-oriented resettlement
- Effective executing organizations that respond to local development needs, opportunities, and constraints
- Public participation in setting resettlement objectives, identifying solutions, and implementing them.

Although the quality of the Bank's resettlement project portfolio has improved, the review also revealed important weaknesses. The actions that have, or will be, taken to achieve further improvements can be divided into four sets of priorities.

Strategic priorities. These include (a) ensuring borrower commitment by agreeing explicitly on policy from the outset and enhancing borrower institutional capacity and (b) improving project design by first avoiding or reducing displacement as much as possible, creating explicit timetables and internal mechanisms that link progress in the civil works with the necessary concomitant progress in resettlement, promoting people's participation, and providing adequate Bank financing. Bank priorities include diversifying project mechanisms so that future infrastructure operations that require the displacement of large numbers of people can be processed as twin projects—one for the civil works and another for the resettlement—and strengthening the Bank's institutional capacity.

Remedial and retrofitting actions. Near-term remedial actions are being taken on active projects that fall short of policy and legal objectives. Some projects may need restructuring, additional financing, or the strengthening of resettlement agencies.

Improving project processing. While responsibility for full compliance with the Bank's procedures and established safeguards rests with the borrower, it is nevertheless essential that the Bank support the process more effectively. Improvements are therefore being made in the analysis of resettlement at appraisal and the design of development packages for resettlers; in the in-house review of resettlement components; and in the staffing and organization of operational units. The Bank will encourage borrowers to carry out pilot schemes to test the adequacy of proposed resettlement operations. The Project Preparation Facility (PPF) and the Institutional Development Fund (IDF) provide additional assistance for technical support and capacity building in the preparatory phases of the project. In major operations—particularly for dams—consideration is increasingly being given in the early identification stages to using a resettlement advisory panel, along the lines of dam safety panels.

Supervision. Supervision of projects, including resettlement, is being improved. Regular supervision missions will take place at least every twelve months and will make greater use of local specialist consultants. In addition, regional units in the Bank will prepare annual reports on projects with resettlement in their portfolio, as part of the Annual Review of Portfolio Performance (ARPP).

Box 2.5. Xiaolangdi Resettlement—A Model for the Future

Xiaolangdi Dam is of critical importance to China. It will provide flood control in the lower reaches of the Yellow River Basin to protect major infrastructure and 103 million people; control siltation in the 800-kilometer downstream channel of the river (so that levees will not have to be raised further for the next twenty years); provide irrigation for 2 million hectares; and generate 1,800 megawatts of hydropower. Constructing the dam and filling the reservoir will necessitate the resettlement of more than 180,000 people, the largest resettlement operations assisted by Bank financing.

A pathbreaking approach was taken to addressing the complexities of this resettlement operation. First, a separate project and a separate Bank credit were created, distinct from the dam project and loan, to ensure a high level of attention, staff inputs, and budgetary resources. The purpose of the project is to restore and improve the resettlers' income. To that end, the project will construct infrastructure and housing for 276 villages and ten towns; develop 11,100 hectares of new land, of which 7,000 will be irrigated; relocate 252 existing small industries and mines; and establish 84 new industries with 20,500 new jobs. The project will benefit about half a million people and create about 75,220 full-time jobs and about 37,400

Progress in these areas began during the past year. Taken together, these measures will help institutionalize standards achieved during the review. Improvements include the following:

- Some projects in the pipeline have been deferred or removed until satisfactory progress in legal and policy frameworks has been achieved.
- During the last two fiscal years, all projects requiring resettlement plans have had them completed by appraisal time. SARs, the basic document presented to the Board for project approval, have had substantially improved reporting on resettlement aspects so that the Board is more fully informed as to how this vital component will be executed.
- The first "twin project" (having a separate project for the resettlement operation so that it receives adequate resources, staff attention, and focus) was approved for the Xiaolangdi Dam in China (see box 2.5).
- Two projects in India have continued to receive supervision and assistance in satisfactorily completing the resettlement operation, even after the project closed.
- Training courses have been carried out for both Bank staff and key borrower countries, including China, India, and Turkey.

part-time jobs. The economic rate of return for the overall project is estimated at 32 percent.

The Chinese have had success in other dam projects since the adoption of new policies and strategies, with Bank assistance, in the mid-1980s. In the nearly completed resettlement of 67,000 people at the Shuikou Hydro-electric project, also in eastern China, resettler incomes exceeded previous incomes by up to 10 percent within a year after transfer. So far, the experience from Xiaolangdi Dam shows that the income levels of the first 2,000 people resettled during the early construction have exceeded their previous incomes by 10 to 60 percent within one year.

Xiaolangdi has the highest resettlement budget per person of any project in China and far above the average among resettlement projects. Unparalleled human resources have been put into the preparation of the extremely detailed resettlement plan. Five alternatives to the Xiaolangdi Dam were considered, but each would have required significantly greater resettlement, ranging from 250,000 to 930,000 people. Although resettlement always remains a difficult and unpredictable task, Xiaolangdi has minimized the number of people to be moved and has taken extensive precautionary measures to prevent impoverishment of the resettlers and, moreover, to improve their lives.

- Drafts of new guidelines for SARs and the Bank's supervision forms are under way and will be issued by the Operations Policy Department.

Furthermore, there is increasing linkage between preparation, supervision, and monitoring information as represented by the SARs, supervision reports, the resettlement database, and the ARPP.

In summary, by supporting resettlement that strives to prevent impoverishment, the Bank promotes policies and approaches that are relevant far beyond Bank-assisted projects. Improving borrower capacity will benefit not only Bank-financed operations but also the much broader resettlement activities of entire sectors, affecting larger numbers of people. Resettlement remains a formidable challenge for borrowers as well as for the Bank, and the Bank recognizes its important responsibility to help borrowers act progressively to improve resettlement whenever displacement cannot be avoided and to extend improved approaches to sector and national contexts.

Note

1. OD 4,00, Annex A, was updated in October 1991 in OD 4.01, *Environmental Assessment*.

3. Building on the Positive Synergies between Development and the Environment

Subsidizing water, while justified in specific situations, promotes waste, almost always benefits the rich more than the poor, and reduces the ability of cash-strapped public utilities to extend service to the poorest peri-urban neighbor-hoods. Imposing water fees encourages the responsible management of water and enables better operation and maintenance of water supply systems.

The principle that concern for social and environmental sustainability must permeate *all* development activity is fundamental to the concept of sustainable development and was accepted universally at the Earth Summit in 1992. To promote this principle, the development community in general, and the World Bank in particular, are changing the way they do business. The World Bank is building its work in environmentally sustainable development on two widely accepted propositions: (a) that reducing poverty and investing in people are essential for environmental sustainability and (b) that promoting the efficient use of resources benefits both the environment and the economy.

The strategies implied by these propositions are consistent with the Bank's central mission—reducing poverty. This chapter is organized around these two propositions. Although it makes no attempt to be comprehensive, by examining examples of activities that are aimed at poverty, population, and the environment or that improve the efficiency of resource use, it provides an indication of how the different activities in the various sectors and departments in the Bank link to create a coherent approach to sustainable development.

Poverty, Population, and the Environment

It is now widely accepted that the links between poverty, high population growth, and environmental degradation are circular and mutually reinforcing. Investing in people, which reduces poverty and population growth, is an urgent moral imperative and is essential, in the long run, for arresting environmental degradation. For many of the poor, earning more income or accumulating needed assets means mining the scant natural resources accessible to them: soil is cultivated without traditional fallow periods, marginal land is tilled, trees are felled, and animal dung and other natural fertilizers are used as fuel, as an increasing number of people seek to feed, shelter, and warm themselves. In many sections of Africa the current consumption of fuelwood exceeds annual growth in supply by as much as 30 to 200 percent. The consequence is that the cycle of poverty, unless broken, condemns poor people to ever-worsening conditions.

The Bank has undertaken research on these links between rapid population growth, poor agricultural development, and environmental degradation, particularly in Africa. This "nexus," first elaborated in a major study in 1992, has been explored further in a series of studies that examine new ways of leveraging these links so as to stop and reverse the cycle.[1] Those published this year focused on land resource management in the Machakos District in Kenya, land rights in Côte d'Ivoire, soil degradation in Ethiopia, and similar issues in Malawi and Nigeria. The analyses present an alarming picture but also illustrate that good policies can make a difference. A study of the Machakos District, for example, illustrates how the nexus links of low income and resource degradation have been turned to advantage through access to markets; considerable investment in education, health, agricultural services, and infrastructure that have contributed to increased per capita agricultural production and income; improvements in natural resource management; and relative economic stability—despite a fivefold increase in population since 1930. Nevertheless, the same initiatives would have produced even better results if the high population growth rate had been reduced.

From a practical perspective, interventions that leverage the environment-development nexus to achieve improvement both in human well-being and in the health of the environment can be divided into three broad categories:

- Resource development interventions that seek to improve the material well-being of the poor and provide incentives to invest in their futures will enable the poor to avoid spending the natural "capital" (rather than only the natural "product") at their disposal.
- Human development interventions, such as those that improve health, nutrition, and education and provide access to better family planning, will help reduce population growth, make people better able to use natural resources efficiently, enable them to make informed choices about how to use resources, and provide them with the means of improving their physical well-being and productivity.
- Social development interventions—which help ensure that the development process reaches down to those who need it most by giving the poor a voice and a role in shaping it—lead to projects that are more sustainable and to a more equitable resolution of the tensions between environmental health and people's aspirations.

These concepts are becoming useful tools for gaining a better understanding of the interaction between the natural and social systems that manifests itself through the various links, and they provide a basis for examining the effect of policy and market failures on these links. From the project perspective, these concepts lay the foundation for developing an integrated package of actions or programs that promote environmentally sustainable development. This conceptual framework has been successfully applied this year in Tanzania in developing the national environmental action plan. Box 3.1 illustrates the application of the nexus principles in Africa.

Box 3.1. Doing Things Differently: Natural Resource Management in the Sahel

A new generation of rural development projects is being developed in the Sahel with financing from IDA and other donors. By bringing together the various approaches to the environment and development nexus, these projects illustrate how Bank practice has evolved. The first such projects are in Burkina Faso and Mali; similar projects will be implemented in Chad, the Gambia, Mauritania, and Niger. The operations, which are based on the strategy of village resource management (*gestion des terroirs villageois*, GTV), combine two critical features: they are participatory, and they are intersectoral.

The projects are based on a social unit, the community's *terroir*, rather than on a physical unit such as a watershed. The communities of beneficiaries have an active role in the preparation, implementation, and evaluation of the projects, and the final objective is the complete control and management by the community of the land, water, and vegetation under its jurisdiction. Under their village resource management plans, rural communities make decisions regarding land allocation for crops, fallowing, grazing, and fuelwood production. For example, they might manage the land, water, and vegetation (and even biodiversity on the land when the *terroir* is near a national park or nature reserve). Such an arrangement often represents an important break from more recent habits of state organization. Thus in Burkina Faso a prerequisite for the GTV approach was the amendment of the land tenure law nationalizing rural land. Although the law was never effectively implemented, it had created uncertainties and discouraged land improvement.

Poverty Reduction and Natural Resource Management

TARGETING POVERTY REDUCTION. The Bank's strategy for reducing poverty (formalized in Operational Directive 4.15: *Poverty Reduction*) involves fostering the efficient use of labor, which is one asset the poor have in abundance; increasing the access of the poor to ownership of physical assets, natural resources, and other forms of capital (by, for example, establishing or regularizing land tenure rights); raising the productivity of different forms of capital in the hands of the poor (by providing infrastructure such as roads and public transport, accessible credit, and technology); developing human capital (by such means as increasing access to and improving the quality of health, nutrition, and education services); improving living conditions (by, for example, providing social services such as clean water and sanitation); and providing safety net protection (by designing social investment funds, for instance).

In pursuing this strategy, the Bank assists borrowers in preparing country-specific poverty assessments and designing country-specific strategies to make sure that Bank programs support and complement the country's own efforts to reduce poverty. Poverty assessments, which increasingly involve beneficiary assessments, are important means of improving the design and implementation of poverty alleviation projects. They typically provide a diagnosis of the scale and structure of poverty—the factual basis needed for proposing actions that will be effective in actually reducing poverty. Twenty-one poverty assessments were completed in fiscal 1994. It is expected that by the end of fiscal 1995, 94 assessments for 83 countries will be completed, and a total of 114 assessments for 101 countries are scheduled for completion by fiscal 1997.

The Bank has continued to expand its lending for poverty reduction. The Program of Targeted Interventions (PTI) provides a valuable way of monitoring targeted lending, but it is only one aspect of Bank support for poverty reduction. Projects in the PTI complement broader macroeconomic and sectoral policies and public expenditures that are also part of the efforts of countries to reduce poverty. As monitored by the PTI, lending for projects that specifically target the poor rose to almost $4.5 billion in fiscal 1994. This was equal to 33 percent of total investment lending, compared with 26 percent in 1993 and 24 percent in fiscal 1992. The total number of projects targeting the poor rose from fifty-eight in fiscal 1992 to sixty-six in fiscal 1994, of which ten are directly targeted at natural resource management. For example, the Tunisia Northwest Mountainous Areas Development Project, described in box 3.2, explicitly addresses both rural poverty and natural resource degradation.

The Bank has also begun to adopt innovative ways of providing the extremely poor with access to credit to improve the management of natural resources. These programs usually encourage the use of nontraditional forms of collateral and promote increased investments in land and water resources. Most of these collateral programs are designed to benefit women, in particular. For example the Agricultural Modernization Project in Egypt will provide credit to women farmers and investors by targeting 350 village banks that will extend loans to women with group guarantees as collateral. In the Benin Community-Based Food Security Project, 50 percent of the financing allocated for income-generating activities will be reserved for groups made up entirely of women. In addition, this year the Bank provided $2 million in grant funds toward setting up the Grameen Trust, which will provide seed capital and start-up funds over the next five years to some thirty or forty microcredit schemes modeled on the Grameen Bank in Bangladesh. (The Grameen Bank is a microlevel program that provides credit to the

---

Box 3.2. Addressing Rural Poverty and Natural Resource Management in Tunisia

The objective of the Tunisia Northwest Mountainous Areas Development Project, supported by a Bank loan of $17.3 million, is to help the population make better use of the limited natural resources available to them in remote mountainous areas. It will help restore sustainable range, forest, and farming activities; reduce soil degradation, erosion, and sedimentation in reservoirs; and increase productivity and incomes for very poor farmers. By using a participatory approach, the project will strengthen the farmers' capacity to plan and implement and will improve the responsiveness of rural service agencies to farmers' needs. The two largest components of this project focus on watershed and rangeland management and on improving the rural infrastructure base. The watershed and rangeland component promotes such measures as rotational grazing to allow regeneration of the vegetation; fertilization grazing areas to improve hay and forage production; and reseeding with native forage species to reestablish rangeland productivity and promote agroforestry. All these measures will help restore natural vegetative cover, reduce runoff and soil loss, and improve soil fertility. The infrastructure component provides isolated villages with access to markets and potable water and improves education and health services by constructing and maintaining such basic needs as rural roads, schools and classrooms, and health centers.

---

extremely poor, almost always women in rural areas. The success of the Grameen Bank has been remarkable and has led to a marked increase in net worth and ownership of resources, higher participation by women in the labor force, and a great improvement in other household welfare indicators such as contraceptive use and the number of children, including girls, enrolled in school.)

USING MARKET FORCES TO IMPROVE RURAL RESOURCE MANAGEMENT. In many countries, both industrial and developing, natural resources such as water are frequently treated as inexhaustible. This ideology discourages charging a price for such resources, with the frequent result that resources are misallocated and used wastefully because access is based on priority or proximity rather than on the value of the resource. In Brazil and Peru, for example, through technical assistance and study tours, the Bank has shown resource managers the advantages accruing to a system in which water rights are vested in users and can be traded in a market. This approach makes water an "economic" good and encourages efficiency and reallocation to higher-value uses. The owners of water can then make better decisions on whether to use the water themselves or sell the use rights to others.

STRENGTHENING AGRICULTURAL RESEARCH AND EXTENSION. Increased crop yields and adoption of new technologies can improve the welfare of farmers, reduce environmental damage, and relieve pressure to convert new land to agriculture. For example, if India had to produce its current wheat harvest with the technologies of twenty-five years ago, farmers would have to bring 40 million *additional* hectares of land of equal quality into production. Because of successes in agricultural research and extension, this tremendous onslaught on fragile lands and forest margins has been avoided.

The forty-eight Bank loans and credits for agriculture sector projects amounted to almost $4 billion in fiscal 1994. They included the Mali Agricultural Research Project, which will make adequate technology available for increasing agricultural growth and reversing the decline in the natural resource base; the Mauritania Agricultural Services Project, which will focus on strengthening the links between extension, research, and agricultural training; and the Viet Nam Agricultural Rehabilitation Project, which will support rehabilitation of the extension system, promote the use of environmentally sound pest management in agriculture, and provide assistance to research institutes. Each project has the objective of an ultimate increase in agricultural efficiency and productivity that will be environmentally sustainable as well.

In addition, the Bank, in cooperation with the Food and Agricultural Organization of the United Nations (FAO) and the UNDP, sponsors the Consultative Group on International Agricultural Research (CGIAR), which the Bank's vice president for ESD currently chairs. CGIAR is a network of sixteen agricultural research centers. At its founding, twenty years ago, the principal objective of the group was to increase the supply of food and so stave off the threat of mass starvation. Since then, the Green Revolution—the development of new high-yielding varieties of wheat and rice—has brought food self-sufficiency and even surpluses to former food-deficit areas. In recent years CGIAR has been shifting its priorities toward improving the sustainability of agricultural development. This goal requires the successful management of agricultural resources to make possible the satisfaction of changing human needs without degrading the environment or the natural resource base on which agriculture depends.

This year the chair submitted a wide-ranging proposal for revitalizing the CGIAR system. A fundamental need is to stabilize the system's financial situation. (The Bank may contribute up to $40 million per year in

1994 and 1995 toward this end and provide additional financing of up to \$20 million to match other donor contributions for the same period). Decisive measures are also proposed for halting the loss of the group's scientific capacity and refocusing the research agenda on approved programs. Reform of governance and management is proposed to ensure predictability, transparency, and accountability. An additional goal is to firmly link the CGIAR programs to participatory programs at the farm level, especially to women's groups and other NGOs. Finally, procedures were proposed for agreeing on a plan of action, including an eighteen-month timetable to formulate and secure endorsement of the new strategies and principles at high government level.

The CGIAR has identified three key areas of focus that will contribute to more sustainable practices:

- Maintaining the productivity of the land and water resources, with less reliance on fertilizers and pesticides, will require diversification of crops and adaptability to different ecological zones. Biotechnology, including accelerated breeding through gene-marking and transgenetic methods, will therefore be a priority area for CGIAR research. These research activities will also need to be linked to farming systems studies and participatory community-based work, with particular attention to the role of women.
- Genetic resource banks, which now include about 600,000 samples, will be maintained and expanded. In addition, the CGIAR will play a role in clarifying new statutes as the implications of the Biodiversity Convention and the General Agreement on Tariffs and Trade (GATT) are factored into national legislation, so that germplasms will continue to be readily available for applications at the farm level.
- Water scarcity, as a central part of natural resource management, remains a key focus of CGIAR. Two new areas that reflect the international nature of CGIAR are aquatic and marine resources and coastal zones.

Women in Ecosystem Management

Targeting projects to benefit women has been an important focus for the Bank in recent years, both for reducing poverty and for protecting the environment. Good natural resource management is particularly important for rural women, whose work is increased as firewood and water become scarcer and soils less fertile—and who are more and more often solely responsible for farming the land. The role of primary agricultural producer may be a traditional one for women (as in Sub-Saharan Africa) or an increasingly important one, as men migrate to urban jobs. Moreover, educating girls not only has a powerful effect in reducing birthrates but also tends to improve the well-being and productivity of the whole household, since women are generally responsible for the health of their families, in addition to being the main providers of food in many rural areas.

The Pakistan Social Action Program Project, approved this fiscal year, benefits women by providing various educational and health services. It will increase girls' enrollment in primary education by recruiting and training more female teachers, promoting coeducation, and providing more schools for girls. It will improve women's health through increased access to health care (by recruiting and training more female medical staff at various levels of service), encourage family planning, improve the quality of rural water supply and sanitation, and expand access to these services through community-based approaches. An increasing number of projects now have women in development (WID) components, and about a third of the projects in fiscal 1994 included gender-related activities. For example, the Lao PDR Forest Management and Conservation Project and the Northwest Mountainous Areas Development Project in Tunisia, both free-standing environment loans, include such activities. In the Lao PDR a WID specialist will be included in each community mobilization training team to ensure women's participation in community planning of the use of forest resources. The Women's Union will also participate in the Lao project. In the Tunisian project female extension workers will be based at each extension and development center to help integrate women into all levels and each aspect of the project's extension activities. Countrywide assessments of WID have now been completed in more than fifty countries.

Agenda 21, adopted at the United Nations Conference on Environment and Development (UNCED) in 1992, places particular emphasis on the role of women in sustainable development. To follow up, in October 1994 the Bank hosted a three-day International Consultation on Women and Ecosystem Management, cosponsored by the Inter-American Development Bank (IDB), the United Nations Development Fund for Women (UNIFEM), the United Nations Sudano-Sahelian Office (UNSO), the UNDP, and the UNEP. The consultation was to encourage joint initiatives among international, regional, and bilateral organizations for engaging women in ecosystem management at the grassroots; to promote the inclusion of women at all levels of society and sectors to advance sustainable ecosystem and equitable development; to support incorporation of policies that would enhance the role of women as ecosystem managers into the deliberations of the Commission on Sustainable Development, the 1994 World Population Conference (held in Cairo in September), the 1995

Fourth World Conference on Women (to be held in Beijing), and the 1995 World Social Development Summit (to be held in Copenhagen); and, finally, to explore ways to improve the effectiveness and cost efficiency of projects that jointly support the advancement of women and ecosystem management through WID and environment cooperation.

The consultation identified the gender issues in ecosystem management in each of five ecosystems: coastal and wetland areas; rivers, groundwater, and lakes; mountains; temperate and tropical forests; and arid and semiarid lands. Although women have different roles to play in each of these ecosystems, the participants at the consultation identified a set of general requirements for women to be effective managers of environmental and natural resources regardless of the ecosystem involved. These requirements include the need for secure rights to land and other natural resources, for access to credit, for full engagement in the process of designing and implementing a project, and for training and environmental education programs. The consultation also emphasized the need to examine the different economic roles of men and women in WID and environment programs and underscored the importance of assessing the microlevel consequences for women (who operate mainly in the informal sector) of macrolevel economic policies.

Social and Natural Resources

There is a growing recognition that the participation of stakeholders in the selection and design of projects can improve decisionmaking, strengthen ownership of projects, and help poor and disadvantaged groups. Over the past year the Bank's Environment Department has coordinated efforts to incorporate social concerns into the Bank's development work, using the techniques of social assessment. Not only are poor people often the primary natural resource managers, they are also the most likely to be affected by, and the least able to avoid, harm from changes in their environment.

SOCIAL FACTORS IN NATURAL RESOURCE MANAGEMENT. Over centuries people build up refined knowledge of the peculiar biological and physical environments around them, techniques for managing those ecosystems, and methods for handling problems that have arisen. The Bank is working to increase knowledge of social factors in natural resource management through a review and synthesis of prior approaches, through action research and testing of new strategies, and through projects that enhance local management capacities rather than disable them. The Bank's recent work in the area of forestry and biodiversity conservation, described in box 3.3, is an example. This year the Bank has also supported work on pastoral associations for sustainable rangeland

Box 3.3. Incorporating Stakeholder Participation into Forestry and Biodiversity Conservation

This year the Bank began developing methodologies for systematically incorporating social and stakeholder-participation issues into sector work and projects in the area of forestry and biodiversity conservation.

- To improve project preparation and sector analyses, the Bank prepared general guidelines for applying the techniques of social assessment to biodiversity conservation projects, in order to provide approaches for reconciling the needs of local populations with biodiversity protection objectives. These approaches are being field tested in Brazil, Ecuador, and India.
- Techniques for promoting stakeholder involvement in forestry sector work and projects were compiled and reviewed in a technical paper for the Participation Sourcebook, discussed in the text. This paper required a more thorough review of the forestry portfolio taking into account best-practice approaches to enhancing stakeholder accountability and participation. The review included thirty-seven forestry projects.
- An evaluation of implementation issues related to the design of integrated conservation and development projects (ICDPs) is being completed. This review examines the key issues in ICDPs, looks at examples of successes and failures, and makes recommendations, where appropriate, on modifying biodiversity protection criteria to accommodate the needs of local populations.
- Ongoing work with indigenous peoples focuses on reducing poverty through legal recognition and protection of access to natural resources. For example, this year the Colombia Natural Resources Management Project is establishing secure rights to 4 million hectares for Afro-Colombian people and another 1 million hectares for Amerindians. In Paraguay the Natural Resources Management Project is demarcating and titling 6,500 hectares for 1,285 Tupi-Guaraní families. (Both projects are discussed in chapter 1.) In all, Bank lending to date is supporting the regularization of more than 13 million hectares of land for indigenous peoples in Latin America.
- In addition, work with indigenous people is being extended to Siberian Russia (for oil development planning), to Asia (particularly for indigenous people affected by large infrastructure and conservation programs), and to Africa (where indigenous people are especially being affected by biodiversity conservation efforts, often in national parklands). In Asia, for example, recent Bank loans and GEF grants to India, the Lao PDR, and the Philippines are based on the strong participation of forest-dwelling indigenous communities in the management of the forest resource.

management in the West African Sahel, particularly where devaluation of the CFA franc has spurred demand for livestock products; such demand will increase pressures on the natural resources on which production is based. Work is also beginning on the social aspects of coastal zone and fisheries management.

PARTICIPATION. This year the Bank has undertaken analytical work and documentation of best practice in participatory approaches and methods of inquiry and training to support participatory development. A Participation Sourcebook is being prepared by the Bank's Environment Department with "how-to" guidelines for participation. In addition, the sourcebook will contain best-practice case studies relating experiences of Bank task managers who have worked with participation in Bank-supported operations. In recognition of the rapidly changing nature of the issue, the sourcebook is not intended to be a definitive product but the first version of an evolving document in looseleaf binder format. The sourcebook draws on the contributions of more than 200 Bank staff. Nineteen chapters have been completed and will be published as separate papers in the Bank Environment Technical Paper Series during the coming year. They will serve as background and in-depth material for the sourcebook itself, which will be published later in fiscal 1995.

PARTICIPATORY POVERTY ASSESSMENT. Analytical work on poverty is being carried out in every IDA country and in many IBRD countries. While this work is exposing the dimensions of poverty, identifying the priority strategies and building the sustainable programs for lifting people out of poverty are best done with poor people themselves. Therefore the Bank has initiated a series of participatory poverty assessments (PPAs) to illuminate the human dimension of poverty. PPAs strive to discover how the poor view public services, particularly health and education but also transport, infrastructure, and administrative institutions in general. This year PPA work has been completed in Benin, Ghana, Guatemala, Kenya, Madagascar, Uganda, and Zambia and is under way in Argentina, Cameroon, Central African Republic, Costa Rica, Ecuador, Pakistan, and South Africa. Future work is being planned for Brazil, Côte d'Ivoire, Gabon, and Mexico. Although few PPAs are at a stage at which their impact on policy formation is visible, it appears that their findings are both complementary to the quantitative work done for poverty assessments and of great potential for improving the relevance and sustainability of policy directed toward poverty reduction.

BENEFICIARY ASSESSMENT. Beneficiary assessment (BA) is a technique for learning the views of people affected by a project at any stage of the project, thus increasing the likelihood that the project design and implementation strategy will be rooted in people's expressed needs. The Bank's Southern Africa Department has been the first to mandate that all operations take account of the views of different client groups, and BAs are being used to fulfill this mandate. Although still incomplete, a BA being carried out on training and visit (T&V) agricultural extension work in Senegal is supplying initial insights about farmer response to extension that have convinced the government implementing agency to increase its use of qualitative methodologies in the future. In Zambia BAs have been carried out on projects in health, education, and social funds. In the case of social funds the findings were particularly useful in showing how different kinds of NGOs had different effects on encouraging the participation of community residents. These findings are being used to assist a subsequent social fund project in Zambia with selecting NGOs for optimal grassroots development.

COMMUNITY-BASED DEVELOPMENT. Existing social organization already has within it tremendous stocks of "social capital"—techniques, trustful relationships, knowledge, organizational skills, confidence, and commitment built from long experience—that can form a foundation for long-term development. Work with indigenous people is one specific area in which development can be community based. In September 1993 a conference on "Traditional Knowledge and Sustainable Development" brought together indigenous people from several continents to educate Bank staff and others about the contributions of traditional or local knowledge to fields as diverse as health, environment, management of natural resources, governance, and local development planning. The Bank, in cooperation with the IUCN Regional Office for Southern Africa, sponsored a series of workshops in Africa for regional NGOs on the use of traditional knowledge in conservation work. In Latin America, with resources available through the Bank's IDF and working with the recently created Hemispheric Indigenous Peoples Fund in La Paz, Bolivia, the Bank began to promote a series of country training programs in development planning and project design for the region's growing number of indigenous organizations. Two programs have been launched so far, in Bolivia and Chile, and seven other countries will soon have similar programs.

Efficient Use of Resources and the Environment

Promoting the efficient use of energy and other resources is the second broad mechanism whereby the Bank influences environmental stewardship indirectly. Policies that encourage efficiency lead to less waste and less consumption of raw materials. Economywide policies also have important effects on how resources are used and on levels of air and water pollution.

Improving Energy Conservation and Efficiency

The consumption of commercial energy in developing countries is rising rapidly and now accounts for 27 percent of the world total. By 2010 energy demand in developing countries is expected to account for more than 40 percent of the total, and energy consumption and efficiency will take on increased importance. Much of this energy is heavily subsidized: overall energy subsidies amount to about $230 billion annually. If, for example, tariffs for electricity alone reflected real costs, an estimated $125 billion per year in savings would be realized.

Encouraging improvements in energy efficiency cannot be pursued in isolation. Efficient use of energy requires a broadly based set of conditions and policies: a stable and open economy (including reforms in pricing, industry, trade, and the financial sector and openness to private investments) is fundamental for achieving economic efficiency in energy production and use. Structural and sectoral adjustment loans and credits (SALs and SECALs) and public enterprise reform loans (PERLs) are the Bank's main instruments for improving macroeconomic conditions.

Since the publication of two energy policy papers in November 1992, the Bank's experience with energy pricing has confirmed that prices and tariffs affect end-use efficiency and, therefore, the environment. In fact, pricing measures typically tap about half of all possible energy savings from demand-side management. But price reform is also an important component of more general structural reform of the sector. A review of countries whose electricity sectors have instituted far-reaching reforms, such as unbundling and the introduction of competition (Argentina, Chile, and Malaysia) shows that revenue from energy sales now cover costs and that the sector is able to generate adequate resources for future investments. In countries where reform is currently under way, prices are not yet in line with costs, but the trend is in the right direction (for example, in China, Morocco, and Pakistan), while in countries that have not embarked on a reform path, prices are generally significantly below costs and the sector must be subsidized from fiscal resources (Nigeria, Turkey, and Ukraine).

Typically, in unreformed countries consumption patterns are heavily skewed toward inefficient use of electricity, while at the same time the quality of supply is low, with frequent brownouts or blackouts and wide swings in voltage and frequency. The Bank plays a significant role in price reform in countries to which it lends for power projects. For example, assistance on price reform is being provided in China, Côte d'Ivoire, India, Indonesia, Morocco, and Poland. Iran's efforts to reduce distortions in resource pricing and improve environmental quality are described in box 3.4.

Two main lessons emerge from recent Bank experience. First, price reform is a component of sector reform, not an alternative to it. In fact, it is questionable whether sustainable price reform can be achieved without addressing the underlying structural problems in the sector. Second, the reform of electricity tariffs involves more than simply adjusting the overall level to cover costs. Just as important is the introduction of differential pricing such as time-of-day tariffs, which will have an important effect on load management and will bring down the cost of electricity generation, and adjustment of prices to different consumer groups to eliminate cross-subsidies. Negative impacts of price reform on poorer segments of the population can largely be mitigated by lifeline tariffs and by innovative financing mechanisms for new connections.

Privatization is an important element in reform of the energy sector: it promotes economic efficiency, and it improves the technical and managerial efficiency of the sector. Projects approved in fiscal 1994 that include restructuring the energy and power sectors and that will encourage private participation range from the Madagascar Petroleum Sector Reform Project to the Pakistan Power Sector Development Project. The Madagascar project will create an appropriate framework for private participation and increase institutional capacity for regulating the sector.

Box 3.4. Win-Win Strategies for Mitigating Environmental Degradation in Iran

Iran's strategy for tackling pollution, environmental degradation, and poor natural resources management rests squarely on market-oriented policy instruments that promote economic efficiency while simultaneously improving the quality of the environment. In the past, heavy subsidies for energy, water, and agricultural chemicals have led to wasteful consumption of resources, more resource-intensive forms of production, and higher pollution levels. For example, low energy prices failed to provide incentives for conserving energy and investing in more efficient processes, and the results were wasteful use of energy and excessive emissions of particulates. Among the win-win options that yield both net economic benefits and environmental benefits are price reforms. It is estimated that efficient energy pricing would reduce premature deaths by about 13,000 a year and would result in fuel savings of $4.7 billion a year.

The Pakistan project has investment and technical assistance components and includes a restructuring and privatization component that will reorganize the Water and Power Development Authority, establish a national regulatory authority, lead to a new pricing policy, and develop a labor-transition program. Other similar projects were approved this year for Hungary, Kazakhstan, Lithuania, Papua New Guinea, Russia, and Zambia.

In addition to promoting efficiency through policy and price reform, Bank lending supports direct intervention and projects affecting fuel choice and technology options. Thus the Russian Federation Second Oil Rehabilitation Project will modernize approximately 1,200 wells, provide measuring facilities, and reconstruct surface facilities (for example, it will replace pipelines and water conduits with corrosion-resistant pipes). Other projects promote the use of cleaner fuels and renewable energy sources. Examples for fiscal 1994 include the China Sichuan Gas Development and Conservation Project (which will substitute coal for gas, thereby reducing emissions of sulfur dioxide, carbon dioxide, and particulates); the Ethiopia Calub Gas Development Project (for mitigating deforestation by replacing woodfuels with liquefied petroleum gas (LPG) in the southeastern region of the country); and the Estonia District Heating Rehabilitation Project (which includes a component to convert small boilers in small towns and counties for use of locally abundant peat and wood rather than the heavy oil used currently). The Estonia project also includes a provision for the sustainable harvesting of the peat and wood (see chapter 1 for details).

Progress with "Clean" Technologies and Practices, Including Renewable Energy

Improving the efficiency with which energy is produced and used will help to abate pollution but by itself cannot reduce it sufficiently. This is especially true in developing countries, where energy demands are growing rapidly and will continue to do so for some decades. Per capita consumption of commercial energy in the low-income economies, which account for 3 billion of the world's population, is less than 4 percent that of the United States; 2 billion people are without electricity and use dung and fuelwood for cooking, a practice that is a major source of environmental damage.

For these reasons, the Bank's economic and sector work on energy is focusing on the use of clean technologies to reduce particulate emissions. The Bank has been active in promoting natural gas for power generation and has financed two 235-megawatt combined-cycle cogeneration units in Hungary and a 300-megawatt combined-cycle gas turbine in Malaysia. Both projects are part of a wider environmental framework that includes, in Hungary, developing an environmental master plan and strengthening environmental management and monitoring capabilities and, in Malaysia, providing technical assistance to the utility's environmental division. The Bank has also been active in the provision of natural gas for domestic and industrial uses; for example, in Egypt it financed a pipeline that will extend the existing gas distribution system to 235,000 additional households, 5,000 commercial enterprises, and 22 industrial enterprises in Cairo, thus displacing liquefied petroleum gas, gas oil, and fuel oil.

Another area of interest is "clean" coal technologies that make use of cost-effective emission controls for removing particulates. In Indonesia, for example, the Bank financed the construction of three 600-megawatt coal units that use low-sulfur coal and are fitted with electrostatic precipitators that remove 99.5 percent of the particulate from the flue gas. Bank financing is also available in other cases where desulfurization is necessary (as in a new plant in Dahanu, India, and an existing plant in Prunerov, Czech Republic).

Such policies and practices, however, still leave unanswered the important questions arising from the dependence on biofuels of 2 billion people who lack access to electricity. That dependence is a source of impoverishment, environmental degradation, and, as *World Development Report 1992* pointed out, ill health. The Bank addresses this problem through two groups of policies and investments.

The first group encourages *more sustainable forms of producing and using biofuels* based on social forestry (for which the Bank has lent approximately $1 billion since 1980), improved soil management practices, and efforts to encourage the wider adoption of improved cookstoves. Improved stove programs have met with mixed results over the years. One recent successful operation was an IDA credit for improved charcoal stoves in Tanzania. The stoves have raised energy efficiency by 50 percent, and adoption rates have been very high—nearly half the population in Dar-es-Salaam use the improved stove. Further studies of rural energy policies are currently under way in Sahelian countries, with the joint support of the Bank and the Dutch government.

The second group *extends modern forms of energy* to a greater share of the world's population. In the past twenty years electricity supplies have been newly extended to a billion people in developing countries—nearly twice the population of the United States and Europe. Although this is a very impressive accomplishment, 2 billion people are still without electricity, and the world population will grow by another 3 billion in the next three or four decades. The situation may be environmentally and socially unsustainable. Efforts must therefore be made to make possible a switch to modern fuels, such as LPG, which emit far less pollution of all forms—sulfur dioxide, particulates, nitrogen oxides, carbon monoxide, and carbon dioxide—and are also more efficient. LPG is five times more efficient a cooking fuel than biofuels, and it is more convenient to use; electric lamps using incandescent light bulbs are ten to twenty times more efficient than kerosene lamps, which are still the most common source of light in rural areas in low-income countries. The Bank therefore continues to support expansion of electricity distribution systems. Since the publication of the policy paper on rural electrification in 1974, for example, the Bank has lent approximately $2 billion for rural electrification. To encourage the wider distribution and use of modern fuels the Bank has encouraged member countries to use pricing policies to promote market expansion.

Renewable energy resources show promise. This year the Bank funded two projects in the Philippines: the Leyte-Cebu Geothermal and the Leyte-Luzon Geothermal (also supported by the GEF), which added a combined 640 megawatts to the country's existing 1,000 megawatts of installed geothermal capacity. Geothermal energy production has much lower carbon dioxide, sulfur dioxide, and nitrogen oxide emissions than fossil fuels, and it helps reduce the country's dependence on imported oil.

Reductions in the costs of solar energy technologies have been substantial. The costs of photovoltaic cells (PVs), for example, have declined from several hundred thousand dollars per unit of peak capacity to less than $6,000 today. Village and domestic lighting, water pumping, battery charging, and electric power for rural health clinics in developing countries are examples of the wide use of PVs. Despite the impressive gains, solar power is still not fully commercial except for small-scale, off-grid applications. However, concerns about global warming produce an impetus for speeding up the process of commercialization. In conjunction with the GEF, the Bank began this year a process of defining a collaborative program among countries on R&D and demonstration projects for solar energy technology. Moreover, under the GEF a number of solar energy projects have begun or are in the pipeline (these are discussed in chapter 4).

Eliminating Subsidies for Use of Resources

Energy is only one of the types of resources that are often subsidized or underpriced and are therefore used inefficiently. Others are water and sanitation and such agricultural inputs as pesticides and fertilizers.

"Implicit" subsidies, such as inadequate stumpage fees for logging enterprises, are also being increasingly recognized.

In the water sector misguided subsidies continue to handicap efforts to provide clean water and sanitation, despite some remarkable achievements. The real costs of water and sanitation supply are rising as a result of the increasing cost of reaching rapidly growing urban populations and the growing scarcity of clean water. A recent comprehensive review of Bank experience in water and sanitation projects documents compellingly that supply costs in developing countries are much higher than they should be, largely because of the low efficiency of water supply agencies (see OED 1992). For example, in Singapore, an excellent performer in this respect, unaccounted-for water (water lost between the distribution point and the users) is 8 percent of total water produced, but in Manila the share is 58 percent and in most Latin American cities is about 40 percent. For Latin America as a whole such water losses cost up to $1.5 billion in forgone revenue every year. Yet in Mexico City subsidies to the water and sewerage services amount to more than $1 billion a year, or 0.6 percent of the gross domestic product (GDP). Subsidizing water has two costs: it promotes waste, and it slows expansion of services to reach growing, and often very poor, peri-urban neighborhoods, as neither the water nor the revenue to finance its provision is readily available.

Data from Latin America and Africa provide clear confirmation that the beneficiaries from water subsidies are almost always the rich. The poor, whose needs are used to justify water subsidies, are often not served and pay street vendors as much as ten times the public price for water, as a recent study in Onitsha, Nigeria, confirms. Eliminating subsidies for irrigation water is also important. The Mexican On-Farm and Minor Irrigation Networks Improvement Project plans to reduce loss and waste of irrigation water through charging water fees. The National Water Commission of Mexico intends to recover 50 to 100 percent of costs for on-farm improvements and 100 percent of running costs from water users, who will also be responsible for operation and maintenance. Other projects with similar components were approved this year in Brazil, Guyana, and Indonesia.

Rational pricing has received attention in the forestry sector, as well as in water and sanitation. Several projects this year include provisions to encourage the improved pricing of wood. Three are free-standing environment projects: the Bhutan Third Forestry Project supports the development and implementation of a new pricing and marketing plan for forest products; the Lao PDR Forest Management and Conservation Project will revise the system of log pricing, which currently encourages tree felling and processing activities; and the Poland Forest Development

Support Project will help develop a new wood-pricing system that will move from rates fixed by the central government to market-based prices reflecting true supply and demand. In addition, the Belarus Forestry Development Project includes a component for implementing macroeconomic and sectoral policy reforms to make the forestry sector more market oriented and will define a new regulatory framework.

Economywide Policies and the Environment

The positive links between economic efficiency, human well-being, and environmental health are clear and widely accepted. However, in practice the effects of broadly based policy reforms are more ambiguous when applied, as they must be, under imperfect circumstances where economies do not function smoothly and distortions persist. Recently, the Bank completed a review of progress made in understanding the links between economywide policies and the environment (see Mohan and Cruz forthcoming). The analysis is based on a comprehensive survey of recent and current Bank case studies. The main findings follow.

- *Removal of major price distortions, promotion of market incentives, and relaxation of other constraints, which are among the main features of adjustment-related reforms, generally will contribute to both economic and environmental gains.* For example, reforms to improve the efficiency of industrial or energy-related activities could reduce both economic waste and environmental pollution. Similarly, addressing the problems of land tenure and access to financial and social services not only yields economic gains but also promotes better environmental stewardship.
- *Unintended adverse side effects may occur when economywide reforms are undertaken even in the presence of neglected policy, market, or institutional imperfections.* Therefore, specific measures that remove such policy, market, and institutional obstacles are not only generally environmentally beneficial in their own right but are also critical complements to broadening economywide reforms. In Morocco, for example, distorted trade policies are projected to lead to a severe water deficit by the year 2020, even though by the same year water sector investments will account for 60 percent of the government budget. The study examined two simulations: raising water prices reduced water use but lowered GDP; liberalizing trade improved household incomes and consumption and allocated resources more efficiently across the economy but also led to increased water use. If complementary increases in water prices were

undertaken simultaneously with trade liberalization, the beneficial expansionary effects of the latter would be largely retained but with substantial reductions in water use. (Another example of policy distortions, in Poland, is described in box 3.5.)

- *Measures for restoring macroeconomic stability will generally yield environmental benefits, since instability undermines sustainable resource use.* For example, stability encourages a longer-term view by decision-makers at all levels, and lower inflation rates lead to clearer pricing signals and better investment decisions by economic agents. These are essential prerequisites for encouraging environmentally sustainable activities.

- *The stabilization process may also have unforeseen, adverse, short-run effects on the environment.* For example, although general reductions

---

Box 3.5. The Need to Address Policy Distortions to Ensure Environmental Gains

In Poland energy intensity and excessive pollution are the fruit not only of the undervaluation of coal in the centralized price system but also of the entire system of state ownership that suppressed market signals and incentives. Previous research has shown how economywide adjustments, including increases in energy prices, contribute to improvements in energy use and pollution in Poland. However, because state ownership encourages output maximization rather than cost minimization, price responsiveness is blunted, and financial losses are simply absorbed into the public budget or passed on to consumers in the form of higher output prices.

In 1990 Poland began an economic transformation program that led to the privatization of many state enterprises. However, the program was adversely affected by a recession and the collapse of trading arrangements linked to the Council of Mutual Economic Assistance. Furthermore, the process of privatization proved to be more complex and lengthy than initially expected, and the government will retain ownership in the energy, mining, steel, and defense sectors in the medium term. Restructuring efforts in the energy sector have accordingly focused on creating an institutional and legal framework that will encourage competition and greater private sector participation in the future. Coupled with aggressive energy pricing reforms, this strategy appears to be making some headway. For example, a recent survey of large state-owned manufacturing concerns found that even without privatization, state-owned enterprises are already adjusting to the transformation program and are reducing their consumption of materials and energy per unit of sales.

in government spending are deemed appropriate, targeting these cutbacks is desirable to avoid disproportionate penalties on environmental protection measures. Another important issue is that the short-term effect of adjustments on poverty and unemployment may increase pressures on fragile and open-access resources by the poor, in the absence of other economic opportunities. In this case, the appropriate measures for addressing the possible adverse social consequences of adjustment receive additional justification, on environmental grounds.

- *Economywide policies will have additional longer-term effects on the environment through changes in employment and income distribution.* Several of the examples confirm one predictable conclusion: that adjustment-induced changes generate new economic opportunities and sources of livelihood, thereby alleviating poverty and reducing pressures on the environment caused by overexploitation of fragile resources by the unemployed. However, although growth is an essential element in sustainable development, it will necessarily increase pressures on environmental resources. Increased efficiency and reduction of waste, as well as proper valuation of resources, will help reshape the structure of growth and reduce these environmental effects. At the same time, sustained longer-run growth will require special attention to eventual tradeoffs between environmental quality and growth.

These findings have implications for decisionmaking, of course. While the relationships between economywide policies and the environment are complex and involve many economic and noneconomic variables, the main concerns may often be limited to a small subset of priority environmental concerns. These are often identifiable by region and certainly by country. Proper recognition of the generally positive environmental consequences of economywide policy reforms could help to build additional support for such programs. At the same time, broader recognition of the underlying economic and policy causes of environmental problems can enhance support for environmental initiatives—both policies and projects. Accordingly, although the Bank's country analyses have historically followed separate economic and environmental tracks, recent progress has been made in integrating the two approaches, especially at the project level. Sector reforms would include cost recovery of operations and maintenance for irrigation water through pricing; liberalization of retail prices for livestock, along with reforms of parastatals and partial privatization of livestock services; soil and water conservation; and land consolidation in rainfed areas.

Note

1. This study, "The Population, Agriculture, and Environment Nexus in Sub-Saharan Africa" by Kevin M. Cleaver and Götz A. Schreiber, was first issued in 1992 in the Agriculture and Rural Development Series (No. 1), Africa Technical Department. The study is included in the authors' forthcoming book *Reversing the Spiral: The Population, Agriculture, and Environment Nexus in Sub-Saharan Africa*.

4. Addressing Regional and Global Environmental Challenges

The costs of solar energy have been substantially reduced in recent years, and through the Global Environment Facility (GEF) a number of solar energy projects are either in progress or in the pipeline. Solar energy is only one of the forms of renewable energy technology in which the GEF and the Bank are investing increasingly.

Some environmental problems—such as loss of biodiversity, damage to international waters, global warming from greenhouse gas emissions, and stratospheric ozone depletion—are neither nationally nor regionally bound. However, as with most other forms of environmental degradation, the poorest in the population are on the front line. Thus, preventing degradation of the regional and global commons falls firmly within the Bank's mandate.

Much of the work described in the previous chapters benefits the regional and global environment. Removing and treating sewage and improving urban transport to reduce carbon dioxide emissions improve the urban environment—and the regional and global commons. The same far-reaching effects are generated by projects for creating and strengthening protected areas or conserving natural resources such as forests. Less directly, but no less importantly, as is argued in chapter 3, investments in people to reduce poverty, improve education, and lower fertility rates, as well as investments to improve the efficiency with which resources are used, will all be beneficial locally and globally.

This chapter begins with a brief discussion of Bank support for regional seas and river basin programs and for the Desertification Convention. The rest of the chapter is devoted to activities the Bank has undertaken as an implementing agency of the GEF and the Multilateral Fund for the Implementation of the Montreal Protocol (MFMP).

Regional Seas and River Basin Programs

A number of environmental programs for regional seas and river basins entered the implementation stage during fiscal 1994 in the Mediterranean, the Black and Baltic seas, and the Danube River Basin. Additionally, the Bank has been instrumental in launching new strategies for the Aral and Caspian seas in Central Asia and for Lake Victoria in Africa.

THE MEDITERRANEAN BASIN. Founded as a pilot program in 1990, the Mediterranean Technical Assistance Program (METAP), is funded by the European Investment Bank (EIB), the Commission of the European Communities, the UNDP, and the World Bank. METAP addresses the need for environmental policy, capacity building, and investments at regional, national, and local levels. Its four main priority areas are solid and hazardous waste management, integrated water resources management, coastal zone management, and marine pollution.

Increasing investment in the environment and seeking new sources of funding are major objectives of METAP. For example, METAP has been successful in linking specific activities to innovative financing sources: Tunisia Marine Pollution—GEF financing; Morocco Al Hoceima Conservation Management Plan—potential EU financing; Cyprus Limassol Municipal Environmental Audit—EIB financing; and Algeria Hazardous Waste Management Options—World Bank financing.

The first three-year cycle of METAP ended in 1992, and a second cycle was launched under METAP II. Follow-on investment for METAP II activities is rapidly being established as well: the recently launched Turkey Solid Waste Management effort has already been linked to the Black Sea Priority Investments Programme.

In 1994 preparation began on the Albania Integrated Coastal Zone Management Project; on a project that will strengthen environmental impact assessment in Algeria; on an oil spill contingency plan in the Occupied Territories; and on a solid waste management project in Turkey. The program also included preparation of an environmental strategy for Lebanon. Institutional development is a central theme of METAP II. The Mediterranean Coastal Cities Network (MEDCITIES) conducted municipal environmental audits in five member cities—Limassol (Cyprus), Oran (Algeria), Sousse (Tunisia), Tangiers (Morocco), and Tripoli/El-Mina (Lebanon)—and began the follow-up action plans. Tirana (Albania) was also added during the fiscal year. The participatory approach and methodologies used in this audit project have inspired other regions to use similar procedures. In addition to the networks, METAP training and direct organizational support are effective in building institutional capacity in the region. Environmental communication, environmental mediation and negotiation, and environmental impact assessment are three main training programs that have been deepened during fiscal 1994. Direct organizational support has also been provided with the creation of an EA in Syria and the completion of the second phase of an EA in Algeria.

THE BLACK SEA. The pollution level of the Black Sea is among the highest in the world. To help reverse the process, the Program for Environmental Management and Protection of the Black Sea will provide the coastal countries—Bulgaria, Georgia, Romania, Russia, Turkey, and Ukraine—with a solid basis for developing long-term policies and investment programs. It will support institution building at the national and regional levels and will foster cooperation among the countries, the scientific community, NGOs, and the private sector. The program is jointly funded by the Bank, the GEF, the EBRD, and several bilateral donors.

During the past year, an urgent investment portfolio (UIP) was identified and agreed on in principle by the countries and donors. Benefits from the UIP investment, largely from human health improvements, will be immediate and direct. The first project, approved in fiscal 1994, is the Bulgaria Water Companies Restructuring Project. Three others—in

Russia, Turkey, and Ukraine—are under preparation, with nine more, in all five countries, to follow. Initial program activities include preparation of a priority investment program and work on biodiversity issues, environmental impact assessment, and integrated coastal zone management (ICZM).

THE BALTIC SEA. Implementation of the Baltic Sea Environment Program is being coordinated by a task force under the leadership of the Helsinki Commission. The task force includes representatives of the countries of the Baltic Sea drainage basin, international financial institutions, selected technical organizations, and NGOs. The Bank is taking an active role in the task force and its various working groups to support implementation of an environmental action plan. During fiscal 1994 the Bank proceeded with the preparation of environmental projects in Estonia, Latvia, and Lithuania. These proposed projects would reduce pollution in the Baltic Sea, promote coastal zone management, and strengthen the management of protected areas. The Bank is also helping to develop projects for improving water and wastewater management in Latvia and Poland in municipalities the program has identified as environmental "hot spots."

In September 1993 the Bank cosponsored a Baltic countries regional workshop, held in Lithuania, on the management of *nonpoint source pollution*. The Bank is an active participant in the Coastal Lagoons and Wetlands Working Group, under the leadership of the World Wide Fund for Nature, and is supporting economic case studies of selected protected areas in the Baltic region.

THE ARAL SEA BASIN. The Aral Sea is bordered by Kazakhstan and Uzbekistan, while the Kyrgyz Republic, Tajikistan, and Turkmenistan form part of the sea's extended basin. The desiccation and salinization of the sea have killed most life in it, destroyed the wetlands in the deltas of the Amu and Syr Darya rivers, engendered salt and dust storms, and hastened the loss of biodiversity. Although it is unrealistic to expect the whole Aral Sea to be restored to life, a small part of the sea may be nearly restored to what it was, some of the wetlands revitalized, much of the ecological damage in those areas mitigated, and the drawdown zone stabilized against salt storms. The Aral Sea Environment Assistance Program was approved by the heads of the five states in January 1994 (see further discussion under "Regional Cooperation," below). The overall coordination of the program will be jointly undertaken by the World Bank, the UNDP, and the UNEP. A Bank preparation mission visited the Aral Sea region to assist the Executive Committee of the Interstate Council for Addressing the Aral Sea Crisis (ICAS) in preparing specific projects. Eighteen projects and a supplementary capacity-building program were selected for Phase I of the program, for an investment of almost $200 million. Of this sum, 20 percent will be in local currency, while foreign exchange funds amounting to about $160 million would be required in the form of loans and credits from the Bank and other donor agencies. The Executive Committee is expected to begin implementation of Phase I projects in fiscal 1995.

THE CASPIAN SEA. At the initiative of the government of Kazakhstan, an international conference was held in Alma Ata on May 26, 1994. At the conference, riparian countries signed the Declaration for Cooperation in the Field of Environmental Protection in the Caspian Sea Region and invited the Bank and other donors to assist in this program. This initiative, which the Bank has agreed to support, has the strong involvement and active participation of private sector oil companies and NGOs. The Bank is now developing a joint work program with the UNDP, the UNEP, and the European Union.

THE DANUBE RIVER BASIN. The Environmental Programme for the Danube River Basin (EPDRB) was initiated by the riparian countries (Austria, Bulgaria, Croatia, the Czech Republic, Germany, Hungary, Moldova, Romania, the Slovak Republic, Slovenia, and Ukraine) and international donors in 1992 and is funded by the GEF and the World Bank's Special Grants Program, EBRD, the European Union, and other donors. The EPDRB is a three-year effort for developing a strategic action plan and a program of institution building and technical support.

EPDRB activities will proceed in two phases. Phase I will focus on short-term actions and the development of a strategic action plan and an investment program and will develop the technical building blocks for environmental planning and management. Phase II will implement the recommendations emanating from Phase I. Under Phase I, eighteen diagnostic assessments and preinvestment studies were conducted in fiscal 1994. Each study covers one tributary basin to the Danube and identifies pollution "hot spots." Nine of the eleven riparian countries in the Danube Basin have also prepared national reviews of their aquatic environments. In addition, an *accident emergency warning alarm system* for the Danube River and its major tributaries has been designed.

The Bank has the responsibility for executing the pre-investment activities funded by a portion of the Danube-GEF grant. Because the worst pollution is found in the tributaries, the Bank has conducted pre-investment studies in the basins of the Chris/Koros, Morava, Nitra, Olt, Osen, Vit, and Zagyva rivers. An action program for high-priority hot spots was completed at the end of fiscal 1994.

LAKE VICTORIA. A pilot Pollution Prevention Project for the Lake Victoria Basin in Tanzania was initiated this year. The lake is the largest body of fresh water in Africa and the primary source of domestic water supply for more than 10 million people. Bordered by Kenya, Tanzania, and Uganda, the Lake Victoria project is an example of a comprehensive approach as advocated in the Bank's policy paper *Water Resources Management*. A description of the many activities included in the project is provided in box 4.1.

Combating Desertification

Land degradation is a worldwide problem, and although the phenomenon is complex, common causes are deforestation, overgrazing, poor farming practices, insecure tenurial arrangements, and population pressure. In addition, inappropriate economic policies such as grain production quotas, subsidies for agricultural inputs, short contractual arrangements for concessions to land, and uncompetitive prices for timber, contribute to the problem. Land degradation is therefore the direct product of poor land management, itself an outcome of inappro-

---

Box 4.1.   Lake Victoria Pollution Prevention Pilot Project

Lake Victoria is a primary source of domestic water supply for more than 10 million people living in its drainage basin, as well as a source of water for agricultural and industrial activities. Lake fish are a vital source of protein for basin residents. The economies of the lake region countries also depend on a sustainable lake ecosystem and its estimated $200-million export fishery.

In recent years, however, the introduction of exotic species of fish (especially Nile perch) and the water hyacinth, coupled with increased sedimentation from soil erosion, discharges of water pollution, and deposition from polluted emissions, have so seriously degraded the lake ecosystem it is near collapse. The urgency of this complex situation cannot wait for intensive research to provide more understanding; comprehensive response is needed right away. Pollution control is one of the initial priorities.

The Lake Victoria Pollution Project is a pilot effort undertaken by the government of Tanzania in conjunction with the Bank. Primary objectives include (a) identification of principal sources of water pollution, (b) estimation of pollution loadings from different point sources, (c) evaluation of costs of different pollution abatement options, (d) utilization of local

priate policies and rural poverty. In the extreme, land degradation results in desertification and the loss of much agricultural output. Reforestation, land desalinization, and programs that encourage alternatives to biomass for fuel are a central part of the Bank's natural resource management projects, in dryland areas in particular—and they all help arrest desertification directly. In Africa, for example, the Bank has committed $50 million to community-based natural resource management programs in Burkina Faso and Mali, and a further $50 million is earmarked for similar programs in Chad, Mauritania, and Niger. Bank-supported programs in the Sahel adopt a *gestion de terroir* (a holistic and participatory system of land management, discussed in chapter 3) approach in which support is provided to communities to identify their constraints and improve land management practices.

As a participant in the Multilateral Working Group on Environment of the Middle East Peace Process, the Bank was requested to assist with the preparation of a regional program to address arid land degradation issues that are common to the region. Participants in the initiative include Egypt, Israel, Jordan, and the West Bank and Gaza. Emphasis will be on applying proven technologies and collaborative networking for dissemi-

experts in conducting the investigations, and (e) implementation of needed pollution prevention measures.

An interdisciplinary team of experts conducted the investigations. They encountered challenges in monitoring point and nonpoint pollution discharges.

Principal point sources of pollution include raw municipal sewage from major urban centers, peri-urban areas, and industries. Nonpoint sources include various agricultural chemicals, animal wastes, eroded soils, and toxic substances (such as mercury) from gold mining operations. Municipal sewage and textile mills are the largest sources of both nutrients and organic loads.

Options for controlling major point sources include rehabilitating the existing sewerage pumping plant and stabilization ponds and extending sewerage treatment to peri-urban and unsewered urban areas, using less costly small-bore sewers. Some of the options for industrial waste minimization are not very costly; they use technologies suited to Tanzanian conditions and should result in an 85-percent reduction in organic pollution.

An important aspect of this pilot project—having a local, multidisciplinary team formulate and carry out the investigation and feasibility studies —resulted in procedures and solutions suited to Tanzania.

nation of best practice; the start-up phase of the initiative has been made possible by a Japanese government grant of $530,000. In addition to the project work on soil degradation, the Bank has participated in the drafting of the Desertification Convention. This convention was begun by the 1992 session of the General Assembly of the United Nations and was completed in June 1994. The Bank was an active observer throughout the proceedings (box 4.2).

The Global Environment Facility

The GEF has emerged as an important catalyst for integrating global environmental concerns into national development goals. By providing grants and concessional funding to developing countries for projects and programs that benefit the global environment, the GEF enables the gov-

---

Box 4.2. The Desertification Convention

The focus of the Desertification Convention is to bring international action and resources to bear on the problem of desertification. Since the convention is the first global instrument to be negotiated after the Earth Summit of 1992 in Rio de Janeiro, many of the issues surrounding the Rio declaration and Agenda 21 are addressed. The convention establishes mechanisms for monitoring and assessment, information dissemination, research and technology development, and drought relief, as well as public participation, awareness, and education on desertification. As a first step, the convention will require the preparation and implementation of national action programs (NAPs) for countries experiencing desertification. However, to reduce duplication of work for already overstretched agencies, the convention encourages the use of existing documents where appropriate. In particular, NAPs often include specific provision to arrest soil degradation.

The Desertification Convention will rely on national bilateral and multilateral funding sources and the establishment of a global financial mechanism. The World Bank has supported many projects and programs in Africa and, increasingly, in Asian countries that contribute, directly or indirectly, to combating desertification. At the same time the Bank has taken an active role in enforcing policy changes, particularly in Africa, in fields such as agricultural and natural resources pricing, land tenure reform, water policy, forest policy, and environmental legislation and institutional development. The Bank will work closely with the Convention Secretariat and the Conference of Parties to bring its experience to assist in the implementation of the convention.

ernments of developing countries to address global environmental issues they would otherwise be unable or unwilling to undertake, and it enables industrial countries to contribute significant resources toward these issues. In doing so, the GEF demonstrates a new approach to global cooperation.

Launched in 1991 as a pilot program, the GEF draws collaboratively on the experience and expertise of three international agencies. The UNDP is responsible for technical assistance and capacity-building activities and is charged with managing the Small Grants Programme for nongovernmental organizations. The UNEP offers expertise in environmental disciplines and supports research. The World Bank plays the primary role in ensuring the development and management of investment projects and acts as trustee of the GEF Trust Fund.

The GEF helps developing countries to address four global environmental problems that have been recognized in recent international treaties and conventions as high-priority issues:

- Global warming, particularly the effects on the world's climate from greenhouse gas emissions resulting from, among other things, the use of fossil fuels and the destruction of carbon-sequestering forests
- Destruction of biological diversity through the degradation of natural habitats and the overuse of natural resources
- Pollution of international waters through, for example, oil spills and the accumulation of wastes in oceans, seas, and international river systems
- Depletion of stratospheric ozone from emissions of CFCs, halons, and other gases.

During the pilot phase, the fourth objective above has been addressed almost entirely through the MFMP, for which the Bank manages the investment operations. However, in its upcoming operational phase the GEF will support the phase-out of ozone depleting substances (ODSs) in countries, such as the Commonwealth of Independent States and the Eastern European states, that are ineligible for Protocol assistance because they consume or produce too many ODSs.

In October 1994 the pilot phase will end, and the GEF will enter its first three-year operational phase. Donors have agreed to make available $2 billion for this phase of the GEF, or almost three times the $750 million available in the pilot phase. Responding to lessons learned during the pilot phase and to the numerous suggestions from donors, recipient countries, and the scientific and NGO communities, this new operational phase involves changes in project identification and selection procedures and in GEF governance (box 4.3).

Box 4.3.   The Global Environment Facility II: Beyond the Pilot Phase

Representatives from more than seventy countries reached an agreement in March 1994 to restructure and replenish the GEF, concluding negotiations that were launched fifteen months earlier in Abidjan, Côte d'Ivoire. The agreement, which came three years after the GEF was launched as a pilot program, builds on the achievements of the Earth Summit of 1992. The lengthy negotiations reflected the determination of governments to avoid the creation of a new bureaucracy.

The GEF will continue to deal with four global environmental problems: climate change, the destruction of biodiversity, the pollution of international waters, and ozone depletion. Furthermore, land degradation—primarily desertification and deforestation—will also be eligible insofar as it relates to one or more of the four main focal areas.

Governance. Decisions will normally be reached on the basis of consensus, but when this is not possible, a vote may be taken. Differences between developing and industrial countries over whether to use the UN system, which is based on one country–one vote, or the Bretton Woods approach, where voting rights reflect economic strength, were eventually resolved with the introduction of a *double majority* system. This requires approval by a 60-percent majority of all member countries as well as approval by donors representing at least 60 percent of contributions—in effect, giving both industrial and developing countries veto power.

The new arrangements represent a unique blend of UN and Bretton Woods practices. They include:

- A universal assembly that will meet every three years to review GEF policies.

The GEF Portfolio

The portfolio of pilot-phase GEF grants that were approved by GEF participants for development and administration by the Bank has grown from an original complement of fourteen projects, totaling $189 million, to fifty-three projects, totaling more than $450 million. The cumulative growth of pilot phase GEF projects administered by the Bank is reflected in figure 4.1.

During the first five tranches of Bank GEF projects, 45 percent of resources from the core fund was earmarked for biodiversity projects, 39 percent for combating global warming, 15 percent for protecting international waters, and 1 percent for controlling ODS emissions. This brings the portfolio to a thematic balance nearly in line with the initial objectives

- A council, constituting the main governing body, that will meet at least twice a year. The thirty-two seats will represent sixteen developing country constituencies, fourteen for industrial countries, and two for economies in transition. Responsibility for conducting the council's business will be shared by an elected chairman (the UN model) and the GEF's chief executive officer (the Bretton Woods model), who will also be the chairman of the GEF.
- A functionally independent secretariat that will be administratively supported by the World Bank but will report directly to the GEF's council. This follows up on one of the main recommendations of a recent independent evaluation of the pilot phase.

Financial arrangement. A parallel negotiating process began in mid-1993 to replenish the GEF, which had committed, by spring 1994, about $750 million to more than one hundred projects throughout the world. Donors agreed to provide more than $2 billion to the GEF's core fund for commitment over three years. This sum, nearly three times larger than the core fund during the pilot phase, is contributed over and above resources channeled to regular official development assistance.

As for burden sharing, it was agreed that contributions would be based on the formula used for the tenth replenishment of the IDA (IDA-10) but with the understanding that the entire issue would be reconsidered in the next replenishment exercise in three years.

Several countries have already pledged voluntary contributions in addition to their shares. The United States will be the largest donor (SDR 307 million), followed by Japan (SDR 296 million), Germany (SDR 171 million), France (SDR 102 million), and the United Kingdom (SDR 96 million).

of 30–40 percent for biodiversity, 40–50 percent for global warming, and 10–20 percent for international waters, with the rest dedicated to ozone depletion projects. A regional breakdown of Bank-GEF core funding in the first five tranches shows that 24 percent of funds allocated is for projects in East Asia and the Pacific, 23 percent for Latin America and the Caribbean, 20 percent for Africa, 12 percent for Europe and Central Asia, 10 percent for South Asia, and 10 percent for the Middle East and North Africa.

As of the end of June 1994, thirty-one projects had been approved by Bank management for implementation (table 4.1), and project funds were being disbursed for fifteen of these. These projects, totaling $280 million of GEF grant funds, include seventeen initiatives approved during fiscal 1994 that are only beginning to disburse funds.

Figure 4.1. GEF Investment Portfolio Development—Overview

Approved GEF Funding (millions of dollars)

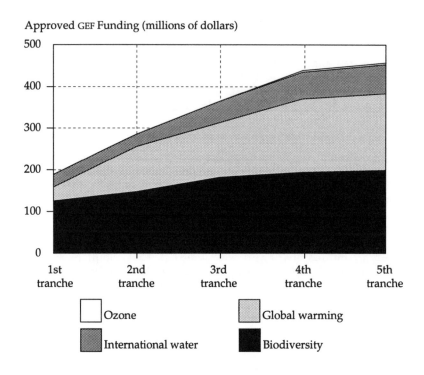

GEF project disbursements to date total more than $20 million, and nearly $30 million of the project preparation advances (PPAs) are included. The rate of disbursement is better than that of average Bank-supported projects. Several factors probably account for this, including the lack of substantive conditionality attached to GEF operations, which allows them to be implemented sooner, and the relatively small size of investments. The rate of project processing has increased rapidly during the past year. During the first two years of the GEF, twenty-three projects were appraised and fourteen were approved by Bank management. By contrast, in fiscal 1994 alone, twenty-six projects were appraised, and seventeen were approved. This points to a steep increase in disbursements in the coming fiscal year.

GEF-Bank operations have encouraged the use of project preparation funds to prepare investments better. PPAs have increased dramatically as a percentage of total allocated GEF funds during the past two years, from less than 1 percent to just under 5 percent in 1993. So far, PPAs have been approved for 26 projects and for initiation of project

Table 4.1. GEF Projects Approved

Country	Project	GEF grant funding (millions of dollars)	Management approval date
Fiscal 1994			
Algeria	El Kala National Park	9.2	4/94
China	Sichuan Gas Development and Conservation	10.0	3/94
Costa Rica	Grid-Integrated Advanced Windpower	3.3	12/93[a]
Czech Republic	Biodiversity Protection	2.0	10/93
Ecuador	Biodiversity Protection	7.2	5/94
Indonesia	Biodiversity Collections	7.2	6/94
Iran	Teheran Transportation Emission Reduction	2.0	10/93
Jamaica	Demand Side Management	3.8	3/94
Lao PDR	Wildlife and Protected Areas Conservation	5.0	2/94
Mexico	High Efficiency Lighting Pilot Project	10.0	3/94
Philippines	Conservation of Priority Protected Areas	20.0	5/94
	Geothermal Energy Development	30.0	5/94
Regional (Caribbean)	Wider Caribbean Initiative for Ship-Generated Waste Oil Pollution Management System for the Southwest Mediterranean Sea	5.5 6.9[b] 5.6[c] 5.8[d]	5/94
Slovak Republic	Biodiversity Protection	2.3	9/93
Ukraine	Transcarpathian Mountains Biodiversity Protection	0.5	7/93
	Danube Delta Biodiversity	1.5	6/94
Total		137.8	
Prior to fiscal 1994			
Belarus	Biodiversity Protection	1.0	9/92
Bhutan	Trust Fund for Environmental Conservation	10.0	5/92
Bolivia	Biodiversity Conservation	4.5	11/92
China	Ship Waste Disposal	30.0	5/92
Congo	Wildlands Protection	10.0	3/93
Egypt	Red Sea Coastal and Marine Resource Management	4.8	11/92
Ghana	Coastal Wetlands Management	7.2	8/92
India	Renewable Resource Management	26.0	12/92
Mauritius	Sugar Bio-Energy Technology	3.3	2/92

(Table continues on the following page.)

Table 4.1 (continued)

Country	Project	GEF grant funding (millions of dollars)	Management approval date
Mexico	Protected Areas Program	25.0	3/92
Poland	Forest Biodiversity	4.5	12/91
Seychelles	Biodiversity Conservation and Marine Pollution Abatement	1.8	11/92
Thailand	Promotion of Electricity Energy Efficiency	9.5	4/93
Turkey	In-Situ Conservation of Genetic Biodiversity	5.1	2/93
Total		142.7	

a. IDB Board.
b. Algeria.
c. Morocco.
d. Tunisia.

studies, and they account for nearly $10 million of advance project development, with nearly one-third of that amount already disbursed. Of PPA funding, 51 percent has been used for biodiversity projects, 23 percent for international waters, 21 percent for global warming, and 5 percent for an ozone project. The high proportion of PPA financing for biodiversity projects reflects the relatively complex preparation work required, including extensive stakeholder consultation and baseline surveys and analyses. Thirty-four percent of approved PPA financing has been for Africa, 30 percent for Europe and Central Asia, 19 percent for Latin America and the Caribbean, and 18 percent for the Middle East and North Africa. No projects in the South Asia or the East Asia and Pacific regions have received funds from the PPA facility. However, seven projects received $6.4 million in project preparatory funds from the UNDP's Pre-Investment Studies Facility, five of which were in East Asia and the Pacific and one each in the South Asia and Africa regions.

Finally, nearly half (twenty-six) of the fifty-three Bank/GEF-supported projects have benefited from being linked with specific Bank lending operations. Associating GEF projects with related Bank initiatives was conceived under the facility as a means not only of benefiting from the Bank's institutional resources, but also—and more importantly—of leveraging significant financial and policy gains. The resulting gains have been substantial for increasing the scope and impact of GEF operations. Additional multilateral and bilateral financing for GEF activities has also been generated for promoting institutional and policy reforms beneficial to global objectives. In addition, GEF leveraging has benefited the Bank's agenda for environmentally sustainable development and has helped promote internal institutional reforms toward greater transparency and accountability.

Local Participation

Although GEF project sites are chosen primarily for their biodiversity values, relative impacts on global climate, or other biophysical criteria, the long-term viability of those projects depends on social, economic, and political factors as well. Local participation is therefore critical to successful project implementation, especially of biodiversity projects, and all GEF projects are required to collaborate closely with local communities and other stakeholders whenever possible.

To assist its task managers and other interested groups, the Bank has prepared Social Assessment Best Practice notes. These notes emphasize the need for identifying all stakeholders (government agencies, local communities, scientific institutions, NGOs, and the private sector) early in project preparation and for engaging in repeated consultation and information exchange throughout project design and implementation. Social assessment and participation are complementary activities that provide crucial sociocultural information on potential areas of conflict and ways to resolve them.

GEF projects have incorporated stakeholder participation through different mechanisms and to varying degrees—from discussion of only a few project components to total delegation of responsibility for protected area management. Most of the experience thus far has come from work on design issues, as the following examples indicate.

- Preparatory work on the India Conservation of Biodiversity through Participatory Management Project used intensive participatory rural appraisal techniques to prepare action plans for eight national parks. A national NGO, the Indian Institute of Public Administration, coordinated fieldwork by training state forestry officials in data gathering and analysis. Workshops held at each site identified community needs, existing tenure and use rights, and the activities that would be compatible with biodiversity conservation goals. In the spirit of ecodevelopment, the participants identified ways to make a living consistent with environmental and resource conservation, such as through regulated harvesting of nontimber products. Extension services for improving water control and soil erosion were also called for.

- The Ecuador Biodiversity Conservation Project provides another example of intensive consultation with local groups. This project ($7.2 million) will strengthen the legal and regulatory system for Ecuadoran protected areas, provide institution building for the main agency responsible for managing protected areas in Ecuador, carry out community activities, and develop protection and conservation infrastructure for eight protected areas. A new government entity, INEFAN, was created by the project to manage Ecuador's forests and national parks and protected areas system. After the government structure and the legislation for boundary demarcation and tourism control were in place, project preparation proceeded with two workshops, for NGOs and the private sector, to identify key critical sites and major issues. Various management schemes were proposed for the priority sites, such as NGO management, private sector investment in sustainable forest management, joint NGO-village management, and local community management (with some state support), in a reserve occupied by indigenous peoples. Decisions on implementing the project will be determined by a regional coordinating committee, composed of representatives of local communities, indigenous peoples, local NGOs, and INEFAN. Education about, and a forum for discussing, natural resource use will be provided not only through the committee's work in approving management plans but also through technical advice to communities in and around protected areas. This technical advice will include how to deal with complex legal questions related to land tenure, land use planning, and negotiations with resource extraction companies.

- The Conservation of Priority Protected Areas Project is unique in that it consists of a grant to the Philippines ($2.9 million) and a parallel grant of $17.1 million to NGOs for Integrated Protected Areas, Inc. (NIPA)—the first Global Environment Trust (GET) grant to be made directly to an NGO. NIPA is a legally incorporated nonprofit consortium of NGOs formed for the purpose of implementing this project. Although project implementation will be coordinated by a government-appointed, joint government-NGO steering committee, project activities themselves will be carried out mostly by NIPA, NGOs, and local communities. A protected area management board will be established for each of the ten protected areas covered by the project. The board will be responsible for formulating the management plan for its protected area and for approving small grants and loans to local community members for financially and environmentally sustainable activities. NIPA will coordinate local NGO activities, provide technical assistance, monitor project implementation, and serve as trustee and manager of a fund for alternative livelihood activities in and around the selected areas.

Sustainable Recurrent Cost Financing

For environmental activities to be sustainable over the long run, reliable sources of financing must be found, and prices must be consistent with the economic value of the resources concerned. Projects currently under implementation are experimenting with a variety of solutions to the problem of sustainable recurrent cost financing—for instance, adapting new energy technologies, finding appropriate taxation and pricing levels of user fees (as part of ecotourism or protected area projects), and establishing biodiversity trust funds.

PRICING AND USER FEES. Sound pricing policies and appropriate market incentives are particularly important in the projects to reduce global warming being carried out by utility corporations, whether publicly or privately owned. This strong link between policy and greenhouse gas reduction is reflected in both the China Sichuan Gas Transmission and Distribution Project and the Jamaica Demand-Side Management Demonstration Project. In the Sichuan project, agreement on gas sector pricing was critical to proceeding with the GEF grant, since activities to reduce methane gas emissions would not be financially sustainable beyond the project period if gas prices did not reach competitive international levels over a reasonable phase-in period. Such agreement and periodic consultations on pricing levels are designed to maintain appropriate pricing signals in this important energy subsector. Similarly, demand side management initiatives, as tested in Jamaica (box 4.4), would not be expandable over the longer term if the overall policy framework were not consistent with GEF goals for energy efficiency and conservation. Agreement on such a policy framework has therefore been an important element of the project preparation process, and implementation is conditional on the adoption of the policy changes.

The importance of appropriate pricing signals is not limited to the global warming field, however. The sustainability of international waters protection is linked to the establishment of pricing and enforcement mechanisms for ensuring that waste producers pay their waste disposal costs. Such mechanisms will be tested in the China Ship Waste Disposal Project, effective in December 1992, after the ship waste facilities have been constructed and the ship monitoring systems are in operation.

Box 4.4. Jamaica: Demand-Side Management Demonstration Project

The Jamaica Demand-Side Management Demonstration Project illustrates institutional and technical means for improving the efficiency of electricity use in the commercial and household sectors of this island nation. Although small by world standards, the activity has become highly visible in the Jamaican energy context and is piloting an approach that could be expanded both domestically and internationally.

The project evolved from a 1990 study, "Power by Efficiency," by the Jamaica Public Service utility organization (JPS). Subsequent studies on energy saving programs such as cogeneration in hotels and efficient lighting in residences were funded by the Rockefeller Foundation. Technical support was provided by the Conservation Law Foundation of New England, the Resources Development Foundation, and the Biomass Users Network. A concurrent UNDP/World Bank Energy Sector Management Assistance Program (ESMAP) on energy savings contributed to a 1991 IDB loan (with a small energy conservation component) to JPS.

All parties agreed on the potential for energy savings, but there was debate about how to promote energy efficiency and capture these savings in practice. Consensus emerged during the eighteen months of project preparation in favor of associating the efficiency program directly with the planning of future generation capacity requirements. Subsequently, JPS reorganized into two major departments—one for planning, energy conservation, and management of transmission facilities and the other for management of the generation plants—with an eye to privatization over the medium term. This paved the way for project appraisal in October 1993 (the appraisal team included two NGO representatives) and approval of the grant in March 1994.

A high level of client commitment and broad participation have been evident throughout project preparation and project launch activities. A full-time Jamaican manager with more than a decade of demand-side management experience in North America was hired to provide leadership and to integrate efficiency goals into the management and planning practices at JPS. Broad participation has been encouraged through outreach activities supported by the Jamaica Environment Trust and conservation awareness programs in the public school system. The project was officially launched at a ceremony presided over by the minister of public utilities, mining, and energy and attended by students, representatives of local NGOs, the media, and the donor community. A national school essay contest on topics related to energy savings will be used by JPS to select the initial test families to receive compact fluorescent lightbulbs under a pilot residential program.

Similarly, discussions are under way with operators of cruise ships plying the Caribbean to agree on an appropriate user fee for vessels discharging wastes at land facilities in the area rather than dumping wastes at sea. Such agreement will be an important element of the proposed Organization of Eastern Caribbean States (OECS) Waste Disposal Project.

Biodiversity conservation and the ability to manage protected areas (including national parks, ecological reserves, and World Heritage Sites) over the long term are also intrinsically linked to appropriate resource costing. This may take a variety of forms—from competitive pricing of timber concessions and stumpage rates, to explicit valuation of watershed protection services and genetic pools, to park user fees that reflect an ecosystem's carrying capacity for human visitors. Approaches are now being tested in national programs and GEF-supported projects to cost resources appropriately and to meet the recurrent costs of maintaining them. For example, the five biodiversity conservation projects in Eastern Europe are studying what level of user fees would meet conservation objectives and still ensure enough park receipts for the operation, maintenance, and investment costs of the park system.

TRUST FUNDS. The establishment of biodiversity trust funds is another possible solution to the problems of insufficient and unreliable local funding. In addition to providing a stable and consistent stream of income to meet the recurrent costs of conservation areas, secondary benefits may include: the funding of smaller and more diverse types of activities than are possible with conventional investment lending; a better match between financial flows and absorptive capacity; promotion of long-term capacity building, broad participation, and local empowerment; and the provision of a flexible mechanism for the cofinancing of conservation.

The GEF has pioneered the trust fund experiment under two quite different conditions, in the Bhutan Environmental Conservation Project and the tri-country Foundation for Eastern Carpathian Biodiversity Conservation. The GET contribution to the Bhutan trust fund was split into two tranches, totaling $10 million. In addition, $3 million in cofinancing was raised from the Netherlands, Norway, and the World Wildlife Fund (WWF-USA). Guidelines for submitting projects have been agreed to, and a review body has been established. For example, resources have been allocated to a community adjacent to the Royal Manas National Park for relieving pressure on wildlife by creating a buffer zone through community reforestation programs, crop production, and aquaculture. Initial returns on investment have not been fully successful, however, and a modest drawdown of the principal was needed to enlarge the conservation program.

The Foundation for Eastern Carpathian Biodiversity Conservation, on the other hand, is an offshore fund involving three countries (Poland, the Slovak Republic, and Ukraine) and several donors, including the World Bank, the MacArthur Foundation, and the WWF-USA. An initial endowment of $600,000 and an additional 100,000 European currency units from the PHARE program of the European Union have been used to begin immediate biodiversity protection investments. Progress has been slow and complicated, only in part because of the number of participants. It would appear that the costs associated with establishing an offshore trust are significant in terms of long legal procedures and requirements that have delayed the trust's effectiveness.

The appeal of trust funds as a means of ensuring the availability of funds to cover recurrent costs has led to burgeoning demand for best-practice guidance from the GEF. In response, this year the Bank produced "Issues and Options in the Design of GEF-Supported Trust Funds for Biodiversity Conservation." The paper argues that experience thus far in GEF projects indicates that despite their appeal, trust funds are not a panacea and have several drawbacks. Trust funds that seek to meet recurrent costs from net income while maintaining the value of their assets in real terms require complex financial and administrative arrangements and, if the initial endowment is small, may generate only small income. Net income may display annual fluctuations as well, requiring considerable management skill for its stabilization. Where grant resources for biodiversity conservation are scarce and biodiversity losses rapid, locking up large amounts of capital that could otherwise be applied to urgent conservation needs may not be the most efficient way to achieve biodiversity conservation. Therefore, GEF experience indicates that trust funds should be chosen only after a review of all other, often simpler, means of securing recurrent cost financing have been examined and deemed nonfeasible or inappropriate.

Nevertheless, despite their financial limitations, trust funds provide an opportunity to build partnerships among local community beneficiaries, local and international NGOs, the private sector, and other stakeholders. Because financial resources are guaranteed in perpetuity and not merely for the life of a project, it is especially important to involve *all* actors and to secure their ownership of the fund's activities. For instance, for the Bwindi Forest Trust Fund of Uganda (approval expected in early fiscal 1995), the Wildlife Clubs of Uganda will represent local NGOs, CARE will represent international NGOs, and Mkerere University will be represented because of its research expertise in the area. The board will allocate 60 percent of the net income of the trust, or about $240,000 per year, to conservation-oriented community development activities proposed by local communities. Such activities would include agroforestry, traditional beekeeping, fruit growing, vine basketry, and operation of onfarm peri-forest timber lots.

Regional Cooperation

Since global environment problems do not recognize political boundaries, a challenge for GEF projects is to develop institutional cooperation and implementation arrangements that reflect the transnational character of some GEF focal problems (such as international waters protection) and to provide a workable basis for problem solving across national borders. In some cases the preferred approach has been to support regional, transnational efforts, working with existing or new regional institutions and providing them with the resources and authority for monitoring, analyzing, planning, and facilitating conflict resolution. In other cases, countries have preferred to work together on a project that is regional in scope but that is executed at the national level, in close coordination with the partner countries.

The Lake Victoria Ecosystem Management Project (preparation to begin in fiscal 1995) is a model for regional cooperation. Preparation will be managed jointly by the three participating countries, Kenya, Tanzania, and Uganda. Each country either is leading the preparatory work in one of the project's focal areas of fisheries management and water quality or is hosting the regional secretariat, with support from the other two participants.

In the Caribbean, two regional initiatives are under way with GEF support to address ship waste disposal problems. Due to differences in project activities and objectives, the institutional and implementation arrangements selected by participating countries for each project also differ. In the case of the Wider Caribbean Initiative for Disposal of Ship-Generated Waste, the goal of the project is to develop a coordinated strategy across the twenty-nine countries of the Wider Caribbean (WC) for ratifying the MARPOL (Marine Pollution) Conventions, with particular reference to Annex V wastes. This involves assessing the legal and regulatory frameworks in WC countries and identifying changes that would be required, identifying potential waste disposal sites throughout the WC, recommending an optimal siting strategy, assessing the current institutional arrangements for managing waste disposal, and recommending the modifications needed for effective management of ship wastes. Given the need for a coordinated approach across countries and for a regional strategy, the countries of the WC opted for a regional project that would be implemented by the International Maritime Organization (IMO), in close consultation with national authorities.

In contrast, the proposed $14-million OECS Waste Disposal Project, covering the six Eastern Caribbean States, has been developed as a regional initiative but will be implemented with financial and technical assistance provided via GET grants and associated loans or credits from the Bank, the EIB, and the Caribbean Development Bank (CDB) to national entities. This approach appeared most appropriate to the participating countries because they have already ratified or are in the process of ratifying MARPOL, and the project funding will support primarily country-specific investments. Where funding will support implementation of a regional component (for monitoring and evaluation or for preparation of a regional sewerage strategy), each recipient country has agreed to contribute its share of funding to a special project unit managed by the OECS secretariat. Thus, implementation arrangements have both national and regional elements within the same project.

Regional cooperation involves breakthroughs in political and technological arenas. A project preparation advance of $0.5 million was approved this year for the International Fund for the Aral Sea. This is a regional institution established by the heads of five Central Asia states (Kazakhstan, the Kyrgz Republic, Tajikistan, Turkmenistan, and Uzbekistan) to finance the Aral Sea Environment Assistance Program and marks the first major effort at collaboration for these newly independent countries. The advance will fund water quality and management feasibility studies, as well as institutional support for the Executive Committee of the Interstate Council for Addressing the Aral Sea Crisis (ICAS), the institution spearheading the Aral Sea initiative.

In coordinating efforts toward biodiversity protection in Eastern and Central Europe, the Bank has worked on building networks, from early project identification to implementation, among five GEF-supported Biodiversity Protection Projects ($10.3 million) in Belarus, the Czech Republic, Poland, the Slovak Republic, and Ukraine. To consolidate the network of project management teams in the region, a meeting took place in November 1993 in Warsaw, Poland, where the members of all five projects had their first opportunity to discuss common concerns and experiences in the implementation of their projects, ranging from administrative to technical and scientific issues. As a result of this initial gathering, the project managers agreed to meet every four to five months thereafter.

To increase the potential for continued cooperation and communication between the five projects, the Ecological Sciences Division of UNESCO is cooperating with the World Bank in developing a computer network between the projects themselves and, through ECONET, with other agencies and organizations working in the field of biodiversity protection. Two of these projects, in Poland and Belarus, already have direct electronic mail connections through the Bank's electronic mail system. The international cooperation displayed between these five nations has attracted wide donor interest, and nearly $10 million has already been generated for Eastern and Central European biodiversity protection efforts, almost matching the $10.3 million GEF contribution.

Institutional Issues and Capacity Building

Successful implementation of environmental projects depends on having realistic, enforceable, and appropriate legislation; strong institutions capable of designing, implementing, monitoring, and evaluating coordinated environmental activities; and well-trained, knowledgeable staff. All too frequently, there are either no national and local institutions responsible for environmental policies and projects, or they are new and inexperienced. These weak institutions are a main reason why project preparation has taken longer in GEF projects than for standard Bank operations. Additionally, training in environmental sciences, natural resource economics, and environmental management is weak in many of the world's least-developed countries, necessitating long-term investments in institution building and training. Consequently, most GEF projects include measures for improving relevant legal frameworks, for institutional strengthening, and for capacity building and training.

LEGAL FRAMEWORK. GEF assistance for assessing and recommending legal and regulatory frameworks for GEF focal areas usually begins in the design phase of a project, with project preparation assistance. Key legal and policy issues are identified, usually in collaboration with work on Bank-funded operations, although few GEF projects insist on policy conditionality. Several GEF projects are associated with Bank projects focusing on policy frameworks, however.

The following projects have examined legal and regulatory frameworks to ensure the long-term sustainability of projects and their effective integration into various national and international policies and strategies:

- The Lao PDR Wildlife and Protected Areas Conservation Project was linked to adoption of new forest laws.
- The Ecuador Biodiversity Protection Project will assist with the assessment of, and recommendations for, legal and regulatory changes to ensure sound management of protected areas, indigenous peoples' rights in protected areas, appropriate pricing for visitor access to national parks, and land use planning policies that encourage sustainable resource use.
- The Wider Caribbean Initiative for Disposal of Ship-Generated Waste will provide support for assessing the current legal and

regulatory frameworks related to waste disposal in the Wider Caribbean countries and for recommending changes to enable participating countries to ratify and fully comply with MARPOL requirements.

- The Southwest Mediterranean Sea Oil Pollution Management Project pays considerable attention to the environmental legislation governing the treatment of oil spills in the three participating countries, Algeria, Morocco, and Tunisia. The project's legal advisers are working closely to harmonize penalties across the three countries for noncompliance with environmental regulations and to ensure consistency in legal recourse.

INSTITUTION BUILDING. As discussed in several contexts in this report, the national entities responsible for environmental policy and project implementation in developing countries are often young and weak. The GEF is financing the establishment or strengthening of environment ministries, national park services, offices of technology assessment, and other relevant institutions in virtually all of its projects. For example, in the Peru Parks and Protected Areas Project, the GEF has been a catalyst for institution building in a country with weak public environmental agencies. Following substantial progress in project preparation, the Peruvian government created PROFONANPE to manage the trust fund that would be established with GET funding (as well as with contributions from other donors, debt swaps, and so forth). The GET's project preparation advance provided support for developing sound financial management and control systems, as well as for strengthening PROFONANPE. Pending the approval of the GET grant, PROFONANPE has been operating for the past year with bilateral contributions.

CAPACITY BUILDING. An important challenge for the GEF is to help build capacity in developing countries, through training courses, for all types of environmental management and research and for creating partnerships between governments, NGOs, and local and academic communities. Therefore, training is addressed in all GEF projects. This may include short courses in economics, forestry, park management, water quality monitoring, project appraisal (especially useful for incremental cost calculations for global warming projects), and other sciences, as well as courses in project management, accounting, and evaluation methodologies. Training is offered to all levels of project personnel, including project and NGO staff, the scientific community, and other personnel directly associated with project implementation. The experience in capacity building in Indonesia (box 4.5) illustrates one form the training can take.

Box 4.5. Indonesia: Strengthening In-Country Use of Biological Information

Indonesia covers only 1.3 percent of the world's surface but supports 10 percent of the world's remaining closed, tropical forests, as well as rich coastal and marine habitats. The 17,000 islands of the archipelago contain an estimated 15,000 to 25,000 species of plants (one-tenth of the world's total), 25 percent of the world's freshwater and marine fish, 17 percent of all bird species, 16 percent of all reptile and amphibian species, 12 percent of the world's mammals, and unknown numbers of invertebrates, fungi, and microorganisms. Many of these species are unique to the Indonesian islands. Indonesias biological resources are economically important, both globally and nationally, yet probably 30 percent of the flora and 90 percent of the fauna are not yet fully described or scientifically documented.

A new GEF project to help restore, rehabilitate, and expand existing botanical and zoological collections in Indonesia will strengthen the countrys scientific capacity and provide a secure national base for biodiversity knowledge. The Biodiversity Collections Project will help Indonesian scientists to catalogue, inventory, and monitor Indonesia's biological resources. The national herbarium and zoological collections were begun in colonial times, and the herbarium collections include more than 1.6 million specimens, the most important botanical collection in Southeast Asia. The project will provide resources to rehabilitate the existing collections and to train national systematists and technicians. The project will also allow Indonesian scientists to access existing biological information held outside Indonesia by strengthening linkages and the exchange of expertise with herbaria and zoological museums in Australia, Europe, and North America. All information will be available on computer databases that allow easy access and dissemination of pivotal information on biodiversity.

At a time when even scientific institutions in industrial countries are short of funds, this project addresses some of the most frequently expressed needs of developing countries: repatriation of knowledge, strengthening and capacity building of local institutions, and improved exchange of biological information.

Team building is an important element in capacity building and is especially relevant for the formerly centrally planned economies and where project staff are reluctant to make decisions. For the Russia Natural Resources Management and Biodiversity Project project preparation advance (PPA) , for example, workshops will be held during project design for scientists and other project personnel to set the main objectives and priority work program.

Partnerships with Other Institutions

GEF projects rely on a broad range of institutions as partners in preparing and implementing project activities. Innovation in financing channels provides an important opportunity to harness the motivation and entrepreneurial vigor of a variety of development actors in partnership with governments. These GEF partners include regional and international organizations and multilateral development banks, as well as special initiatives with the IFC. Additionally, with GEF grant resources, the usual requirement for government guarantees of loans is unnecessary, making possible more flexible arrangements for channeling resources directly to NGOs, local communities, and the private sector.

REGIONAL AND INTERNATIONAL ORGANIZATIONS. These organizations have been tapped for their expertise in analyzing and resolving global environmental issues. For example, the IMO has collaborated with the Bank in developing the Wider Caribbean Initiative for Disposal of Ship-Generated Waste and will be the executing agency for the implementation phase. The OECS also provided regional support for development of the OECS Waste Disposal Project, and a specialized project management unit will direct project activities that are regional in scope during the implementation phase.

Multilateral organizations are working in association with the Bank in developing pilot-phase GEF projects. For example, the IDB, working closely with the Costa Rican national utility company, submitted the Costa Rica Grid-Integrated Project to the participants as part of the pilot-phase program to reduce global warming. During preparation, the IDB performed the functions the World Bank would normally execute as a GEF implementing agency (technical advice, appraisal, negotiations, and approval). During implementation, the IDB will be responsible for project supervision, management of disbursements, and audit review. This collaboration has provided valuable experience for the future structuring of operational relationships between the Bank and regional development banks during the permanent phase of the GEF in order to maximize the benefits of decentralization while ensuring accountability to the participants.

An emerging method for building partnerships between the government and NGOs in GEF project design and implementation has been to support either *alternative livelihood* activities (as part of integrated conservation and development programs) or *direct conservation* activities by local communities and NGOs. These two approaches feature in the Bank's GEF portfolio, with some variation in the local management arrangements project by project.

Alternative livelihood funds are included in GEF biodiversity conservation projects in Congo, Ghana, Lao PDR, the Philippines, and Romania's Danube Delta. For example, the IUCN has been authorized by the government of Congo to administer alternative livelihood funds totaling $700,000 for the Nouabale-Ndoki, Conkouati, Dimonika, and Lake Tele protected areas to encourage biologically sustainable economic activities by communities in the buffer zones around the protected areas; these include production of nontimber forest products and medicinal plants and developing limited ecotourism. WWF-USA will help design a conservation trust fund, to be financed outside the project, and will train Congo nationals to manage it. Assistance will be provided to strengthen the administrative capacity and skills of local NGOs to expand beyond government implementation capacity for conservation actions.

Small grants for direct conservation activities are included in the Bank-GEF Czech and Slovak biodiversity projects. For example, the first round of grants has already been made to the Slovak Republic's GEF Biodiversity Conservation project from the small grant fund administered by the government's project management unit. For the eight grants made, $235 has been provided to the Bratislava Section of the Slovak Union (a national NGO) for protection programs for the spring migration of frogs, and $2,220 has gone toward protecting endangered waterfowl near the Danube River.

Combating Ozone Depletion

The Montreal Protocol on Substances That Deplete the Ozone Layer was adopted in 1987 by more than twenty countries. Parties to the Montreal Protocol (MP) agreed to institute control measures for eliminating the production and consumption of ozone depleting chemicals by 1996, with developing countries having a ten-year grace period. The Montreal Protocol has been ratified by more than a hundred countries, and its provisions have already significantly decreased the amounts of ozone depleting substances (ODSs) emitted into the atmosphere.

The World Bank is in its third year as an implementing agency of the Multilateral Fund for the Implementation of the Montreal Protocol (MFMP). The Bank and its clients have operations in fourteen countries around the world, and operations are forthcoming for many more. The grant portfolio approved by the MFMP Executive Committee has grown from less than $5 million in 1991 to close to $80 million as of the end of fiscal 1994. To date the Bank has reached agreement with twelve countries for fourteen projects, committing almost half of the grant resources. The majority of commitments have been in East Asia, South Asia, and Latin America. Several activities are also under way in Europe, the

Middle East, and North Africa, and efforts have been made to initiate work in Sub-Saharan Africa. In fiscal 1994 Bank management approved seven project packages for implementation, totaling $26 million in commitments. Through June 1994, $6 million had been disbursed; however, as almost 80 percent of MFMP-approved resources were committed by the Bank in fiscal 1994, disbursements are expected to increase rapidly during fiscal 1995. Table 4.2 shows all MFMP projects approved by Bank

Table 4.2. MFMP Projects Approved by Bank Management through Fiscal 1994

Country	Project	MFMP grant agreement amount (millions of dollars)	Management approval date
Fiscal 1994			
Brazil	Ozone Depleting Substances Phaseout I	$2.9[a]	12/93
China	Ozone Depleting Substances Phaseout I	$6.9	11/93
China	Ozone Depleting Substances Phaseout II	$4.9	5/94
Ecuador	Ozone Depleting Substances Phaseout I	$1.6	10/93
Jordan	Ozone Depleting Substances Project I	$1.5	9/93
Tunisia	Ozone Depleting Substances Project I	$1.8	6/94
Turkey	Ozone Depleting Substances Project I	$6.2	1/94
Total		$25.8	
Prior to fiscal 1994			
Chile	Ozone Depleting Substances Phaseout I	$1.2	6/93
Malaysia	Ozone Depleting Substances Phaseout I	$1.6	11/92
Mexico	Mobile Air Conditioning Recycling	$0.2	3/92
Mexico	Ozone Protection	$4.0	11/92
Philippines	Ozone Depleting Substances Engineering	$0.4	1/92
Thailand	Ozone Depleting Substances Engineering	$0.4	1/92
Venezuela	Ozone Depleting Substances I	$1.3	4/93
Total		$34.9	

management through fiscal 1994. Examples of the fund's activities and projects in the pipeline follow.

- The Bank has assisted the government of Argentina with the preparation of its country program for the phaseout of ODS and with the identification of a pipeline of projects totaling over $40 million.
- In China the Bank is working with the National Environmental Protection Agency to prepare the third ODS Phaseout Project ($80 million), which will consist of an umbrella agreement expected to cover MP projects for two to three years. The projects will support technology transfer in all of the sectors that use substances regulated by the Montreal Protocol: aerosols, domestic and commercial refrigerants, and foams and solvents.
- In Jordan, a project to produce a replacement for CFC propellant will use a hydrogenation process that has never been used in a developing country. This project will allow aerosol manufacturers to introduce locally made non-ODS substitutes.
- In Turkey a compressor and refrigerator manufacturer has significantly reduced the use of CFC-11 in refrigerator walls. The company has also re-engineered its line of compressors to rely on non-ODS substances and is currently field testing these new compressor designs.
- In Venezuela the first MP project to be fully implemented by one of the Bank's clients will result in the phaseout of over 250 tons of CFC-11 a year.

PART 2

Equipping the Bank and Reaching Out

Part 2 addresses how the Bank is better equipping itself for achieving the goals of its environmental agenda described in Part 1. Actions have been taken to increase environmental staff and improve both training and the World Bank's dialogue with outside partners.

5. Building Capacity for the Task

Over the past year the Environment Department has coordinated efforts to incorporate social concerns into the Bank's development work. In particular, a "Participation Sourcebook" is being prepared to help Bank task managers include and learn from the views of people affected by projects, such as these villagers in Mali.

Chapters 1 through 4 have described the World Bank's large and growing environmental agenda. This chapter addresses how the Bank is equipping itself for the task in two respects. The first involves internal capacity building, through improved staffing, training, and management practices. The second involves the Bank's external relationships and includes (a) partnership building with official and nongovernmental organizations and (b) improved communication and openness. These two elements are addressed in turn.

Building Internal Capacity

Skills Mix and Numbers

The past year has provided an opportunity to strengthen the Bank's skills mix in line with the reorganization of 1993 (box 5.1) and a Bank-wide assessment of environmental staffing needs. That assessment found a shortfall in a number of critical skills areas and resulted in the creation of twenty-seven new positions for technical environmental specialists and twelve new positions for social scientists throughout the Bank. Environmental skills were enhanced in the biological sciences (especially biodiversity and terrestrial, freshwater, and marine ecology), environmental engineering (in air and water quality and hazardous waste management), forestry and protected areas management, and environmental economics and indicators. Social skills were strengthened in the sociological and anthropological fields dealing with indigenous peoples, resettlement, social impact analysis, and community participation.

As part of the Bank's general strategy of moving more specialists to country operations, the number of full-time environmental specialists and long-term consultants within country departments grew to around ninety, from some thirty last year. In addition, by year's end the central Environment Department and the four regional environment divisions comprised 162 higher-level staff and long-term consultants. The new Environment, Agriculture, and Infrastructure research division in the Policy Research Department (created in 1993) also was strengthened during the year. And other support units of the Bank, including the Legal Department and the EDI, maintained or increased their environmental staff levels. Taken together, more than 300 high-level staff and long-term consultants are now working on environmental matters in the Bank. This does not include the significant number of technical specialists working in water and sanitation, energy, health, economics, and other areas related to the environment. Nor does it reflect the total number of staff-years involved in environmental work, since all task managers and

---

Box 5.1. Improved Structure to Enhance Bank Priorities

The Bank modified its structure in 1993 to strengthen delivery of services to borrowers. The changes involved replacing the central vice presidency for Sector and Operations Policy with three new vice presidencies: ESD, Human Resources Development and Operations Policy, and Financial and Private Sector Development. These central vice presidencies were charged with providing policy guidance, operational support, and dissemination of good practices to assist member countries and improve project performance. Regional technical staff also were realigned to better provide specialized services for project preparation and supervision.

The ESD vice presidency encompasses three existing departments: the Environment Department (ENV), the Agriculture and Natural Resources Development Department (AGR); and the Transport, Water, and Urban Development Department (TWU). ENV continued to be responsible for coordinating the Bank's overall environmental policies and associated development approaches. The department was reorganized and expanded from three divisions to four: the Land, Water, and Natural Habitats Division; the Pollution and Environmental Economics Division; a new Social Policy and Resettlement Division; and the Global Environment Coordination Division (the coordinating unit for all GEF investment projects managed by the Bank, as well as projects implemented with resources from the Montreal Protocol Multilateral Fund).

Other departments in ESD also maintained or expanded their environmental roles. In the Agriculture and Natural Resources Department, a new Natural Resources Division was established to better promote sustainable management and use of soil, water, and forest resources. The TWU Department continued to lead the Bank's work in sanitation and water supply, urban management, and transport-related environmental issues.

---

country officers and some finance and external relations staff now spend time on the environment as an integral part of the Bank's core agenda.

During the year the three departments of the vice presidency for Environmentally Sustainable Development—the Environment Department, the Agriculture and Natural Resources Department, and the Transport, Water, and Urban Development Department—dramatically increased their level of direct operational support to the regions in natural resources, pollution control, social issues, and urban environmental management. In the Environment Department alone, through staff increase and substantial staff redeployment, support to operations tripled, with the highest demands coming from Eastern and Central Europe (including the republics of the former Soviet Union) and Sub-Saharan Africa.

Similarly, country departments within the regions continued to adjust and refine their structures to better support borrowers in the environmental aspects of projects and sector work. All twenty-two country departments have environmental coordinators, and most now have operational units or sections dedicated to environmental work, often in conjunction with another prominent sector. Going one step farther, the Indonesia country department created an Environmental and Social Impact Unit in Jakarta, the first such effort at the level of a resident mission.

As country departments' expertise has grown, the regional environment divisions have undertaken more regionwide initiatives, including strategic work and pilot projects, in addition to maintaining formal project environmental review and clearance functions.

- The Asia Technical Department Environment and Natural Resources Development Division (ASTEN) gave high priority to producing a major environmental strategy for Asia, as outlined in *Toward an Environmental Strategy for Asia* (Brandon and Ramankutty 1993). ASTEN also began to implement the Asia Biodiversity Strategy completed in 1993, created a regional environmental working group on industry and energy, and, through the MEIP, initiated local demonstration projects on community management, sanitation, and environmental protection.
- The Latin America and Caribbean Department Environment Division (LATEN) emphasized regionwide capacity building for EA, indigenous peoples, and resettlement issues. Its new EA guidelines for privatization loans have been adopted Bank-wide. Aiming to better integrate environmental work within operations, the region also decided at the end of fiscal 1994 to create environmental divisions in each country department still lacking one, in order to enhance technical assistance and operational support to borrowers preparing EAs, strengthen environmental country and sector dialogue, and manage the growing environmental portfolio.
- The Europe and Central Asia/Middle East and North Africa Technical Department Environment Division (EMTEN) sought to further strengthen country departments' environmental skills and shifted toward demand-driven, specialized support for country department strategies. A highlight of EMTEN's fiscal 1994 work program was the completion of the regional Environmental Action Programme for Central and Eastern Europe, endorsed at the Lucerne Environment for Europe ministerial conference and published in the second half of the fiscal year (see chapter 1). In parallel, the Middle East and North Africa region organized a major environ-

mental conference in Casablanca, focusing on regional environmental issues.

- The Africa Technical Department Environmentally Sustainable Development Division (AFTES) gave clear priority to assisting countries in building their national environmental capacity. Since the Africa region has the majority of active IDA borrowers, this region placed particular emphasis on technical assistance and dialogue concerning the national environmental action planning process in each country. Several of these planning efforts led to identification of environmental or natural resource investment projects (see chapter 1). In some cases in which local capacity was particularly limited, the Bank's support included producing country environmental strategies as background for the NEAP process. Special attention also was paid to providing technical assistance for national biodiversity conservation strategy studies, and work began toward a post-UNCED strategy for Sub-Saharan Africa.

In the Policy Research Department, an Environment, Infrastructure, and Agriculture Division (PRDEI) was created to study environmental issues. Its completed and recently initiated work includes studies on pollution, health issues, and deforestation.

- Using a massive U.S. data base, comprehensive estimates of marginal and average abatement cost by industrial sector for several major air and water pollutants were calculated. Although U.S. estimates are broadly representative at the sectoral level and hence can be used to analyze pollution regulations in other countries, future work will focus on using data from developing countries.
- On the benefit side of pollution control, a study measured the health effects of particulates and ozone on acute respiratory illness in Taiwan, China. A contingent valuation study estimated that people there were willing to pay $10, on average, to avoid a day of minor respiratory illness. A similar study is planned for Delhi, India.
- In additional work on health, staff of PRDEI collaborated with other PRD staff to collect survey data on and begin analyzing living standards of households in Tanzania hard hit by the AIDS (acquired immunodeficiency syndrome) epidemic. The analysis focuses on the effects of premature adult mortality and on the costs and benefits of alternative policies to reduce these effects.
- A series of research studies is examining the sources, nature, and impact of tropical deforestation. The first studies, currently under way in Belize and Thailand, will analyze in an economic and geographic framework how land characteristics, government poli-

cies, agricultural markets, roads, timber extraction, and population distribution interact to affect deforestation in tropical countries.

Environmental Training

A 1993 assessment of the Bank's training programs recommended more systematic core environmental training for Bank nonenvironmental staff, along with continued upgrading of economic and technical skills. In line with this, some 70 to 80 percent of operations staff have been targeted to receive basic environmental training over the next two years. Central to achieving this goal was the establishment of a new flagship course, "Fundamentals of Environmental Management." This course provides an overview of ecological and economic principles and a number of technical, social, and institutional issues important for the Bank's work in EA, NEAPs, and environmental project preparation.

More specialized Bank-wide environmental courses in specific sectors and issues continue to be offered. Overall in fiscal 1994, the Training Division sponsored twenty-one courses, averaging two days each and reaching more than 550 staff throughout the Bank (see table 5.1). These courses were built on good-practice cases, highlighting analytical techniques and emphasizing the operational aspects of Bank policies and procedures. The EA courses continued to reach the greatest number of sectoral staff, but environmental economics courses remain particularly popular among economists and noneconomists alike. A new annual course, "Principles of Environmental Institution Building," was introduced to address special institutional issues in environmental management. These courses are all led by Bank specialists, increasingly in collaboration with developing country practitioners who lend valuable field experience and firsthand knowledge.

In addition to Bank-wide training offered by the Training Division, numerous specialized courses, workshops, and seminars continued to be given within the regions and country departments to address special environmental issues or project-related training needs. For example, the Latin American region has begun regional training on social assessment and participation in Bank-assisted operations as groundwork for introducing social assessments into project preparation. The Africa and Asia regions also have made special training available to their staffs, and staff from the Middle East and North Africa region attended a week-long program on natural resources, the environment, and social issues at Duke University.

The Friday Environment Seminar Series, initiated in October 1993, provides a forum for Bank staff and outside guests to discuss environmentally sustainable development. Topics have ranged from

**Table 5.1. Internal Training Courses for Bank Staff
on Environmental Issues, Fiscal 1994**

Flagship course
Fundamentals of Environmental Management

Sector-specific courses
Environmental Assessment for Agriculture Staff
Environmental Assessment for Transport Staff
Environmental Assessment for Water and Sanitation Staff
Environmental Assessment for Urban Staff
Environmental Assessment for Industry and Energy Staff
Urban Environment Strategies and Action Plans
Forestry Symposium
Water Resources Seminar
Critical Success Factors for Implementing Energy Efficiency Improvement
    Programs

Environmental economics and impact analysis
Introduction to Environmental Economics
Economic Analysis of Environmental Impacts
Economywide Policies and the Environment

Special issues
Principles of Environmental Institution Building
National Environmental Action Plans: Issues and Options
Indigenous Peoples and Economic Development
Involuntary Resettlement Workshop
Environmental Information Systems
International Environmental Law and the GEF
Legal Aspects of Resettlement in Bank Projects
Regional Seminar on Environment

"Sharks, Sea Slugs, and the World Bank" to "Ecological Tax Reform,"
and speakers have included distinguished academics, practitioners,
and politicians.

Thematic Teams and Collaboration across Work Units

Increasingly, environmental issues are recognized as crossing depart-
mental lines. As part of the 1993 reorganization, thematic teams were
established within the ESD vice presidency in six areas: water, land
management, the urban environment, social policy, indicators of ESD,
and the "nexus" between poverty, population, gender, and the environment. These teams worked primarily to shape policy and provide conceptual and methodological guidance for Bank operations.
    Among the most active of the teams was that on the urban environ-
ment, which moved its focus beyond the brown agenda toward a more

cross-sectoral and multijurisdictional approach to urban environmental management. The team began analyzing the urban aspects of NEAPs and EAs, and it is helping prepare for the World Bank's Second Annual Conference on Environmentally Sustainable Development, "The Human Face of the Urban Environment," to be held in September 1994. Bank-wide development of social assessment methodologies continued to be guided by the social policy team, and regional water strategies by the water team. The land management team focused on information exchange, with early analytical work particularly in land property rights and land degradation. The work of the indicators team is described in the next section.

Cooperative efforts were expanded across vice presidencies as well. For example, the Environment Department increased its interaction with the Population, Health, and Nutrition Department on environmental health issues and with the Education and Social Policy Development Department on environmental education. In the area of energy and the environment, the Industry and Energy Department is cooperating with the Environment Department on a computerized information and decision support system, the "Environmental Manual for Power Development," which will be available in 1995. Publication of an occasional paper on policy instruments for pollution control and analysis of energy and transport environmental issues from an energy sector perspective is also under way.

Better Tools and Indicators

One aspect of the Bank's plan to improve project performance has been increased attention to operations policies and related tools that guide staff in project design and supervision. Among the findings of the Bank-wide portfolio performance review was the need for a simplified and more user-friendly system of operational policies and procedures, in tandem with better guidance on performance indicators and technical issues and increased learning from ex-post evaluation of Bank operations. During the year the Bank began implementing this new system, preparing guidance on the use of indicators of environmental performance, and developing additional operational technical manuals and handbooks in environmental and social issues. The Operations Evaluation Department (OED) also expanded its environment-related evaluation work.

POLICIES AND PROCEDURES. The new system of operational policies and procedures, which went into effect during fiscal 1994, divides the old operational directives into three categories of statements: (a) Operational Policies (OPs), which are short, focused statements of policies considered mandatory for Bank-financed projects; (b) Bank Procedures (BPs), which spell out mandatory, common procedures or documentation for projects to ensure consistency and quality across regions; and (c) Good Practice (GP) statements, which contain explanatory and advisory materials for helping staff carry out Bank policies. At year's end existing environmental and social policies were in the process of being converted or revised according to this new system, and all operational directives were expected to be converted during fiscal 1995. New policies, such as the forest and water policy, were issued as OPs. (See annex A for a list of documents on major environmental policies.)

INDICATORS OF ENVIRONMENTALLY SUSTAINABLE DEVELOPMENT. Compiling sector-specific environmental performance indicators is part of the Bank's plan for improving tools for project performance monitoring and portfolio management information systems. During the past year the Environment Department took the lead in organizing this work directly and through the thematic team on indicators, methodologies, and concepts. The Environment Department is proceeding on three tracks. First, it has drawn up and widely circulated a framework for indicators for twelve environmental issues, such as urban environmental quality, forestry, water, and soil, that are important for environmentally sustainable development. This framework was compiled from (a) existing data sources—for example, the FAO, the Global Environment Monitoring System (GEMS), the UNEP, and the World Conservation Monitoring Centre (WCMC); (b) national-level indicators of existing conditions (and subnational-level indicators where available, as in forestry); and (c) information on appropriate targets where there is already serious degradation. Recognizing that there is no internationally agreed framework for environmental indicators, the Bank is using as a baseline the *OECD's Core Set of Indicators for Environmental Performance Reviews* (OECD 1993). To adjust the rough indicators to reality, the team is circulating this information to sector specialists and task managers of Bank projects and requesting feedback on the relevance of the indicators for specific project sites. Finally, in a few areas in which environmental issues cut deeply across conventional sectoral lines (for example, in pollution abatement and biodiversity), the Environment Department is taking the lead in producing detailed performance indicators. This work is now in a pilot phase. The goal of this long-term and complex process is to make environmental performance indicators as routine in project monitoring as economic and social indicators now are. An initial set of national indicators on biodiversity has also been drafted by the GEF, with advice from the World Resources Institute (GEF 1993).

MANUALS AND HANDBOOKS. Improved technical guidance materials in the form of handbooks and manuals were in preparation for a number of key environmental and social topics. These materials built heavily on lessons from operational support and good-practice cases. The Social Policy Division of the Environment Department managed the production of the "Participation Handbook," a compendium of Bank experience that provides task managers with advice on tested methods of promoting stakeholder and beneficiary assessment in Bank work (see chapter 3). Led by the GEF division of the Environment Department (see box 5.1), work is well advanced on "Rapid Biodiversity Appraisal Guidelines," and preparation has begun on the "Natural Resource Management Sourcebook," which will supplement other technical materials on natural resource management such as the "EA Sourcebook." (For other environmental documents issued during fiscal 1994, see the bibliography.)

EX-POST EVALUATION. The OED evaluates completed projects to help improve the design and performance of new lending operations. In any given year, the OED undertakes more than 400 evaluations and related studies, including annual reports, annual reviews, performance audits, and impact evaluation studies. This year, in addition to its continual auditing of Bank investments that have environmental components and operations that have environmental impacts, the OED contributed to an independent review of the pilot phase of the GEF. Other OED evaluations with significant environmental implications during fiscal 1994 are summarized in box 5.2. The general conclusion emerging from this work is that improvement in environmental conditions and the management of natural resources is dependent on clear environmental benefits that will motivate all relevant parties to act. At the national level, this means that Bank-supported actions should be backed by strong government commitment so that the necessary financial resources are provided and the necessary laws and regulations are enacted and enforced.

Improving Openness and Accountability

The Bank's experience clearly indicates that the quality of Bank operations benefits when staff and governments consult and share information with participants of projects, and expanded access to information strengthens the Bank's links with all its partners in the development community. In addition, increased focus on accountability during 1993 led the Bank to examine country experience with inspection function and to consider whether a new inspection unit was needed to augment the Bank's existing supervision and evaluation procedures. A separate issue

---

Box 5.2. The Operations Evaluation Department and the Environment

Major studies undertaken or completed by the Operations Evaluation Department (OED) over the past year included the evaluation of environmental aspects of Bank operations in several areas.

Urban review. A study entitled "Twenty Years of Lending for Urban Development (1972–92): An OED Review" (OED 1994) analyzed 162 urban projects that, among other things, addressed the phenomena of rapid urban growth, housing finance, municipal development, disaster recovery, and urban transport. With the growing recognition of the importance and complexity of the urban environment, Bank experience shows that urban environmental improvement and pollution-control actions need to be integrated with cost recovery and institutional development measures. Borrowers and the Bank have begun to adopt better-targeted and more innovative approaches in recently approved projects. Completed urban projects resulted in environmental improvement in cities in all regions through provision of clean water, solid waste collection and disposal, sanitation, and drainage (although older projects rarely referred to such improvements as "environmental"). Few completed urban projects contributed substantially to cleaner air in cities, although traffic management and other components of urban transport operations sought in part to reduce congestion-related pollution.

Indonesian transmigration. The Transmigration Program in Indonesia, one of the largest land resettlement schemes in the world, aims to improve

---

was whether the Bank had easy access, when needed, to a reliable source of independent judgment about specific projects that may be facing severe implementation problems. These developments resulted in two major new procedures for communicating with the public.

Expanded Access to Information

In January 1994 the Bank issued a new, expanded policy on disclosure of information, which became effective immediately (see World Bank 1994c). Under the policy four types of environmental documents are available. *Environmental data sheets,* also available through the Internet network, are prepared by Bank staff and briefly describe major environmental issues in Bank-financed projects and proposed mitigative actions. The other documents are prepared by the borrowers. *Environmental assessments* (for category A projects likely to have significant adverse environmental impacts) are publicly available from the Bank, with borthe living conditions of poor landless families from the inner islands by moving them to the less-populated outer islands. A study of five Bank-supported projects within the program reviewed (among other issues) their effects on incomes, living standards, women, and the environment. Although incomes rose and the large majority of resettlers were satisfied with the projects, significant weaknesses were found in certain areas of environmental management (including the negative environmental impact of removing tree cover and clearing steeply sloping lands at some sites).

Maharastra Petrochemical Impact Study. The Maharastra (India) Petrochemical Complex was designed in the early 1980s at a time when neither the Bank nor the borrower were as environmentally conscious as they are today. This year the OED conducted an environmental impact evaluation for the petrochemical facility at Nagothane, focusing on the resettlement and environmental aspects of the project. The team that visited the site found that the project has had a very satisfactory outcome. The corporation has a serious attitude and does not cut corners. Staff are constantly reminded of their responsibilities through seminars, publications, and training seminars. Project managers concluded that it is cheaper to take environmental concerns into account at the outset and to respond to problems at the earliest possible time rather than to wait for major problems to develop. For example, the complex has in place air-quality monitoring stations that automatically transfer air-quality data to a central information processing station. After aggregation, these data are sent to the Maharastra Pollution Control Board.

rower consent, once they are officially cleared. For some category B projects (projects with more limited environmental impacts), a separate *environmental analysis report* may be produced by the borrower and made available. (Environmental assessments and analyses, which have been required since October 1989, are normally officially submitted to the Bank prior to project appraisal.) *Environmental action plans*, also prepared by borrowers, are made publicly available once they are officially received and the Bank has obtained the government's consent for release.

A new Bank document, the project information document (PID), has been created to present information concisely to interested parties during project preparation. The PID, which provides a brief factual summary of the project's main elements (objectives, probable components, costs and financing, and environmental and other issues), is available through Internet.

These and other materials are available at the Bank's new Public Information Center (PIC), established in January 1994 at Bank headquarters in Washington, D.C., as the central contact for people seeking access to Bank documents.[1] The PIC has a public reading room, and inquiries may also be submitted through Internet, through the Bank's offices in Paris, London, and Tokyo, and through Bank field offices. As of June 1994 the PIC was responding to more than 250 requests for documents and approximately 3,000 Internet queries for environmental data sheets each week.

Creating an Independent Inspection Function

Following the comprehensive review of evaluation functions carried out in 1993, the Bank concluded that its interests would be best served by the establishment of an independent Inspection Panel to complement the Bank's standing supervision, audit, and evaluation activities. The Panel would provide an opportunity, independent from Bank management, to investigate the claims of parties charging that they have been adversely affected by Bank-financed projects on the grounds that the Bank has not followed its policies or procedures in project identification, appraisal, or implementation. The Bank's executive directors approved creation of the panel in September 1993, and the Panel's three members were appointed in April 1994, to start work on the 1st of August.

The motivation for establishing an inspection panel stemmed from the desire to ensure compliance with Bank policies and procedures in the design, preparation, and implementation of Bank-supported projects. In addition, the inspection function would strengthen the Bank's system of accountability before the executive directors decide on the course of action to be followed, especially in environmental and social matters.

The Inspection Panel will consider requests for inspection of a project from affected parties (not single individuals) in the territory of the borrower, and will recommend to the Bank's Board whether the inspection should take place. Following the Board's decision, the Panel will conduct an inspection and submit a report to the executive directors and the president of the Bank. This report will consider all relevant facts and include findings on whether the Bank has complied with its own relevant policies and procedures. The Bank's management will then report to the executive directors on its response to the findings.

International Cooperation

International cooperation on environmental policy has become an increasingly vital part of the Bank's work program, particularly since UNCED and the follow-up to Agenda 21. In addition, to build working partnerships for improved projects and for future replenishment negotiations, there has been a marked increase in outreach to bilateral agencies, NGOs, and local groups on the Bank's internal policies, issues of disclosure of information, and project quality. These outreach efforts increasingly use environmental specialists to support external relations staff. During the past year the Bank's environmental outreach strategy has had four objectives: (a) to raise awareness of ESD issues and lessons from Bank experience and thus promote support for the Bank and for sustainable development in general; (b) to listen to views and criticisms of those outside the Bank, with the purpose of improving Bank activities; (c) to create a more accurate picture of the Bank's activities on environmental issues; and (d) to build partnerships with donors, nongovernmental groups, and the private sector.

Interagency Activities

Within the United Nations system, priority was given this year to collaborating on international environmental policy through the new United Nations Commission on Sustainable Development and the Inter-Agency Committee on Sustainable Development, which was established to improve coordination and cooperation within the UN system in implementing Agenda 21. For the second meeting of the commission, in June 1994, the Bank was requested to provide information about its priorities and programs in some fifteen areas. Topics included financing, water resource management, science and technology, transfer of environmentally sustainable technology, control of hazardous wastes, and international environmental law. The Bank was also represented by senior environmental managers at the annual meeting of the commission, several Inter-Agency Committee meetings, and related initiatives following the 1992 Earth Summit. As an example of the last point, the Bank actively participated in the two-week Global Conference on Sustainable Development of Small Island States convened by the United Nations in May 1994 in Barbados. This meeting produced a Programme of Action for small-island developing states (to be monitored by the Commission on Sustainable Development), as well as the Barbados Declaration reaffirming support for various international agreements.

Priority also was given to monitoring and participating directly in deliberations of major international conventions. For example, the Bank sent technical specialists to the meetings of the Climate Change and Biodiversity Conventions and provided technical input for negotiations on the draft Desertification Convention (see chapter 4).

The Bank sponsored the first environmental working meeting of representatives of the fourteen members of the MFI group. This meeting, which included technical specialists from the development banks, focused on environmental assessment policies and procedures.[2] The outcome was that the members reached consensus on holding annual meetings under the auspices of an environmental subgroup of the MFI Cofinancing Group chaired by the Bank. The next annual meeting of this group will bring together multilateral and bilateral agencies that are undertaking a parallel initiative within the OECD to harmonize EA requirements in development projects.

Bilateral Collaboration

In the past year the Bank has continued to work closely with bilateral donor agencies and legislatures on the environmental dimension of the development agenda. To further promote communication and share experience, Bank senior management made it a priority to visit donor countries for meetings with parliaments, government officials, NGOs, and the media on topics such as follow-up activities to the Earth Summit and Agenda 21, the Bank-wide Resettlement Review, and the Bank's broader lending program. The Bank encouraged and participated in a number of seminars on the Bank and the environment, cosponsored by governments and NGOs, in Canada, Italy, Germany, Norway, Sweden, and other countries. It continued to be an active observer-member of the OECD/DAC Working Party on Development Assistance and Environment, working particularly with its Task Force on Capacity Development in Environment.

The bilateral agencies have become increasingly important partners in supporting the Bank's environmental work and cofinancing free-standing environmental projects and projects with environmental components. Of the twenty-five free-standing environmental projects listed in annex C, five had bilateral cofinancing, frequently of technical assistance. Donor consultant trust funds remained an important source of financing for environmental initiatives. In fiscal 1994 environmental activities continued to receive the most bilateral trust fund support by volume of funds—about $7.9 million, up from $6.7 million in fiscal 1993.

During the year six consultant trust funds (CTFs) specifically targeted for environmental purposes were replenished (two trust funds each by Norway and Sweden, one by Canada, and one by the Netherlands). In addition, CTFs from Australia, Belgium, Denmark, Finland, France, Italy, Japan, Korea, and Switzerland provided selective funding for environmental projects and activities. These funds facilitated the exchange of environmental specialists and increased the opportunities for transferring experience among institutions on approaches and best practice in environmental policy and project work.

In addition, project activities under the special trust fund for the Pilot Program to Conserve the Brazilian Rain Forest moved toward implementation. This program, under World Bank trusteeship, was launched at the request of the Group of Seven (G-7). As of June 1994, about $290 million had been pledged for the program by the G-7 countries, the European Union, and the Netherlands. In May and June 1994 the first two grant agreements for pilot program projects were successfully negotiated. The first agreement, for demonstration projects, is a small-grants program for local communities, local NGO networks, and local and state governments to fund subprojects aimed at reducing pressure on native forests. Project implementation is expected to begin in July. The second agreement, the Science Centers and Directed Research Project, will promote generation and dissemination of scientific knowledge for conservation and sustainable development activities in the Amazon region.

A continuing source of donor financing targeted to the environment is the Policy and Human Resources Development Fund for technical assistance, funded by the government of Japan. In fiscal 1994 thirty-four grants totaling $22.3 million were approved to fund technical assistance for the preparation of Bank-financed projects on the environment.

Environmental Training for Borrowers

As environmental and social issues occupy a growing part of Bank dialogue and project work with borrowers, borrower interest in training in environmental policies and technical issues has significantly increased. The Bank's EDI continues to be a major vehicle for training government officials and others from borrower countries. The EDI's environmental program, which started in earnest three years ago, was formalized last year with the designation of an Agriculture and Environment Division to handle environmental training and provision of additional resources, including three environmental specialists. A fourth specialist was added in 1994. This year's environmental training program, which is usually organized on a regional basis, had two major objectives: (a) to teach and disseminate ways of integrating environmental issues into national policies and plans; and (b) to teach and disseminate ways of assessing the environmental impact of programs and projects. To support the first objective, courses were conducted on structural adjustment and the environment, environmental economics, national environmental action plans, and biodiversity conservation and agriculture. Courses on EA and project appraisal addressed the second objective. In total, more than twenty workshops and seminars reached some 750 participants worldwide during the year (see table 5.2).

As part of the EDI's longer-term strategy, the institute also develops programs to help countries carry out environmental valuation of economic and sector policies and investments. A major initiative during

Table 5.2. Environmental Training Activities of the Economic Development Institute, Fiscal 1994

Date	Location	Seminar or workshop for borrowers	National/regional (N/R)
1993			
July	Paraná, Argentina	Workshop on Environmental Impact Assessment	N
July	Harare, Zimbabwe	Seminar on Water Resources Management for Southern Africa	R
July	Gabarone, Botswana	Seminar on Energy Investments and the Environment for Southern Africa	R
August	Moscow, Russia	Course on Energy Projects Analysis for FSU Countries (including environmental assessment)	R
August	Choluteca, Honduras	Workshop on Environmental Impact Assessment	N
September	Hyderabad, India	Seminar on Involuntary Resettlement and Rehabilitation	N
October	Kandi, Sri Lanka	Seminar on Sustainable Forestry Management for Resource-Poor Asian Countries	R
October	Abidjan, Côte d'Ivoire	Seminar on Energy Policy Analysis, Planning, and the Environment for West African Countries	R
October	Varna, Bulgaria	Seminar on Economic Development and Environment Management for Eastern European Countries	R
November	Nanjing, China	Seminar on Economic Policies, Planning, and Implementation for Reservoir Resettlement	N
November	Istanbul, Turkey	Seminar on Resettlement and Rehabilitation Policies, Planning, and Implementation	N
November	Dakar, Senegal	Seminar on Structural Adjustment, Trade, and the Environment for West and Central African Countries	R
November	Nairobi, Kenya	Seminar on Environmental Economics for National Environmental Action Plans (NEAPs) for East and Southern African Countries	R

1994 was the development of a training program for government officials in Central and Eastern Europe on the linkages between economic policies and the environment in addressing industrial pollution. The program's objectives and activities are guided by the Central and Eastern Europe Environmental Action Programme (see chapter 1), have been designed

Date	Location	Seminar or workshop for borrowers	National/ regional (N/R)
1994			
January	Washington, D.C.	Course on Project Analysis for FSU Countries (including environmental assessment)	R
February	Abidjan, Côte d'Ivoire	Seminar on Economics for an Environmental Strategy for West and Central African Countries	R
February	Washington, D.C.	Course on Energy Projects Analysis for FSU Countries (including environmental assessment)	R
March	Tunis, Tunisia	Seminar on Water Resources Management for the Maghreb Countries	R
April	Hakone, Japan	Seminar on Strategies for Managing Urban Environments for Asian Countries	R
April	Montpellier, France	Workshop to Develop Training Materials on Energy Policy and the Environment	R
May	Guri, Venezuela	Workshop on Environmental Assessment of Development Projects	N
June	Lima, Peru	Workshop on Environmental Assessment	N
June	Moscow, Russia	Course on Energy Projects Analysis for FSU Countries (including environmental assessment)	R
June	Hyderabad, India	Seminar on Resettlement and Rehabilitation Policies, Planning, and Implementation	R
June	Tunis, Tunisia	Seminar on Sustainable Development Strategy for North African Maghreb Countries	R
June	Washington, D.C.	Program Development Workshop on Environmentally Sustainable Development for the Central Asian Countries	R

in collaboration with the Foundation for Advanced Studies in International Development, and are funded by Japan. The first seminar of the program was held in Bulgaria in late 1993.

New initiatives in environmental training for borrowers also were undertaken directly by regional environment divisions and country departments. For example, the Bank cosponsored, with the German Agency for Technical Cooperation (GTZ) and the International Academy for the Environment, two environmental communication workshops for Turkish officials and NGOs from municipalities in the Mediterranean and Baltic regions. The workshops focused on the use of mass media to convey environmental information for policymaking and projects and covered communication theory, mechanisms of environmental communication planning, and the effective use of public communication and participation tools to change attitudes and behavior for environmental action.

Working with Nongovernmental Organizations

During the year the Bank's interaction with NGOs expanded in operational collaboration and in substantive dialogue on policy issues. Two trends have emerged regarding NGO involvement. The first is the increasingly strong role of NGOs in reflecting the perspectives of local people in project design. Some NGOs have conducted surveys of local concerns that have influenced design; others have helped set up community-based organizations that work with project authorities to ensure that local views are reflected or have trained existing popular organizations for such activities.

The second trend is NGO involvement at the local level in the supervision process to help improve implementation. For example, in the Andhra Pradesh Forestry Project in India—a participatory project stressing the involvement of local people in joint forest management—NGOs will be represented on the forestry committees at local, district, and state levels and will assist in the capacity-building efforts for the community organizations to ensure the smooth transition of the management of forest plantations to local communities. In a new initiative, approved this year by the Global Environment Trust Fund, a project for the Philippines will go directly to a coalition of NGOs for implementation (see chapter 4).

The Bank-NGO dialogue has involved a variety of often controversial subjects, including the links between adjustment and the environment, the preparation of NEAPs, resettlement, and public access to information. The ESD vice presidency has taken a lead within the Bank in much of the NGO policy dialogue, and the Bank has gained valuable experience and information from these meetings. The NGOs have welcomed the Bank's increased effort toward openness.

Examples of NGO policy dialogue include an intensive two-day international consultation in May in Washington, D.C., to discuss a draft review of forest policy implementation that will be presented to the Board in fiscal 1995. The majority of the forty-seven non-Bank participants (representing all regions) were from NGOs; academics and other specialists were also present. Similar, smaller meetings were held in London and in Libreville, Gabon. This process substantially influenced the revision of the paper. During the year the Industry and Energy Department also initiated informal consultations with NGOs on issues relating to energy and the environment. These are expected to lead to more formal meetings with a broader range of NGOs on energy efficiency and other special issues of mutual interest.

Although much of the dialogue has been with NGOs in industrial countries, increased dialogue with developing country NGOs has been a major objective. In Mexico, for example, the preparation of a resource conservation and forest sector review provided a unique opportunity to involve NGOs, both in the consultation workshops and in preparing some of the working papers. Dialogue with NGOs in both developing and industrial countries on specific, controversial high-profile projects—such as the Arun Dam Project in Nepal, the Bangladesh Flood Action Project, and the Rondônia Natural Resource Management Project in Brazil—has been helpful.

Conferences

The Bank hosted or cosponsored several major international conferences related to environmental and social issues in 1994. The World Bank's First Annual Environmentally Sustainable Development Conference, hosted by the new ESD vice presidency, was held in Washington, D.C., in the fall of 1993. The conference, entitled "Valuing the Environment," brought together leading experts concerned with the environment and development. Among the speakers were Nitin Desai, director-general of the United Nations Commission on Sustainable Development; Kamal Nath, minister of environment and forests, India; underwater explorer Jacques-Yves Cousteau; and World Bank president Lewis T. Preston. Technical discussions centered on the question of how to identify the costs and benefits of alternative uses of natural resources. The conference highlighted the need for better management of natural resources in the face of worsening shortages and increasing pollution and stressed the need for greater involvement of local communities affected by development. The target audience included key government officials attending the Annual Meetings of the World Bank and the International Monetary Fund (which preceded the conference), environmental NGOs, and Bank staff; about 500 people from around the world attended the event. The second annual ESD conference, in September 1994, will focus on urban issues and is entitled "The Human Face of the Urban Environment."

In March 1994 the Bank sponsored the Conference on Sustainable and Equitable Development, a series of symposia held in Australia. These discussions attracted the participation of high-level representatives from government, academia, the private sector, the media, and nongovernmental organizations in Australia.

Joint events with other agencies included a three-day International Consultation on Women and Ecosystem Management in October 1993, cosponsored with the IDB and several United Nations agencies (discussed in chapter 3). Participants considered the role and capacities of women as environmental managers in the context of five ecosystems: coastal and wetland areas; rivers, groundwater, and lakes; mountains; temperate and tropical forests; and arid and semiarid lands. The key findings were that women require (a) secure rights to land and other natural resources; (b) access to credit, training, and environmental education; (c) full and effective engagement in designing and implementing projects and in making decisions about relevant technologies; and (d) opportunities for entrepreneurial activities that encourage sustainable production practices.

Another jointly sponsored conference, "Overcoming Global Hunger— A Conference on Actions to Reduce Hunger Worldwide," drew hundreds of development experts, government officials, and representatives from international and nongovernmental organizations. NGOs from both developing and industrial countries actively participated in preparation and follow-up. The interrelationship between poverty, hunger, and economic and environmental policies was the overriding theme, and the conference produced commitments by the Bank and several participating organizations to increase efforts to reach the extremely poor with programs that would support productive—and environmentally sustainable—investments. The Bank made a grant of $2 million to the Grameen Bank in Bangladesh (discussed in chapter 3), which offers very small loans to the very poor, and it announced that it would work with other donors to fund similar credit organizations in the developing world.

In June 1994 an international conference on "Development, Environment and Mining" cosponsored by the United Nations was hosted by the Bank. The conference drew some 300 participants from fifty-five (mostly developing) countries, including environmental specialists, policymakers, and representatives of mining companies. It focused on the role of mining in economic development and the challenge of environmentally sustainable mining. Environmental protection in the process of privatization was also discussed, particularly the sharing of responsibilities between the public and private sectors for past and ongoing contamination problems.

In the spirit of the United Nations International Year of the World's Indigenous Peoples and with the support of the Swedish International

Development Agency, the Bank hosted the Second Annual Workshop on Indigenous Peoples and Development in Latin America, which brought together five international development agencies and ten indigenous organizations. This conference led to a regional Indigenous Peoples' Development Initiative in the Bank's Latin American region. Under the initiative, the Bank will work with indigenous peoples' organizations on training seminars that focus on defining their own development agendas, building capacity in project administration, and strengthening negotiation and planning skills.

Finally, the Bank had an active role in the preparation of the 1994 International Conference on Population and Development in Cairo, the third in a series of United Nations conferences that started in Bucharest in 1974 and continued in Mexico City in 1984. This year's conference focused on population trends and how they relate to economic development, poverty reduction, and the environment.

Broader External Relations and Communications

External relations staff continued to give high priority to environmental issues and to communicating broadly the Bank's environmental and social initiatives. Information outreach centered on parliamentarians, academics, NGOs, the media, and the private sector. Public forums for discussing environmental issues and exchanging views were organized for senior Bank managers in North America, Australia, Europe, and Japan, as well as at several Bank field offices. Written materials, films and other background information, and topic-specific information briefs were produced to illustrate the Bank's continually expanding work on the environment. Press briefings were held, including several on the Bank's Resettlement Review and one on protection of global marine biodiversity, cosponsored by the Center for Marine Conservation. The Bank also published several reports in the Environment Papers and GEF Working Paper series (see bibliography).

World Bank News, a weekly newsletter distributed free and published in English, French, and German, expanded its coverage of environment-related projects and activities, and *Report to Students* provided a vehicle for the president of the World Bank to communicate with students around the world who express concerns about the environment and other major development issues. The *Environmental Data Book*, aimed at high school students, and a *Teaching Guide* were published and exhibited at several conferences and workshops.

In an effort to use a wider range of information technologies, a television feature on land management in Burkina Faso, coproduced with the UNDP for the Azimuths series, aired in 172 countries. Film footage was prepared for possible videos on air pollution in Mexico; environmental pollution in Volgograd, Russia; pollution and sewage treatment in Shanghai, China; the Red Soils project in Jiangxi, China; and water supply in Oaxaca, Mexico. Videos prepared during fiscal 1993 and currently available include "Rondônia: The End of the Road," a 30-minute documentary on attempts to contain destruction of the Amazon and achieve sustainable development, and "Orangi: Streets of Hope," about a community's efforts to provide good sanitation facilities. A continuing effort, the International Multimedia Consortium for Environment and Development, has finished the first version of a prototype CD-ROM for an interactive educational video.

In addition to these formal productions, the number and volume of more informal Bank newsletters on the environment grew this year. The "Environment Bulletin" produced by the Environment Department continued to be the most widely disseminated such publication, with a demand-led circulation growing to 30,000. A new series of two-page "Dissemination Notes," designed to present economic and technical information in a concise format, was established. Seven Dissemination Notes, on topics as diverse as forestry values, measurment of health impacts, and environmental indicators, were produced during the year and disseminated widely, both within and outside the Bank. The EA Sourcebook Updates continue to be popular and now reach some 2,000 subscribers in 170 countries (see chapter 2). In addition, all of the regional environment divisions now produce newsletters highlighting their work and regional events; sector-specific newsletters (for example, on forestry and urban management) are also becoming more available.

Notes

1. The Public Information Center is located at 1776 G Street, N.W., Room G-C1-300, Washington, D.C. 20433. Telephone: (202)458-5454, telefax: (202)511-1500. The e-mail address is pic@worldbank.org.

2. See "Proceedings of the EA Technical Workshop for Multilateral Financial Institutions" (World Bank, Environment Department, Washington, D.C. September 29, 1993).

PART 3

Strengthening the Private Sector's Role

The private sector has a critical role to play in improved environmental stewardship. This chapter explains how the International Finance Corporation and the Multilateral Investment Guarantee Agency are helping to meet this challenge.

6. Strengthening the Private Sector's Role: The IFC and MIGA

MARTYN RIDDLE

Many industrial plants in the formerly centrally planned economies of Eastern Europe are both heavily polluting and economically inefficient. The Kunda Nordic Cement plant in Estonia, for example, is responsible for a third of the total particulate emissions in the country. An IFC-supported project will reduce plant emissions by 98 percent, as well as generate significant economic benefits for the regional economy.

The International Finance Corporation (IFC), the member of the World Bank Group that promotes private sector development, helps businesses to pursue environmentally sound operations as they plan for expansion, new ventures, or the privatization of government services and enterprises. During fiscal 1994 the IFC approved 231 projects involving $2.5 billion in debt, equity, and quasi-equity financing by the IFC and total project costs of $15.8 billion. Like a private financial institution, the IFC prices its financing and services in line with the market, to the extent possible. The corporation seeks profitable returns and shares full project risks with its partners. In addition to making direct investments, the IFC mobilizes additional project funding from other investors and lenders, either in the form of cofinancing or through loan syndications, the underwriting of debt and equity securities issues, and guarantees. The IFC offers advisory services in such areas as capital market development, corporate restructuring, risk management, and project preparation and evaluation. It also advises governments on creating an environment that encourages the growth of private enterprise and foreign investment.

The Multilateral Investment Guarantee Agency (MIGA), established in April 1988 as part of the World Bank Group, promotes foreign direct investment for economic and social development in member countries. It guarantees investments against political risks, helps countries create an attractive investment climate, and provides promotional and advisory services. These services are offered directly through the agency's Investment Marketing Services (IMSs) unit and indirectly through the Foreign Investment Advisory Service (FIAS), which is operated jointly with the IFC and the Bank.

The Trend toward Ecoefficiency

Profound changes are occurring in industries and markets around the world because of stricter environmental regulations and enforcement, public pressure, consumer demand for "green" products, more realistic input pricing that takes account of environmental costs, and growing competition. Businesses and governments, aware of the high cost and potential liabilities of poor environmental performance, are increasingly considering environmental factors when they make decisions about production, investment, privatization, and trade. The private sector is more frequently being called on to provide environmental goods and services, once the domain of the public sector.

Forward-looking companies have made a strategic shift from merely complying with environmental regulations to recognizing that environmental factors affect most aspects of their operations. By becoming ecoefficient—reducing energy usage; minimizing resource use, waste, and pollution; improving the workplace environment; and identifying new environmentally driven products and services—they are increasing efficiency, reducing the cost of cleanup and disposal, and capitalizing on new business opportunities. Ecoefficiency has become the hallmark of good management and profitability.

In response to these challenges, the IFC has developed a comprehensive environmental program that addresses not only the physical effects of private sector activities but also the socioeconomic and cultural aspects. The IFC seeks to safeguard the cultures of indigenous peoples and advocates measures that promote worker health and safety.

The Environment Division in the IFC's Technical and Environment Department is the focal point for the corporation's environmental activities. During fiscal 1994 the division increased its staff to accommodate growth in its activities, which include

- Ensuring that IFC- and MIGA-financed projects are environmentally sustainable
- Strengthening the environmental capability of project sponsors and financial intermediaries by providing training and technical assistance
- Helping project sponsors to improve projects by using efficient, clean technologies and taking measures to enhance environmental and socioeconomic benefits
- Promoting investments in the environmental business sector
- Assisting with revision of the Bank's guidance materials on industrial pollution control
- Addressing global environmental challenges by participating in the GEF, the Multilateral Fund for the Implementation of the Montreal Protocol (MFMP), and other international initiatives.

Demand for the IFC's expertise and financing has grown steadily, particularly in techniques for environmental risk management, capital investments in environmental projects, and the impact of global issues on the private sector. The areas in which increased effort has been noteworthy are highlighted here.

- *Environmental risk management:* environmental review of projects; project monitoring and supervision; training to strengthen the capacity of IFC staff, project sponsors, and financial intermediaries in environmental risk management; and liaison with the World Bank on informational materials for industrial pollution control and related matters
- *Environmental business sector:* identification of environmental projects; development of bankable environmental projects; and plan-

ning and assessment of the feasibility of equity and venture capital funds to preserve biodiversity, reduce emissions of greenhouse gases, and promote energy efficiency and the use of alternative energy resources

- *Global environmental activities:* development of private sector projects eligible for grants from the GEF and from the MFMP to phase out the use of ozone depleting substances; promotion of carbon-offset investment projects; and increased communication and liaison with multilateral and bilateral development agencies, environmental businesses, and NGOs on the environment and development.

Environmental Risk Management

All projects financed by the corporation have to meet stringent environmental standards. To ensure that proposed projects are environmentally sustainable, a project sponsor must submit an environmental analysis as part of its proposal to the IFC. During the appraisal, IFC staff review the environmental analysis to ensure that the project is environmentally sound and sustainable and that it complies with host country requirements and World Bank policies and guidelines. For financial intermediaries that finance subprojects with IFC funds, verification is required that the intermediaries are both capable of and committed to carrying out environmental reviews.

The IFC's environmental risk management activities cover environmental review of all projects, including those financed by the IFC's Africa Enterprise Fund. In fiscal 1994 the Environment Division reviewed about 450 projects, of which 231 were approved by the Board of Directors. Of the projects approved, 8 fell into category A, 123 into category B, and 69 into category C; the remaining 31 were in the category of financial intermediaries.[1] Box 6.1 identifies the category A projects approved during this fiscal year. Box 6.2 highlights a recent category B project illustrating the kind of environmental action that the IFC is supporting in developing countries and the newly independent states of Eastern Europe.

Under a mutually agreed arrangement with MIGA, the IFC acts as environmental adviser for MIGA projects. At MIGA's request, IFC staff review MIGA projects and provide comments and guidance on environmental matters. This process ensures that MIGA is aware of relevant environmental guidelines that may apply to a project. The IFC conducted twenty industrial project reviews for MIGA in fiscal 1994.

Once a project is approved by the Board, it is monitored and supervised to ensure its continuing compliance with local and national requirements and with World Bank policies and guidelines. Monitoring

Box 6.1. Category A Projects Approved in Fiscal 1994: Key Environmental Issues

Brazil

Rio Capim Quimica, S.A. (development of a kaolin open-pit mine; remediation and transport facilities). Key environmental issues include loss of forest habitat, fugitive dust, disposal of solid and liquid wastes, control of erosion and siltation, and socioeconomic impacts. The EA provides for the establishment of a forest reserve, which will add 4,000 net hectares of forestland, and an ecological station. The company is working with local NGOs and local governments to deal with the socioeconomic impacts.

Guatemala

Basic Petroleum International, Ltd. (corporate loan; oil pipeline construction). Key environmental issues include environmental performance at the company's facilities and the potential effects of the oil pipeline on rain forests, archaeological sites, and residents along the right-of-way. The sponsor completed an environmental audit of all of its facilities and has prepared a plan to bring all facilities into compliance with the environmental requirements of the Guatemalan government and the World Bank. The EA prepared for the oil pipeline made several recommendations intended to mitigate adverse impacts on rain forests, archaeological sites, and residents along the right-of-way.

India

GVK Industries, Ltd. (gas and naphtha-fired combined-cycle power plant). Key environmental issues include air emissions, land use modification at the plant site and along the right-of-way for pipelines and transmission lines, and discharge of cooling water. The EA prepared by the project sponsor indicates that the project will be well within local standards for emissions and ambient air quality. Because the project site is barren land, no sensitive ecological resources are affected. Gas and water pipelines will be constructed in the dry season and will be buried, allowing farmers to continue to crop the right-of-way.

ST-CMS Electric Company (lignite-fired thermal power plant in Neyveli, Tamil Nadu State). Key environmental issues are air-quality impacts as a result of sulfur dioxide, nitrogen oxide, and particulate emissions, and impacts on water resources. The EA demonstrated that the use of low-sulfur lignite as a fuel, low-nitrogen-oxide burners, and electrostatic precipitators will result in ambient air quality that is well within World Bank requirements. The project will be supplied with water from the dewatering program and the adjacent lignite open-cast mine, and a closed cycle is planned for water use during project operation.

Kazakhstan

Kazgermunai Company (oil field development). Key environmental issues are management of produced gas, land disturbances, and potential impacts on groundwater resources in the project area. The project sponsor's EA demonstrates that produced gas will be captured to produce electricity, and land disturbances will be minimized by utilizing directional drilling and prohibiting the use of off-road vehicles. Pits will be lined to prevent contamination of groundwater, and the project sponsors have initiated a large-scale groundwater study to create an inventory of the region's resources.

Nepal

Himal Power, Ltd. (run-of-the-river power plant). Key environmental issues include effects on fish resources and fisheries; the cumulative effects of a second phase providing expanded capacity; land acquisition and compensation; and social impacts. The EA prepared by the project sponsor deals with these issues satisfactorily, and the sponsor has collaborated in an exemplary program to work with local residents and community leaders to arrive at a mutually satisfactory compensation and relocation package for each of ten households displaced as a result of the project.

Peru

Minera Yanacocha Expansion (Maqui Maqui project to expand existing gold mining). Key environmental issues include potential land disturbance, water quality, and land compensation. The project sponsors' EA addresses all these issues satisfactorily. An extensive archaeological survey and planned systematic excavations are being undertaken with the Peruvian National Culture Institute, and inventories of flora and fauna are being made. An extensive land compensation program is included for landowners who will lose grazing lands. Annual environmental audits will be conducted to ensure that the project's environmental management, including monitoring, is operating according to plan.

Zimbabwe

Sable Safaris (Private), Ltd. (upgrading and modernization of two existing safari camps and construction of two new camps adjacent to a national park). Key environmental issues include the impacts on sensitive ecosystems and endangered species, increased pressure on local resources such as water, the potential for secondary development in the area, waste disposal, fire protection, and occupational health and safety. The sponsor prepared an EA and conducted an environmental audit of the existing facilities. Each camp is limited to twenty to thirty beds, to minimize impacts on local ecological resources. Game population and movement will be closely monitored to determine game trail clearing and trail use; these activities will be closely coordinated with the national park authorities.

Box 6.2. Kunda Nordic Cement A/S, Estonia

Kunda Nordic Cement A/S (KNC) is the first IFC project in Estonia. The KNC plant is thought to be the country's single largest source of particulate emissions; at 140,000 tons a year, its emissions account for one-third of all particulate emissions in the country. Implementation of the project will reduce plant particulate emissions by 98 percent.

KNC, which is located on the Gulf of Finland, about 100 kilometers east of the capital, Tallinn, is jointly owned by the government of Estonia and Atlas Nordic Cement, a consortium of foreign cement producers that includes Scancem International, Holderbank of Switzerland, and Atlas Cement of the United States. The feasibility study for the project was partially financed by the IFC through its Finnish and Swiss trust funds. The total project cost is estimated at $44 million, about $7.5 million of which is earmarked for environmental improvements. The IFC is making a $6 million loan and a $4 million equity investment in KNC.

The IFC's investment will finance modernization of the KNC plant, which was constructed in the 1960s with Russian technology. The first phase of the modernization includes improving pollution and environmental control systems, upgrading plant equipment to meet competitive production standards, reducing energy consumption, and developing a new port facility that will reduce port handling costs by about 90 percent.

The IFC's Technical and Environment Department provided guidance for the development of an environmental management plan that integrates the environmental, health, and safety concerns identified in an environmental audit completed before project appraisal. The plan serves as a vehicle for assessing progress in KNC's environmental improvements. Equipment will be installed to reduce emissions from the kilns, cement mills, and oil shale mills to comply with World Bank guidelines.

KNC has employed an environmental manager to oversee implementation of the environmental management plan, which includes the environmental, health, and safety program for reducing air emissions and treating liquid effluents; disposing of solid wastes; preventing spills; monitoring impacts associated with the dredging of the port facility, the disposal of dredged material, and the potential impact on fisheries; and preventing accidents and employee exposure to dust and noise.

The project is expected to generate significant economic benefits for the regional economy, including environmental and health benefits for KNC's employees and the local population. Additional benefits, such as increased yields from agriculture, livestock, and forestry, could result from cleaner air. The IFC is conducting a study to quantify the expected economic benefits to the region from the environmental improvements yielded by the KNC project. The Finnish IFC Trust Fund, KNC, Finnfund, and NEFCO, the Nordic Investment Bank's environmental affiliate, are also supporting this study.

and supervision by IFC staff ensure that adverse environmental impacts do not jeopardize new investment projects and that unanticipated environmental damage during project implementation is arrested quickly. In addition, project sponsors must submit annual implementation updates, enabling the Environment Division to monitor the sponsor's compliance with, and progress on, actions recommended by the IFC.

During this fiscal year, the Environment Division staff and other IFC technical specialists made numerous site visits to appraise projects, visiting all those in category A and several in category B. Problems were investigated, recommendations were made for their resolution, and a timetable was agreed on for addressing problems or outstanding issues. The IFC's experience with monitoring and supervision revealed that solid waste management and occupational health and safety, which can be improved to some extent by training, need more attention and resources from project sponsors. The social impact of projects also warrants better planning on the part of project sponsors.

In fiscal 1994 the IFC instituted practices designed to achieve greater rigor and transparency in the environmental aspects of its investments. A revised environmental review procedure was established for proposed projects. Key changes were expanded public disclosure requirements for category A and B projects, including release of environmental information on proposed projects (environmental assessments for category A and environmental review summaries for category B) at the Bank's Public Information Center. The IFC also requires that sponsors of category A projects consult with local affected groups and interested parties during preparation of the EAs.

Under the IFC's Technical Assistance Trust Funds program, launched in mid-1988, resources from bilateral and multilateral donor agencies were used to assist project sponsors. Trust funds financed the technical assistance needed to carry a project idea through the preparatory stage to a well-designed proposal able to meet the investment criteria of the IFC and prospective investors. Trust fund donors included Australia, Canada, the Commission of European Communities, India, Italy, Finland, Japan, the Netherlands, Norway, Sweden, Switzerland, the United States, and the UNDP.

Environmental Performance

Improved environmental performance was noteworthy in several areas and countries. For example, in their site visits during this fiscal year, IFC staff found substantial improvement in the environmental performance of Argentina's oil and gas industry, in part achieved through privatization and more active enforcement of environmental requirements by the government. The IFC played an important role by requiring that its investments in the oil and gas sector comply with applicable World Bank policies and guidelines (or, in their absence, international best practice), as well as with the Argentine government's requirements. An oil and gas industry association and several companies requested assistance with training and the transfer of expertise and technology, and the companies themselves have made substantial investments to improve their environmental performance. In many companies the senior management has internalized the concept of ecoefficiency, and an active dialogue on regulatory issues continues between the Argentine government and the oil and gas industry.

The IFC's environmental review process and investment practices assisted the privatization of formerly state-owned enterprises in Central and Eastern Europe, producing considerable improvement in environmental performance. Investments were made in new waste treatment systems, and waste minimization, recycling, fuel switching, and energy-efficiency improvements were achieved. Examples include the following.

- A formerly state-owned lighting manufacturer in Poland, through a joint investment by the IFC and Philips Lighting of the Netherlands, modernized and upgraded its operations. Outmoded machinery was replaced, and new machinery made possible a more careful dosing of the mercury used in fluorescent lamps, thereby reducing the danger of mercury contamination and permitting the safe recovery of mercury from lamps broken and rejected during manufacture. Air emissions were reduced significantly, and a sophisticated wastewater treatment facility was installed. Philips Lighting Poland, the successor private company, now produces 14 million highly efficient compact fluorescent lamps annually, for domestic use and for export.
- In the Czech Republic, Moravia Glass, a formerly state-owned company, was modernized and expanded through a joint investment by the IFC and Vetropack, a leading Swiss glass- and plastic-container firm. At the new company, Vetropack Moravia Glass (VPMG), a highly efficient glass-melting furnace will replace obsolete and highly polluting furnaces. The new furnace is expected to increase energy efficiency by about 13 percent. VPMG is also exploring container glass recycling to replace virgin raw materials in glass manufacturing.
- Fibranova's medium-density fiberboard plant in Cabrero, Chile, is a state-of-the-art installation that produces more than 100,000 cubic meters of high-quality reconstituted wooden panels a year,

for domestic use and export (about 75 percent). The panels are used to make furniture, subflooring, construction panels, and toys, and they can be substituted for particle board, plywood, hardboard, and wood used in making moldings. The raw materials are wood from pine plantations and green or wet sawmill waste. Additional environmental installations recommended by the IFC and put in place include a water deaeration tank and civil works to ensure proper drainage and to capture waste, such as oil and other hazardous materials. Supervision and monitoring by IFC staff in fiscal 1994 revealed satisfactory plant operations.

In fiscal 1993 the IFC conducted an independent energy audit of the dyeing, printing, and finishing operations of Arvind Mills, a leading textile manufacturer in Ahmedabad, India, in which the IFC had invested. The audit was supported by the U.K. Overseas Development Administration. As of mid-1994 several of the audit's energy-saving and efficiency recommendations were being implemented. For example, machinery for dyeing and finishing was being enhanced with energy control equipment; lignite was being partially replaced with coal to obtain more fuel efficiency; and compressor leakages were being controlled to save energy. Arvind Mills' management was examining the feasibility of additional recommendations. The IFC supervised the project in fiscal 1994.

The monitoring and supervision of environmental aspects of IFC projects are also illustrated by the Phase I audits of several smaller projects in Sub-Saharan Africa. The audits were conducted during fiscal 1993 and 1994 (see boxes 6.3 and 6.4).

Expanded Training in Environmental Risk Management

In late fiscal 1993 and early fiscal 1994 the IFC conducted a needs assessment of the training and tools required by project sponsors to establish an environmental risk management system. A representative sample of project sponsors was interviewed to determine how the IFC could strengthen its support and enhance two-way communication on environmental matters. Discussions with clients revealed a number of areas in which communications and support could be reinforced. It became clear that financial intermediaries needed training to establish an effective environmental risk management system for their investments. Sponsors of category B projects needed better tools and techniques to improve their communications with IFC staff on the measures to be implemented to correct environmental issues and problems. As a result

---

**Box 6.3. Environmental Audits: The Africa Project
Development Facility and the Africa Enterprise Fund Project**

The Africa Project Development Facility (APDF), founded in 1986, advises
African entrepreneurs who are seeking to start new ventures, or to expand,
modernize, and diversify existing ones, in a wide range of industries. It
helps them formulate project proposals; carry out feasibility, marketing,
and technical studies; and identify domestic and foreign financial and
technical partners. By the end of 1993 the APDF had assisted 163 projects
and helped project sponsors raise about $188 million in financing. The
APDF is cosponsored by the IFC, the African Development Bank, and the
UNDP and receives additional funding from fifteen donor countries. The
Africa Enterprise Fund (AEF) was launched by the IFC in 1989. It finances
smaller projects with costs ranging from $250,000 to $5 million, in all types
of industries owned or managed by local entrepreneurs. By mid-1994 the
fund had approved $69.7 million in debt and equity financing for 110
projects in twenty-four countries.

Between May and July 1993 the IFC carried out environmental audits of
thirty-nine projects financed through the AEF or assisted by the APDF. The
objectives of the audits were to assess project compliance with World Bank
occupational health, safety, and environmental (OHS&E) guidelines; to
evaluate the guidance that project sponsors receive on OHS&E issues; to
advise on measures for improving the OHS&E status of the sponsor companies; to recommend ways of improving the IFC project review system to
ensure compliance with OHS&E requirements; and to identify what additional assistance the IFC could provide.

The project sites visited were in Benin, Côte d'Ivoire, Ghana, Kenya,
Mauritius, Swaziland, Uganda, and Zimbabwe. They included nine plantations; seven food processors; four projects each in tourism and property
development; three each in vegetable oil and fat processing, other agrifood

---

of these expressed needs, an expanded program of internal and external
training was designed and is being implemented by the IFC.

To strengthen its staff capability in the environmental area, early in
fiscal 1994 the IFC launched an intensive training program in environmental risk management and the revised environmental review procedure. Half-day workshops were conducted for all investment
departments, the Legal Department, and the Economics Department.
About 250 staff participated in the workshops, including department
and division managers. The workshops continue to be offered on a
quarterly basis.

industries, wood and wood product manufacturing, and metalworking; and two in the plastics industry. For projects (one in Botswana and nine in Nigeria) that could not be visited, the potential environmental issues for each industry or manufacturer were identified by means of desk reviews.

The audits recommended various measures to mitigate environmental problems. Eleven projects (or 28 percent) required significant corrective measures, and nineteen projects (or 49 percent) needed minor corrective solutions. The principal environmental problems related to the use or handling and disposal of hazardous materials and wastes; effluent treatment and disposal, including spill prevention; the potential for resource and energy conservation; waste minimization and pollution prevention, including recycling; attention to water quality; use of safety equipment such as gloves, masks, and boots; worker training; and sustainable management of resources such as hardwood forests and fish stocks.

The audits estimated that about 80 percent of the problems identified could be corrected through better management practices, without additional capital expenditures. These practices include upgraded plant operation, improved worker training, and incentives to workers to use safety equipment. Only three projects would need significant spending for additional equipment to solve the environmental problems—about $10,000 or less in each case. Audit reports were sent to each of the project sponsors, and corrective action plans have been requested from them. The IFC will maintain close contact with the sponsors to make certain that the recommended measures are implemented, and Environment Division staff are available to provide technical support, including site visits, as necessary.

The audits also revealed that the IFC could provide more assistance in the form of training for IFC, AEF, and APDF regional staff and for representatives of the sponsor companies. In addition, IFC staff work with counterparts in the World Bank on encouraging institutions and governments to pay more attention to OHS&E issues.

An innovative training program was initiated for financial institutions in developing countries and for the newly independent countries in Eastern Europe that are current or prospective clients. Through the Environmental Risk Management workshops, investment officers were trained to screen proposed investments for any unacceptable risks to the environment that could jeopardize the investments and make them inviable, both for the companies and, ultimately, for the financiers. The several risks that could stem from environmentally unsound projects are credit risk (delayed payment or writeoff of interest and principal), position risk (devaluation of company's securities), security risk (defunct or devalued collateral), legal risk (liability for cleanup costs after foreclo-

---

**Box 6.4. Addressing the Environmental Implications
of the Chiparawe Farms Project**

Chiparawe Farms (Pvt.), Ltd., is a 3,500-hectare mixed-farming operation
in Marondera District, Zimbabwe, 100 kilometers southeast of Harare. In
1992 the project sponsors airfreighted vegetables worth $1.8 million di-
rectly to U.K. supermarket chains, making them the single largest grower
and exporter of vegetables in Zimbabwe. An irrigation dam and a 10.5-
million-megaliter reservoir on the Inyangui River are being constructed to
meet Chiparawe's increasing demand for water, shortages of which have
severely constrained increases in production. Key potential impacts of this
category B project include loss of grazing land, effects on riverine hydrol-
ogy, an increase in waterborne diseases, and the impacts of construction.
The land being flooded is nonarable, rocky scrubland void of human
settlements.

The sponsors plan to replant indigenous plant species on land that is
likely to be disturbed by the dam construction. In addition, they will
contribute to the river fishstocks by introducing native fish species to the
reservoir, and they will allow farm workers and local inhabitants to fish
the reservoir on a noncommercial basis. A 900-hectare wildlife conservation area is being established adjacent to an existing 735-hectare conservation area, with the reservoir forming a natural protective boundary to the
west that will provide a safe haven for the region's wildlife. Local school-
children will be allowed to come to the conservation area to study the
environment and animals.

The farms employ 550 people and produce maize, tobacco, soybeans,
wheat, and horticultural crops, including sugar snap peas, passion fruit,
and snow peas. The reservoir will provide sufficient irrigation to meet
anticipated growth of horticultural exports by expanding the cultivated
area from 311 hectares to 550 hectares over ten years and further diversifying production to include perennial blueberries, raspberries, asparagus,
and other vegetables. The reservoir will also benefit other farms and
subsistence farmers downstream by maintaining year-round flow of the
Inyangui, which often slows to a trickle during dry seasons. The project
costs of $1.87 million are being supported by a loan of $0.79 million from
the Africa Enterprise Fund.

---

sure), and funding risk (reduced access to, and increased cost of, capital
from international markets). IFC techniques for environmental risk management enable financial institutions to gain competitive advantage by
assessing and managing environmental risk as part of the regular credit
review process. Financial officers identify projects with unacceptable
environmental risks and either reject them or make them acceptable by

lessening the risks, to the extent feasible, through environmental analysis and transfer of the remaining environmental risks to third parties—for example, through environmental insurance.

A pilot training module was developed early in the year and was tested in India with the management and staff of a venture capital firm and a leasing company. Building on the results of the pilot training, the IFC conducted workshops for an additional ninety-six financial institutions located in Argentina, Brazil, Colombia, Indonesia, Mexico, Peru, the Philippines, Russia, Singapore, Slovenia, Tanzania, Thailand, and Ukraine. More than 350 staff from the financial institutions were introduced to techniques for appraising the environmental aspects of investment projects (including opportunities for pollution prevention, waste minimization, and energy efficiency) and managing environmental risks by working alongside project sponsors to address outstanding environmental issues.

During the year the IFC completed a project designed to help the sponsors of small and medium-size projects meet high environmental standards cost-effectively and to contribute to the efficiency of project appraisal and monitoring by the IFC and its financial intermediaries. In late fiscal 1993 and early fiscal 1994, with funding support from the Norwegian Agency for Development Cooperation, IFC and Norwegian consultants developed forms and guidance materials to facilitate the exchange of environmental information about projects between the IFC and project sponsors. The expanded training program in environmental risk management for IFC staff and financial intermediaries was also an outgrowth of this effort. Two brief reports, "Environment Management Systems" and "Environmental Improvement Techniques," were prepared to provide additional guidance to project sponsors on improving the efficiency of their environment-related activities.

The Environmental Business Sector

The worldwide market for environmental goods and services is expected to grow rapidly, and the IFC estimates that it could double from roughly $300 billion in the early 1990s to $600 billion by 2000. For the past several years the IFC has actively encouraged investments in environmental projects in such areas as water supply and wastewater treatment, solid and hazardous waste management, the manufacture of clean production technology and pollution control equipment, recycling, and ecotourism.

In screening project proposals, the IFC considers a variety of factors, such as the host country's support for private investment and the project sponsors' record, management capability, and ability to mobilize financial resources for the project. It also carries out a preliminary assessment of the project's viability. Projects that prove satisfactory in these respects are closely followed, and the IFC provides technical assistance, as necessary, to help the sponsors strengthen the project. In cases where projects do not meet the IFC's criteria, the IFC can, at the request of the sponsors, help identify weaknesses in the business plan and offer guidance on ways to improve the project's viability. The Environment Division identifies promising environmental projects and works with project sponsors to develop them into bankable projects as needed. It works closely with the IFC's investment departments—in particular, with the Infrastructure Department—in carrying out this activity.

Over the past year the IFC received more than 100 expressions of interest in financial participation in environmental projects, of which forty were considered appropriate for possible IFC involvement. About 73 percent of the project proposals were in Asia and Latin America. The largest number of projects considered bankable by the IFC originated in Latin America. Twenty-nine of the project proposals that the IFC seriously considered during fiscal 1994 are for areas with which the private sector in industrial countries already has substantial experience, such as water supply, wastewater treatment, and waste management. Companies from France, the United Kingdom, and the United States sponsored the largest number of waste management and water supply projects.

In fiscal 1994 the IFC approved its first wastewater project, a 750-liter-per-second wastewater plant to serve Puerto Vallarta, Mexico, an international tourist destination. In developing the financial structure required to attract foreign investors, the IFC worked closely with the sponsor, Mexican financial institutions, and the government of Mexico. The project is serving as a model for financing other private sector environmental projects in Mexico.

The second environment project was an investment in Aguas Argentinas, the private sector consortium that will operate, improve, and expand water and wastewater services in metropolitan Buenos Aires. This project represented the largest privatization of water services outside Western Europe. Aguas Argentinas serves a population of nearly 9 million in an area of more than 500 square kilometers. Capital requirements, all to be raised privately, are significant. In the first five years of the thirty-year concession, Aguas Argentinas will invest $1 billion in improvements and construction of new facilities.

The IFC encourages the use of clean technologies and processing modifications to reduce energy consumption. For example, during fiscal 1994 it supported a project that will help EDENOR, a recently privatized Argentine company that provides electricity distribution services to the greater Buenos Aires area, to improve electricity distribution, decrease energy waste and loss, and lower prices. In Thailand the IFC provided financing for the Star Petroleum Refining Company to build a new refinery that will help significantly in meeting increased domestic demand for clean, high-quality petroleum products. The IFC also made a $4 million loan to the Alliance ScanEast Fund, for investments in Central and Eastern European companies that will promote more efficient energy use, finance environmental technologies, reduce pollution in the pulp and paper industries, and modernize oil refineries to produce cleaner fuels than current fuels with high sulfur and benzene levels.

A project identification and development study on waste paper generated in the countries of the European Union was financed through the European Union Asia Trust Fund and carried out for the IFC by an independent consultant. The study, completed in 1994, proposed, as a cost-effective way of making use of unsorted, mixed waste paper, that the paper be exported to paper- and fiber-scarce countries in South and East Asia, where recycled wastepaper would help meet rapidly growing demand for high-value paper goods. A promising venture of this type—one that would help solve a waste-disposal problem in industrial countries while saving resources in developing countries—is likely to emerge in the near future. "Papermaking Opportunities Using Recycled Fiber," a summary of the study, was issued February 1994 by the IFC in conjunction with the European Union.

During fiscal 1994, the IFC engaged the major international private sector water and waste management companies in discussions on improving the number, quality, and diversity of projects for possible IFC financing. IFC staff are also assessing the feasibility of developing venture capital and equity funds aimed at the environmental business sector, as well as at activities that promote biodiversity, at ecotourism, at energy efficiency, and at alternative energy and renewable resource use. A biodiversity equity fund is being explored, and discussions are under way with potential partners. Within the context of a new programmatic activity using GEF funds along with IFC investments, the Environment Division is appraising several projects for sustainable commercial forestry. In addition, a number of small-scale ecotourism ventures are being examined for possible financing.

IFC staff made presentations on environmental business opportunities at numerous conferences and seminars. These presentations enabled staff to respond to inquiries from companies about IFC investments in environmental projects and other projects that minimize environmental risks. Staff also fielded questions about appraisal methodology, industry-specific environmental issues and problems such as the management of hazardous wastes and energy efficiency, and eligibility for grant funding through GEF and MFMP mechanisms.

Global Environmental Activities

Concern about the depletion of the earth's nonrenewable resources and the limited capacity of the earth to absorb or recycle wastes is rapidly changing the way business is conducted. The replenishment of the GEF and recent international agreements such as the Framework Convention on Climate Change, the Convention on Biological Diversity, and the Montreal Protocol on Substances that Deplete the Ozone Layer demonstrate a growing awareness that efforts to address these issues need to be continued and that global cooperation is essential.

The widely accepted international conventions mentioned above give the IFC a unique opportunity to participate in business developments that promote the objectives of these conventions, such as increasing energy efficiency, developing renewable sources of energy and cleaner production of energy, reducing natural gas flaring, and phasing out the use of chlorofluorocarbons (CFCs), halons, and other ozone depleting substances.

Among the sources of multilateral grant funds for eligible private sector projects are the GEF and the MFMP. The money available is limited to specific types of projects and allowable incremental costs. The IFC seeks to leverage these funds to obtain additional private sector investments. IFC consultants funded by the GEF and the MFMP are working with staff to identify private sector projects and activities that would be eligible for GEF and MFMP grants. GEF grants are being sought for projects in energy efficiency, reduced gas flaring, renewable energy utilization, "clean coal" and coalbed methane, and unconventional wastewater treatment.

One of the proposed IFC projects is a small-scale enterprise project fund of $4 million–$6 million to provide incremental risk capital directly to smaller ventures or through financial and other intermediaries (banks, NGOs, and venture capital companies). Funding would range from hundreds of thousands to perhaps $2 million to optimize global environmental benefits while maintaining essential profitability. IFC staff have identified a wide range of potential business deals, including energy-efficiency projects, nontimber forest products, and ecotourism ventures.

The IFC has also proposed a $5 million GEF private sector energy-efficiency project in Poland to catalyze the adoption of compact fluorescent lamps (CFLs) and related lighting equipment through a direct manufacturer wholesale price reduction program and utility promotion program. Improved lighting is expected to directly decrease the coal-fired baseload and peak electricity demand in Poland. Project participants would include local manufacturers of CFL and related equipment (including Philips Lighting Poland and other lighting manufacturers), the Polish

Power Grid Company, the Warsaw and Gliwice electricity distribution companies, the Polish Foundation for Energy Efficiency, and the IFC.

Investigations are being carried out to find avenues for promoting investment in the preservation of biodiversity and in sustainable development practices. At present, ecotourism ventures and projects to preserve endangered plant and animal species are often unattractive to potential sponsors because of their small size. Thus, one avenue being explored is the creation of an equity or venture capital fund that would package together for investment a number of small projects in different countries.

The Bank and the IFC also have begun to explore, independently of the GEF, the establishment of venture capital funds for biodiversity and renewable energy and energy efficiency projects in developing countries. Although these funds have been defined only conceptually at this stage, the IFC and the Bank are examining the feasibility of implementing these initiatives in partnership with private venture capital funds, private foundations, and interested bilateral donors.

During fiscal 1994 the IFC expanded its activities related to the Montreal Protocol. It is working with its clients in several countries to phase out the use of ozone depleting substances. Reviews of the IFC portfolio in India and Turkey have already been conducted, and several projects have been identified for appraisal during fiscal 1995. Potential opportunities in Latin America and Sub-Saharan Africa are also being pursued. In Eastern Europe the IFC, with funding from the GEF, is assisting two Slovakian companies in phasing out these chemicals.

The IFC is engaged in a wide range of activities with businesses and NGOs worldwide to promote environmentally sound business practices and to encourage communications on a variety of environmental issues. Among others, the IFC is in contact with the Business Council for Sustainable Development and its regional networks; the World Industry Council for Environment, organized by the International Chamber of Commerce; the Foundation for Sustainable Development in Latin America; the International Network for Environmental Management; the International Institute for Energy Conservation; and the Earth Council. A dialogue continued during fiscal 1994 between the IFC and leading environmental NGOs on working more effectively with the private sector to achieve environmentally sustainable development.

During the year the IFC also discussed project proposals with the four major regional development banks—the African Development Bank, the Asian Development Bank, the EBRD, and the IDB—and with a number of other multilateral and bilateral development institutions. In addition, discussions were held on ways in which increased collaboration and consultation between the IFC and these institutions could foster environmentally sound private sector investments to achieve the goal of sustainable growth.

Future Directions

The IFC plans to expand its activities in four areas over the short and medium term. First, it will undertake more training activities to strengthen its capabilities in environmental risk management. Increased training will benefit both IFC staff and the staffs of financial intermediaries and project sponsors, expanding their knowledge and skill in analyzing and managing environmental risk. Second, the IFC will pay greater attention to project supervision, monitoring, and implementation, particularly for projects that have significant environmental components and possible impacts requiring sustained attention and greater capacity on the part of project sponsors. Third, the IFC will step up efforts to develop new environmental initiatives funded through the GEF and the MFMP. Such projects will focus on reducing ozone depleting substances, offsetting carbon emissions, and promoting energy saving and efficiency, biodiversity conservation, and ecotourism in eligible countries. The corporation will also seek to improve the quality, diversity, and geographic distribution of environmental projects that it might finance. Fourth, the IFC will continue to explore the feasibility of new financing mechanisms for environmental projects, such as specialty funds established with other multilateral banks and private groups, venture capital funds, and specialized credit lines to financial intermediaries.

Note

1. IFC projects are categorized according to their potential impact on the environment in the same way as Bank projects. These categories are described in chapter 2. In addition, the IFC adopts a fourth category, that of financial intermediaries, for projects that include numerous subprojects for which a financial intermediary must conduct environmental reviews.

Annex A. Environment- and Social-Related Operational Policies and Bank Procedures

Beginning in fiscal 1993 existing Operational Directives (ODs) began to be revised and incorporated into a new system of operational policies and Bank procedures. The new system comprises three categories of outputs: Operational Policies (OPs), Bank Procedures (BPs), and Good Practices (GPs). Where the policies listed below have already been converted and reissued, the new citations are given. Where conversions are under way, the new citations are annotated in parentheses as "to be issued."

Primary Statements on Environment and Social Issues

OD 4.01   Environment Assessment (to be issued as OP/BP/GP 4.01)

This document outlines Bank policy and procedures for the environmental assessment and environmental analysis of Bank lending and operations. All environmental consequences are recognized early in the project cycle and are taken into account in project selection, siting, planning, and design.

OD 4.02   Environmental Action Plans (to be issued as OP/BP/GP 4.02)

This document outlines Bank policy and procedures relating to the preparation of country environmental action plans by IBRD and IDA borrowing governments. The Bank encourages governments to prepare environmental action plans and supports this work. The action plan identifies key environmental problems, sets priorities for dealing with them, and leads to a comprehensive national environmental policy and programs to implement the policy. The Bank reflects the findings and strategies of the country's plan in Bank work and encourages periodic revision of the plan as needed.

OD 4.03   Agricultural Pest Management (to be issued as OP/BP/GP 4.03)

The Bank promotes effective and environmentally sound pest management practices in Bank-supported agricultural development. Any Bank loan that provides substantial funding for pesticide procurement or increases the use of pesticides in the project area must include specific measures to achieve this aim and to promote safety in pesticide handling and use.

OP 4.07   Water Resources Management

The policy promotes economically viable, environmentally sustainable, and socially equitable management of water resources. It includes the provision of potable water, sanitation facilities, flood control, and water for productive activities. Among priority areas for Bank assistance and involvement are the development of a comprehensive framework for designing water resource investments, policies, and institutions; adoption of appropriate pricing and incentive policies for water resources; decentralization of water service delivery; restoration and preservation of aquatic ecosystems against overexploitation of groundwater resources; avoidance of water quality problems associated with irrigation investments; and establishment of strong legal and regulatory frameworks to enforce policies. In cases where borrower progress in priority areas of water resources management areas is deemed inadequate, Bank lending is limited to operations that do not draw additionally on a country's water resources.

OD 4.20   Indigenous Peoples (to be issued as OP/BP/GP 4.10)

This policy ensures that (a) indigenous people benefit from development projects, and (b) potentially adverse effects of Bank projects on indigenous people are avoided or mitigated. An Indigenous Peoples Development Plan is prepared, as appropriate, in tandem with the main investment project.

OD 4.30   Involuntary Resettlement (to be issued as OP/BP/GP 4.12)

This document outlines the Bank policy and procedures covering Bank staff and borrower responsibilities in operations involving involuntary resettlement. Any operation that involves land acquisition or is screened as a category A or B project for environmental assessment purposes is reviewed for potential resettlement requirements early in the project cycle to protect the livelihood of people who lose their land, their houses, or both. The objective of the Bank's resettlement policy is to assist displaced persons in their efforts to restore or improve former living standards and earning capacity. To achieve this objective, the borrower is required to prepare and carry out resettlement plans or development programs.

OP/GP 4.36   Forestry

Bank lending in the forest sector aims to reduce deforestation, enhance the environmental contribution of forested areas, promote afforestation, reduce poverty, and encourage economic development. Sector work should examine the legal and institutional basis for ensuring environmentally sustainable development of the forest sector. The Bank expects governments to have in place adequate provisions for conserving protected areas and critical watersheds and for establishing environmental guidelines and monitoring procedures. The Bank does not provide financing for logging in primary tropical moist forests.

OD 9.01   Procedures for Investment Operations under the Global Environment Facility (to be issued as OP/BP/GP 10.20)

This policy describes the steps, in addition to standard Bank investment lending procedures, required to process GEF operations. Other GEF operational procedures, including those for environmental assessment, generally follow standard Bank procedures for investment lending.

OD 4.00, Annexes B-B4   Environmental Policy for Dam and Reservoir Projects (to be issued as OP/BP/GP 4.05)

The Bank's environmental policy for dam and reservoir projects aims to avoid, minimize, or compensate for adverse environmental impacts wherever possible, using project design features (for example, modifying dam location or height) and measures implemented as part of the project. The potential project impact is determined at an early stage with the advice of environmental specialists.

Operational Policy Note 11.02   Wildlands: Their Protection and Management in Economic Development (to be issued as OP/BP/GP 4.04 under the title Natural Habitats)

The Bank supports the protection, maintenance, and rehabilitation of natural habitats. The Bank does not finance projects that involve the conversion of designated critical natural habitats. Where there are no feasible alternatives for projects that convert natural habitats, mitigation and restoration are included in the project to minimize habitat loss. In addition, the Bank may require that the project include the establishment and maintenance of an ecologically similar compensatory area.

Operational Policy Note 11.03   Management of Cultural Property in Bank-Financed Projects (to be issued as OP/BP/GP 4.11 under the title Cultural Property)

The Bank's general policy regarding cultural properties is to assist in their preservation and to seek to avoid their elimination. The Bank normally declines to finance projects that will significantly damage nonreplicable cultural property, and it assists only those projects that are sited or designed so as to prevent such damage.

Statements Supportive of Environment

OP/BP/GP 8.41   Institutional Development Fund (IDF)

The Institutional Development Fund is a grant facility designed to fill gaps in the Bank's set of instruments for financing technical assistance for institutional development work associated with policy reform, country management of technical assistance, and areas of special operational emphasis, particularly poverty reduction, public sector management, private sector development, and environmental management.

OD 14.70   Involving Nongovernmental Organizations in Bank-Supported Activities (to be issued as OP/BP/GP 14.70)

This policy sets out a framework for involving NGOs in Bank-supported activities and provides staff with guidance on working with NGOs, bearing in mind their potential contribution to sustainable development and poverty reduction. NGOs heighten awareness and influence policy concerning environmental degradation, involuntary resettlement, and tribal people.

Statements with Environmental References

OD 2.00   Country Economic and Sector Work (to be issued as OP/BP/GP 2.00)

Country economic and sector work analyzes the macroeconomic and sector development problems of borrower countries. As the long-term quality and sustainability of development depend on other factors in addition to economic ones, country economic work may also focus on questions of the environmental effects of alternative policy options.

OD 2.11   Country Assistance Strategies (to be issued as OP/BP/GP 2.11)

Country assistance strategies (CASs) for IDA and IBRD borrowers are analytic and issue-oriented statements that provide information on historical perspective and recent economic and portfolio performance; the country's external environment in terms of external trade, investment, and financial policies; and the Bank's CAS. CASs are reviewed regularly by the Bank's Executive Directors. The CAS presents the main objectives of the Bank's program of assistance for the country, including efforts to reduce poverty and sustain the environment.

OD 2.20   Policy Framework Papers (to be issued as OP/BP/GP 2.20)

Policy framework papers are vehicles for governments to reach agreements with the Bank and the International Monetary Fund on the broad outline of medium-term programs to overcome balance of payments problems and foster growth. The papers should maintain an adequate balance in the coverage of macroeconomic, sectoral, social, environmental, and institutional aspects. In the diagnoses of the current situation, any long-term constraints on development, including the environment, should be covered briefly.

OD 4.15   Poverty Reduction (to be issued as OP/BP/GP 4.15)

Sustainable poverty reduction is the Bank's overarching objective. Maintaining the environment is critical if gains in poverty reduction are to be sustained and if future increases in poverty are to be avoided. In sector work, particular attention is paid to the impact of sector policies on the links between environmental issues and poverty.

OD 7.50   Projects on International Waterways (to be issued as OP/BP/GP 7.50)

The Bank recognizes that projects involving the use of international waterways for development purposes may affect relations between the Bank and its borrowers and also between states, whether members of the Bank or not. The international aspects of Bank-supported projects on international waterways are brought to the fore and are dealt with through notification of other riparians; determination of the proposed project's potential to harm the interests of other riparians through deprivation of water, pollution, or otherwise; and negotiation and agreements between states at the earliest possible opportunity.

OD 8.40   Technical Assistance (to be issued as OP/BP/GP 8.40)

Technical assistance (TA) for policy and project preparation includes support for environmental action plans, project preparation, and environmental assessment. Institutional development TA addresses the need to strengthen capacity for environmental analysis and enforcement.

OD 8.60   Adjustment Lending Policy (to be issued as OP/BP/GP 8.60 under the title Adjustment Lending)

Analysis of adjustment programs considers implications for the environment. Bank staff review the environmental policies and practices in the country. The design of adjustment programs takes into account the findings and recommendations of such reviews.

OP/BP/GP 10.00   Investment Lending: Identification to Board Presentation

During project identification, Bank staff decide on the environmental category assigned to a project, the type and timing of any environmental assessment, and the environmental and natural resource management issues to be examined. The project identification document and staff appraisal report on or track these same points. The memorandum and recommendation of the Bank's president discusses the project's environmental impact, the main findings of the environmental assessment, consultation with affected groups, and feedback to these groups on the findings of the assessment.

OP/BP/GP 10.04   Economic Evaluation of Investment Operations

This policy includes consideration of global externalities as part of economic evaluation of investment operations when there is an international environmental agreement in force on related topics (whether or not the country is a party to that agreement) and where the country project is receiving GEF funding.

OD 13.05   Project Supervision (to be issued as OP/BP/GP 13.05)

A supervision plan should be prepared and discussed for each project with the borrower during project appraisal. The plan should cover the entire supervision period and include aspects of the project that require special Bank attention during supervision, such as environment. In addition, in the project implementation summary the project is to be rated in terms of both the implementation of any environmental component included and any unforeseen environmental deterioration resulting or threatening to result from the implementation of the project.

OP/BP/GP 13.55   Implementation Completion Reporting

This policy requires an implementation completion report (ICR) for each lending operation the Bank finances. The ICR assesses the degree of achievement of the project's major objectives (including environmental objectives); prospects for the project's sustainability; Bank and borrower performance; project outcome; and the plan for the project's future operation. Special attention is given to evaluation of environmental and other objectives, in order to improve project performance in these areas and build a store of information for expanded evaluation. For projects requiring an environmental assessment, the ICR evaluates specific concerns raised in the environmental assessment process, including environmental impacts anticipated in the EA report; the effectiveness of the mitigation measures taken; and institutional development and training regarding the environment.

Annex B. Guidance on Identification of World Bank Environmental Projects and Components

This annex indicates the criteria used to identify Bank projects and project components having primarily environmental objectives. For the most part, it is organized according to the traditional areas and sectors of Bank lending (urban development, transport, industry, agriculture, health, and so on). However, certain specific types of environmental interventions, such as watershed management or conservation and those involving cross-cutting environmental activities, are also distinguished. It should be noted that this is a working list that will be periodically reviewed and updated as Bank initiatives in support of country environmental management continue to evolve.

Project sector	Examples of environmental project objectives or components
Infrastructure and urban development	
Urban (planning, sites and services, housing)	Urban institutions and planning for pollution control, monitoring, and regulation and enforcement; environment-based land use planning; slum upgrading; wastewater and solid waste treatment, management, and disposal; reduction of urban air, water, and noise pollution
Transport (roads, airports, traffic engineering)	Traffic management for reduced congestion; vehicle fuel efficiency and modification; reduction of vehicle emissions; emission standards; incentives for higher occupancy vehicles; mass transit; reduction of marine pollution, ships' waste, and spills; port environmental safety and cleanup; reduction of noise pollution; institutional strengthening

Project sector	Examples of environmental project objectives or components
Water supply and sanitation	Water quality management (ground and surface); water pollution abatement; wastewater and sewage treatment, management, and disposal; water pricing and conservation incentives; standard setting, regulation, monitoring, and enforcement for quality management; institutional strengthening
Disaster relief and reconstruction	None
Telecommunications	None
Industry and finance	
Industry	Increased plant efficiency; reduction of waste and emissions; clean technologies; end-of-pipe pollution abatement; recycling; control and prevention of air and water pollution; hazardous waste treatment, management, storage, and disposal; standard setting, regulation, monitoring, and enforcement for quality management; institutional strengthening
Industrial development finance	Lending for pollution abatement; support to financial intermediaries to conduct environmental assessment
Natural resources management	
Agriculture and livestock	Soil management, conservation, and restoration; extension for environmentally sound land management; surface and groundwater management; pasture and grazing management; pesticide management such as integrated pest management; multisectoral water allocation; input pricing for water and agrochemicals; institutional strengthening; research extension
Forestry	Natural forest management, plantation development, and reforestation; management and afforestation for noncommercial uses (for example, social forestry, extractive reserves); conservation management, including biodiversity; institutional strengthening

Project sector	Examples of environmental project objectives or components
Watershed management	Watershed and river basin protection, management, and rehabilitation; multisectoral planning and allocation; institutional strengthening
Land management	Land mapping, titling and tenure, and transfers; land restoration and reclamation; institutional strengthening
Fisheries and marine resource management	Management of marine and freshwater resources; coastal zone management; biodiversity conservation; marine and riverine fisheries management; institutional strengthening
Conservation, including biodiversity	Conservation of terrestrial and aquatic biodiversity; protected areas; ex-situ conservation; financing mechanisms; training and institutional strengthening
Energy	
Energy and power sectors	Supply-side energy efficiency; demand-side management and conservation; reduced emissions; alternative and renewable energy technologies; removal of energy subsidies; institutional strengthening; standard setting, regulation, monitoring, and enforcement
Population and human resources	
Population	None
Public health and nutrition	Environmental health components
Education	Environmental awareness and education; environmental extension services; environmental research, science, and technology
Social	Resettlement associated with biodiversity projects; preservation of cultural property
Cross-cutting environmental activities	Environmental assessment National Environmental Action Plans Institutional development for environmental policy; regulation, monitoring, and enforcement; research

Project sector	Examples of environmental project objectives or components
	Natural resource accounting; environmental indicators; environmental valuation
	Transfer of clean technology
	Environmental technical assistance and training (Bank and borrower)
	Environmental information systems, including natural resource monitoring and geographic information systems
SALs (monetary, fiscal, exchange rate, trade policies)	Reduction of subsidies for natural resource use

Annex C.   Projects with Environmental Objectives and Components Approved in Fiscal 1994

This annex provides details on projects approved by the Bank's Board of Directors between July 1, 1993, and June 30, 1994, that have environmental objectives or components. The list illustrates the broad range of environmental concerns addressed by Bank projects. It includes both projects with primarily environmental objectives (table C.1) and projects with significant environmental components (table C.2). The dollar figures provided for projects with primarily environmental objectives represent the Bank share (IBRD loan or IDA credit) of the total project cost.

Table C.1. Projects with Environmental Objectives Approved in Fiscal 1994

Country	Project	Project description
Africa		
Gambia, The	Capacity Building for Environmental Management Technical Assistance ($2.6 million)	Aims to develop and guide an effective system for environmental planning and management within the National Environmental Agency (NEA) and other relevant agencies. Supports institutional and policy development of the Gambia Environmental Action Plan, development of a public awareness strategy, electronic and print media campaigns, an environmental information and monitoring system, and development of a disaster awareness and contingency planning system.

Country	Project	Project description
Togo	Togo Urban Development ($26.2 million)	Promotes improvement of the urban environmental management and environmental and sanitary conditions of the Bè Lagoon and supports community development. Supports capacity building of institutions in the area of urban management; improvement of the environment of the Bè Lagoon through antierosion, dredging of the Bè Lake, drainage of two pilot zones, and disposal and treatment of wastes; community participation through training programs in environmental management; construction of public latrines; miniprojects aimed at improving the urban environment; and improvement of transport and traffic conditions.
Asia		
Bhutan	Third Forestry Development ($5.4 million)	Seeks to develop and implement an approach for sustainable protection, management, and use of forest resources by involving rural communities in improving and managing local forests related to their livelihood, as well as increasing the level of economic activity through social forestry practices; supports adoption of multiple-use management of forest lands, rehabilitation of degraded forests to maintain their economic and environmental benefits, and improvement of the planning and implementation capacity of the Department of Forests.

Country	Project	Project description
China	Forest Resource Development and Protection ($200 million)	Seeks to develop institutional capacity and enhance biodiversity conservation through establishment of protected forests and nature reserves; establishment of multiple-use protection forests; afforestation models that promote biodiversity and reduce the incidence of disease damage; promotion of development of different canopy levels; and development of multitiered vertically stratified canopies to minimize soil erosion and water runoff. Supports institutional strengthening of sectoral institutions such as the Division of Nature Reserves through preparation of national management plans, related technical assistance, preparation of policy studies, and strengthening of information and research services on key issues related to biodiversity conservation.
	Shanghai Environment ($160 million)	Aims to improve and protect drinking water and halt the rapid deterioration of surface and groundwater quality in Shanghai through construction of a major raw water supply intake, pump stations, and a multiple-barrel low-pressure supply main; improvements in existing water treatment facilities and distribution networks; protection and improvement of water quality through construction of a wastewater conveyance system; wastewater collection and treatment in Songjiang Town; construction of a water quality monitoring facility; and development of solid waste and nightsoil management strategies. Supports institutional strengthening through technical assistance for development of a water supply master plan and geographic information systems, workshops, feasibility studies, and preparation of future projects.

Country	Project	Project description
China *(continued)*	Loess Plateau Watershed Rehabilitation ($160 million)	Aims to reduce erosion and inflows of sediment to the Yellow River by encouraging sustainable crop production on high-yielding level farmland; planting of the slope lands with a variety of trees, shrubs, and grasses for land stabilization; afforestation of degraded agricultural lands in the project area; and improved livestock management. Provides institutional support such as training, technological transfer, and research support to the Upper and Middle Reach Bureau to strengthen its capacity as a leading agency for soil and water conservation in the Yellow River Basin.
India	Forestry Research Education and Extension ($47 million)	Supports research on and development of methods for the conservation of biodiversity. Components include development and implementation of programs for ecodevelopment around two protected areas; financing of a range of ecodevelopment activities and concurrent improvements in the planning and management of the two protected areas; support for research aimed at improving protected area management and the implementation of ecodevelopment; and a program to monitor socioeconomic and ecological changes. In addition, supports the involvement of local communities in the planning and implementation of ecodevelopment programs.

Country	Project	Project description
India *(continued)*	Andhra Pradesh Forestry ($77.4 million)	Aims to maintain and improve biodiversity and develop sustainable management systems that foster participation and sharing of benefits by individuals and village communities, particularly in forest areas that are home to tribal groups. Supports forest regeneration and rehabilitation; improvement of adaptive forestry research and silviculture management; and joint forest management training in participatory rural appraisal. Provides institutional support to the nature conservation program through development of an integrated protected areas system; studies; boundary demarcations; fire protection; upgrading of roads; habitat improvement; captive breeding programs; and ecodevelopment in and around selected parks and sanctuaries.
Indonesia	Surabaya Urban Development ($175 million)	Seeks to improve urban environmental quality by assisting the local government's capacity to plan, implement, and operate infrastructure in an environmentally sound fashion and by enhancing community participation through strengthening the management, staffing, and financial viability of the local government water authority for both water supply and human waste disposal; protecting and improving water quality in the Kali Surabaya; improving onsite wastewater disposal; providing offsite sewerage; demonstrating and evaluating the potential for conventional and low-cost offsite sanitation and cost recovery in human waste services; and increasing and improving waste collection and landfill disposal techniques with improved services. In addition, the project will protect the rights of resettlers affected by the project.

Country	Project	Project description
Indonesia *(continued)*	National Watershed Management and Conservation ($56.5 million)	Aims to raise the living standards of poor upland farmers by improving and restoring the productive potential of their resource base and at the same time to improve watershed environmental quality and protect downstream watershed resources. Provides institutional strengthening through improvement of planning, management, and natural resource information systems. Supports the creation of a multidisciplinary upland research program and training and extension; development of a critical watershed on West Java; and investment for regreening and reforestation.
Korea, Republic of	Environmental Technology Development ($90 million)	Aims to strengthen selected national research institutes to adequately address environmental issues and to undertake environmental R&D activities. Provides institutional support to the policy and planning role of the Ministry of Environment by providing overseas training, visiting experts, and library materials, as well as equipment and equipment-related inputs and civil works to house the equipment.
Lao PDR	Forest Management and Conservation ($8.7 million)	Assists with the introduction of a more sustainable natural resource management system and conservation of the country's forest resources through support of an institutional framework and formulation of the regulatory framework for the forestry sector; implementation of national programs on forest resource inventory and planning; sustainable forest management and protection; establishment and management of protected areas; and provision of the necessary technical assistance and human resource development.

Country	Project	Project description
Pakistan	Balochistan Natural Resource Management ($14.7 million)	Represents the first phase of long-term support to improve Balochistan's protection of its environment and management of its natural resources. Aims to strengthen the principal environmental institutions through formulating environmental policy, legislation, and regulations; monitoring natural resource management; and providing training, technical assistance, and support staff. Supports site-specific methods of rehabilitation and development of degraded forests, watersheds, rangelands, coastal areas, and natural habitats. Supports the efficient, sustainable use of groundwater, especially by eliminating government subsidies for drilling tubewells.

Europe and Central Asia; Middle East and North Africa

Country	Project	Project description
Algeria	Water Supply and Sewerage Rehabilitation ($110 million)	Promotes water conservation by charging the true economic cost of the services to consumers; supports rehabilitation of a number of existing wastewater treatment plants to prevent the spread of water pollution that is damaging to the natural environment as part of a larger water supply and sewerage restructuring project.
Estonia	District Heating Rehabilitation ($38.4 million)	Promotes energy efficiency and economy by supporting the conversion and replacement of small boilers for use of peat and wood, to be harvested and used in an environmentally sustainable manner; reducing wastewater in the district heating systems; installing new substations with regulators and heat meters; and strengthening and restructuring the district heating institutions.

Country	Project	Project description
Poland	Forest Development Support ($146 million)	Assists the government in executing its Program for the Development of Selected Forestry Branches and Protection of Ecosystems in National Parks, thereby ensuring the protection of Poland's forest ecological capital, providing for social benefits, and accommodating sustainable forestry. Supports institutional strengthening of the General Directorate of State Forests through development of a strategy for environmentally sound forest use to balance environmental and economic considerations. Goals include increasing the vitality of forest stands and their ability to overcome the effects of present and future air pollution; the restoration of pollution-damaged forests to protect watersheds and prevent soil erosion; afforestation of land moving out of agriculture; a genetic conservation and improvement program; and the creation of an information system including a geographic information system integrated with the planning system.

Country	Project	Project description
Tunisia	Northwest Mountainous Areas Development ($27.5 million)	Aims to arrest degradation of the natural resource base through active participation of village communities. Supports improvement of the management and productivity of range and farm land; measures to reduce erosion, runoff, and reservoir sedimentation; and increased involvement of village organizations. Supports strengthening of the technical and implementation capability of the executing agency and the planning capability of village committees through technical assistance and training.
Latin America and the Caribbean		
Colombia	Natural Resource Management Program ($39 million)	Aims to arrest the ongoing degradation of natural renewable resources through development of a national forest policy and a strategy for natural resource management in the Choco Region; ecological zoning; establishment of an environmental monitoring system; titling and demarcation of indigenous reserves; titling and demarcation of land in Black communities; and institutional support to Black and Amerindian communities. Supports local projects to protect and rehabilitate watershed areas through technical assistance for preparation of annual plans. Strengthens the capacity of the National Parks Service to protect threatened ecosystems through funding of staff, infrastructure, and technical assistance. Promotes forestry and environmental education, training, research, and project management.

220

Country	Project	Project description
Ecuador	Mining Development and Environmental Control Technical Assistance ($14.0 million)	Aims to support systematic development of the mining industry, promote environmentally sound mineral production, arrest mining-related environmental degradation, and mitigate the damage caused by the use of primitive and inadequate technology by informal miners. Supports the establishment of applicable environmental standards and a monitoring system; helps contain and possibly detoxify mining-related hazardous wastes. Other components are monitoring mining-related health issues in mining communities; improving institutional structures, staffing coordination, and preparation of environmental standards; assisting the National Directorate of the Environment in establishing and implementing an extensive mining pollution monitoring program; and developing a phased feasibility and implementation program to contain and neutralize hazardous mining wastes in a critical drainage area.
Mexico	Northern Border Environment ($367.8 million)	Aims to improve the environmental quality on the U.S.-Mexican border, reverse past degradation, and reduce health risks. Supports institutional strengthening by improving the capabilities of the municipal, state, and federal governments for more effective environmental management, planning, and enforcement. Supports priority investments and action plans for preservation of the environment; a strategy to implement the government's national policy on toxic and hazardous materials and a pilot program to test the use of transportable hazardous waste treatment units; and initiatives on protection of ecological areas and biodiversity. Assists the development of an environmental emergencies program; supports the supervision of environmental audits and the development of a media public awareness campaign to increase public interest and participation in improving and conserving the environment.

Country	Project	Project description
	Second Water Supply and Sanitation Sector ($350 million)	Aims to improve the management of water resources and the environment by supporting water quality programs. Supports the National Development Bank for Public Works and Service in enforcing environmental regulations and carrying out environmental impact assessments; addresses environmental concerns through strengthening the major federal institutions that manage water resources; develops the planning and environmental capabilities of the Autonomous Water Utilities and Operating Agencies; and finances subprojects that rehabilitate waste-water collection and treatment facilities such as laterals, trunk sewers, pump stations, primary, secondary, and advanced wastewater treatment plants.
Mexico (continued)	Second Solid Waste Management ($200 million)	Aims to improve solid waste services, strengthen the capacity of relevant institutions to appraise and supervise solid waste projects, and provide technical assistance to municipalities and states. Supports improvement and updating of the legal and regulatory framework and cost recovery mechanisms of the sector and training of professionals in environmental fields. Provides technical assistance for final engineering designs and environmental impact assessments. Supports reduction of health hazards caused by inadequate collection and disposal systems; institutional strengthening for the government development agency (SEDESOL) and the national development bank (BANOBRAS); development of a national recycling strategy and a public awareness campaign; implementation of integrated solid waste management plans including least-cost final disposal facilities, strict environmental control measures, and closing of the current dumpsite; and a retraining and education program for open-dump-site scavengers.

Country	Project	Project description
Paraguay	Natural Resources Management ($50 million)	Aims to establish the institutional framework to deal with the major agricultural and natural resource problems of the project area, generate information through research, assist small farmers in the establishment of sustainable agricultural production systems, and encourage the direct participation of the local population in project implementation. Supports planning and implementing actions designed to slow and reverse the degradation of soils and other natural resources; to protect, conserve, and restore the genetic diversity of the area; to develop activities of research, reforestation, and technology generation; to strengthen environmental legislation and institutions involved in this area; to strengthen the institutional presence in existing forestry reserves and national parks; and, through the Natural Resources Conservation Fund (FOCORN), to make available grant resources to correct damages such as erosion and soil degradation caused by the indiscriminate conversion of land for agricultural production.
Uruguay	Natural Resources Management and Irrigation Development ($41 million)	Aims to develop and implement a soil and water management strategy by supporting environmentally sound investments in rehabilitation and development of irrigation and drainage schemes and related service infrastructure and by supporting the development of pilot microcatchment areas to gain experience in the management of ecologically fragile zones and establish soil and water management demonstration farms in selected agroecological zones where potential soil degradation problems have been identified. Includes priority applied research and technology transfer subprojects and provides technical assistance for forestry development and nontraditional agricultural export activities.

Table C.2. Projects with Environmental Components Approved in Fiscal 1994

Country	Project	Environmental component
Africa		
Ghana	Urban Transport	Finances construction of dedicated nonmotorized transport paths connecting low and middle-income residential areas to commercial and business districts and initiates an integrated bike path network study.
Mali	National Agricultural Research	Supports research programs and extension on natural resource management and other appropriate agricultural activities.
Uganda	Small Towns Water	Rehabilitates and constructs sewers and sewage treatment works and provides assistance to strengthen the capacity of institutions responsible for water supply and sanitation improvements.
Asia		
China	Songliao Plain Agricultural Development	Provides soil and water conservation measures, including watershed management, afforestation, an environmental monitoring program, and training for farmers.
	Sichuan Gas Development and Conservation	Includes rehabilitation and environmental upgrade of gas transmission and distribution systems to reduce gas leaks and provides technical assistance and training in this area.
	Second Red Soils	Implements vegetative and structural soil and water conservation treatments and supports development of watersheds through planting forests and crops.
	Second Shanghai Metropolitan Transport	Invests in public transport system and provides technical assistance to support an environmental action plan for vehicle inspection and maintenance and reduction of emissions.

Country	Project	Environmental component
India	Haryana Water Resources Consolidation	Provides technical assistance and training for environmental management and beneficiary participation.
Indonesia	Integrated Swamps	Supports coastal zone land use management by creating a natural resource database, strengthening park management, and establishing interdepartmental implementation committees.
	Java Irrigation Improvement and Water Resources Management	Includes long-term integrated water resource management for municipal, industrial, agricultural, and other demands; strengthens institutional base for water management (water and cost accounting systems, water rights system, and a water service fees framework).
Philippines	Subic Bay Freeport	Carries out an environmental baseline survey to develop basic information on environmental conditions in the area, provides environmental monitoring equipment, and gives institutional support to establish sound environmental infrastructure.
	Leyte-Cebu Geothermal	Replaces coal burning with geothermal plants and reduces carbon dioxide emissions.
	Leyte-Luzon Geothermal	Replaces coal burning with geothermal plants, reduces carbon dioxide emissions, and recruits advisers to strengthen environmental and social engineering departments.

Europe and Central Asia; Middle East and North Africa

Albania	Durres Water Supply	Reduces water loss by rehabilitating current plumbing systems and installs a demand management program for water supply and sewerage through metering. Includes a customer education program in water conservation and a collector to prevent sewerage overflows into the Durres harbor.

Country	Project	Environmental component
Belarus	Forestry Development Sector	Supports implementation of a forest ecology policy for biodiversity preservation, assessment of the ecological impact of forestry harvest and maintenance systems, and planning for wetlands, drained wetlands, and Chernobyl-contaminated forest resources.
Bulgaria	Water Companies Restructuring and Modernization	Provides technical assistance to build capacity for water resource management and sewerage investment to reduce pollution in sensitive watercourses where upstream pollution prevents downstream use of natural resources (such as drinking water) or results in irreversible environmental damage (for example, to biodiversity or beaches).
Egypt	Agricultural Modernization	Provides for training and technical assistance to the agriculture bank for environmental loan appraisal, management, and monitoring capacity.
Hungary	Energy and Environment	Contains an environmental management component for environmental training, monitoring, technical assistance to develop an environmental master plan, and mitigation to deal with problems identified in the environmental assessment.
Jordan	Energy Sector Adjustment	Adopts environmental guidelines and regulations; designates monitoring and enforcement authority within the government; and improves energy conservation by removing energy subsidies and strengthening electricity demand management, power plant efficiency, and institutional support mechanisms.
Romania	Petroleum Sector Rehabilitation	Implements environmental action plans to introduce environmental abatement measures in gas and oil production, transmission, and transport systems.

Country	Project	Environmental component
Latin America and the Caribbean		
Belize	Belize City Infrastructure	Provides for traffic management to reduce congestion and improve sidewalks and bicycle lanes. Also includes a coastal zone management component.
Bolivia	Municipal Sector Development	Includes pilot program to improve the environmental management capabilities of the River Basins Department of the La Paz municipality, which is in charge of controlling soil erosion and flooding and surface water quality in the area.
Brazil	State Highway Management II	Builds the institutional capacity of the state road agencies for the preparation and enforcement of environmental guidelines by adding professional staff to their environmental units and conducting training for staff responsible for environmental assessment review and enforcement of standards.
	Minas Gerais Municipal Management and Environmental Infrastructure	Strengthens local environmental enforcement agencies, encourages regional cooperation water basin authorities, and prepares long-run marginal cost pricing studies to revise user charges. Invests in environmental infrastructure in the areas of water and sewerage treatment, solid waste collection, paving and control of erosion caused by drainage, and efficient lighting.
Guyana	Water Supply Technical Assistance and Rehabilitation	Includes technical assistance for the Guyana Water Authority to establish financial, accounting, and management systems (billing and collection) and improved cost recovery schemes.
Mexico	On-farm and Minor Irrigation Networks	Trains farmers in management and monitoring of water use from overexploited aquifers.
Nicaragua	Agricultural Technology and Land Management	Contains program to promote environmentally sound and effective pest management practices (integrated pest management).

Country	Project	Environmental component
Panama	Roads Rehabilitation	Provides technical assistance to strengthen the institutional capacity of the Ministry of Public Works to address environmental issues.
Paraguay	Eighth Highway	Provides technical assistance and training to strengthen the Environmental Unit of the Ministry of Public Works.
Peru	Transport Rehabilitation	Contains a pilot subproject for nonmotorized transport, including construction of bicycle lanes, provision of credits for purchase of bicycles, and promotional and educational campaigns.
Venezuela	Urban Transport	Invests in traffic management and mass transit to relieve congestion in major transport corridors and central areas, resulting in lower emission of pollutants per vehicle-kilometer.

Annex D. Ongoing Environmental Projects under Implementation

This annex lists projects with primarily environmental objectives that were approved by the Bank's Board of Executive Directors prior to July 1, 1993, and were under implementation throughout fiscal 1994. The annex identifies projects for urban environmental management and pollution control (table D.1), natural resource management (table D.2), and environmental institution building (table D.3). Each table specifies whether the project is being financed through an IBRD loan, an IDA credit, or both and indicates the fiscal year in which the project was approved (shown in parentheses), the Bank Group's financial contribution, and the total estimated project cost.

Table D.1. Projects for Urban Environmental Management and Pollution Control (31 Projects)
(millions of dollars)

Country	Project (year approved)	Loan or credit	World Bank Group contribution	Total project cost
Angola	Lobito-Benguela Urban Environmental Rehabilitation (92)	C	46	59
Brazil	Water Quality and Pollution Control—São Paulo/Paraná (93)	L	236	494
	National Industrial Pollution Control (92)	L	50	100
	Minas Gerais Water Quality and Pollution Control (93)	L	145	308
	Second Industrial Pollution Control (88)	L	50	100
Burundi	Energy Sector Rehabilitation (91)	C	23	23
Chile	Second Valparaiso Water Supply and Sewerage (91)	L	50	142
China	Ship Waste Disposal (92)	C	15	64
	Beijing Environment (92)	C + L	125	299
	Tianjin Urban Development and Environment (92)	C	100	195
	South Jiangsu Environment Protection (93)	L	250	584

Country	Project (year approved)	Loan or credit	World Bank Group contribution	Total project cost
Czech Republic	Power and Environmental Improvement (92)	L	246	246
Côte d'Ivoire	Abidjan Environmental Protection (90)	L	22	50
Cyprus	Limassol Amathus Sewerage and Drainage (90)	L	25	69
	Southeast Coast Sewerage and Drainage (92)	L	32	103
India	Industrial Pollution Control (91)	C + L	156	236
	Renewable Resources Development (93)	C + L	190	440
Korea, Republic of	Pusan and Taejon Sewerage (92)	L	40	130
	Kuangju and Seoul Sewage (93)	L	110	530
Mauritania	Water Supply (92)	C	11	15
Mexico	Transport Air Quality Management (93)	L	220	1,087
	Solid Waste Management (86)	L	25	50
Niger	Energy Project (88)	C	32	79
Poland	Heat Supply Restructuring and Conservation (91)	L	340	739
	Energy Resource Development (90)	L	250	590
Tunisia	Energy Conservation Demonstration (87)	L	4	4
Turkey	Bursa Water Supply and Sanitation (93)	L	130	258
	Izmir Water Supply and Sewerage (87)	L	184	522
	Istanbul Water Supply and Sewerage (88)	L	218	570
	Ankara Sewerage (90)	L	173	557
Portfolio total			3,498	8,643

Table D.2. Projects for Natural Resource Management (49 Projects)
(millions of dollars)

Country	Project	Loan or credit	World Bank Group contribution	Total project cost
Algeria	Pilot Forestry and Watershed Management (92)	L	25	37
Bangladesh	Forest Resources Management (92)	C	50	59
Benin	Natural Resources Management (92)	C	14	24
Bolivia	Eastern Lowlands (90)	C	35	55
Brazil	Rondônia Natural Resource Management (92)	L	167	228
	Mato Grosso Natural Resource Management (92)	L	205	286
	Minas Gerais Forestry Development (88)	L	49	308
	Land Management I—Paraná (89)	L	63	138
	Land Management II (90)	L	33	72
Burkina Faso	Environmental Management (91)	C	17	25
Central African Rep.	Natural Resource Management (90)	C	19	34
Côte d'Ivoire	Forestry Sector (90)	L	80	147
Ecuador	Lower Guayas Flood Control (91)	L	59	98
Egypt	Matruh Resource Management (93)	C	22	31
Gabon	Forestry and Environment (93)	L	23	38
Ghana	Forest Resource Management (89)	C	39	65
Guinea	Forestry and Fisheries Management (90)	C	8	23
Haiti	Forestry and Environmental Protection (92)	C	26	29
India	Uttar Pradesh Sodic Lands Reclamation (93)	C	55	80
	Maharashtra Forestry (92)	C	124	142
	Integrated Watershed Development (Hills) (90)	C	75	75
	Integrated Watershed Development (Plains) (90)	C	55	55
Indonesia	Second Forestry Institutions and Conservation (90)	L	20	33
	Integrated Pest Management (93)	L	32	53
	Yogyakarta Upland Area Development (91)	L	16	25
	Forestry Institutions and Conservation (88)	L	30	63
Kenya	Forestry Development (91)	C	20	65
	Protected Areas and Wildlife Services (92)	C	61	143

Country	Project	Loan or credit	World Bank Group contribution	Total project cost
Madagascar	Antananarivo Plain Development (90)	C	31	69
	Forests Management and Protection (88)	C	7	23
Malaysia	Sabah Land Settlement and Environmental Management (89)	L	72	203
Malawi	Fisheries Development (91)	C	9	16
Mali	Natural Resource Management (92)	C	20	32
Morocco	Second Forestry Development (90)	L	49	100
Nepal	Hill Community Forestry (89)	C	31	45
Pakistan	Northern Resource Management (93)	C	29	40
	Fordwah E. Sadiquia Irrigation and Drainage (93)	C	54	71
	Second Scarp Transition (91)	C	20	49
Paraguay	Land Use Rationalization Project (92)	L	29	41
Philippines	Environmental and Natural Resource Management (91)	C + L	224	369
Rwanda	Second Integrated Forestry (88)	C	14	20
Seychelles	Environment and Transport (93)	L	5	7
Sri Lanka	Forest Sector Development (89)	C	20	31
Sudan	Southern Kassala Agriculture (89)	C	20	35
Tanzania	Forest Resources Management (92)	C	18	26
Tunisia	Second Forestry Development Project (93)	L	69	148
Turkey	Eastern Anatolia Watershed Rehabilitation (93)	L	77	121
Venezuela	National Parks Management (93)	L	55	96
Yemen	Land and Water Conservation (92)	C	33	48
Portfolio total			2,308	4,021

**Table D.3. Projects for Environmental Institution Building
(13 Projects)**
(millions of dollars)

Country	Project	Loan or credit	World Bank Group contribution	Total project cost
Bolivia	Environmental Technical Assistance (93)	C	5	5
Brazil	National Environment (90)	L	117	166
Chile	Environment Institutions Development (93)	L	12	33
China	Environment Technical Assistance (93)	C	50	70
Ghana	Environmental Resource Management (93)	C	18	36
Indonesia	BAPEDAL Development Technical Assistance (92)	L	12	15
Korea, Republic of	Environmental Research and Education (93)	L	60	97
Madagascar	Environment Program (90)	C	26	86
Mauritius	Environmental Monitoring and Development (91)	L	12	21
Mexico	Environment and Natural Resources (92)	L	50	127
Nigeria	Environmental Management (92)	C	25	38
Pakistan	Environmental Protection and Resource Conservation (92)	C	29	57
Poland	Environment Management (90)	L	18	27
Portfolio total			434	778

Annex E.   Projects with Full Environmental Assessment Approved in Fiscal 1994, Category A Projects

Since October 1989 Bank staff have been required to screen all proposed new investment projects with respect to their potential environmental impacts and to classify them accordingly. Category A projects are those considered likely to have significant environmental impacts that may be sensitive, irreversible, and diverse. Such projects require a full environmental assessment (EA). This annex lists all category A projects approved by the Bank's Board of Directors in fiscal 1994. For each, the annex indicates the estimated total cost and the IBRD or IDA financing, and provides a brief description of the project and the contribution of the environmental assessment.

Country	Project	EA description	Total project cost/Bank financing (millions of dollars)
Africa			
Ethiopia	Calub Gas Development	Aims to augment the availability of Ethiopia's indigenous energy resources such as biomass, natural gas, and geothermal energy in an economically viable and commercially and environmentally sustainable manner. The EA demonstrated how the expanded supply of liquid petroleum gas and kerosene in urban areas is expected to reduce firewood consumption, thereby slowing the unsustainable rate of deforestation. The EA recommended sound industrial environmental practices, such as reinjecting unused natural gas into the reservoir to minimize hydrocarbon emissions, which will be incorporated in the design, construction, and operation of the Calub plant. Pollution control measures that meet international industry standards will also be incorporated in the design of the plant. An Environmental Monitoring System to assess the project's impact on the cultural heritage and socioeconomic systems in the concerned areas was established.	$130.81/IDA $74.31

Country	Project	EA description	Total project cost/Bank financing (millions of dollars)
Guinea-Bissau	Agricultural Land and Environment	Aims to enhance the environment by promoting conservation, reforestation, and family planning and reducing the ongoing environmental destruction in the country. The EA earmarked potential environmental problems such as land use management plans that may lead to intensive land use, weak institutions, and negative effects from the construction and operation of the Tabanca Pilot Centers (TPC). Mitigation measures ensure that all project-related activities such as construction and operation of TPCs follow acceptable standards. The National Environmental Council and the Department of Forestry will be strengthened, and environmental management and training will be provided. In addition, monitoring of the project will be established as standard procedure.	$8.9/ IDA $8.0
Asia			
Bangladesh	Jamuna Bridge	Supports construction of the Jamuna bridge to connect the eastern and western parts of the country. The environmental issues that were identified were bridge construction, soil and water pollution, negative impacts on fisheries, and induced settlements. Measures for mitigation include a compensatory fisheries development program; environmental guidelines for construction-related activities, to minimize human health and ecology impacts; a wildlife action plan; a land use master plan, particularly for the areas around the bridge, to support environmentally acceptable economic and urban development; and monitoring of groundwater levels should adverse situations arise.	$696/ IDA $200

Country	Project	EA description	Total project cost/Bank financing (millions of dollars)
China	National Highway	Aims to relieve transport congestion and to promote free flow of goods between Hebei and Henan. The EA identified air pollution and impacts during construction as environmental problems. Mitigation measures include establishment of emissions testing at the expressway's toll plazas in both provinces and the restriction of permitted land uses along the roadway. Potential noise impacts during the construction phase of the project will be mitigated by restrictions on construction activities. Cultural heritage identified will be salvaged to avoid adverse impacts during construction.	$894.7/ IBRD $380
	Sichuan Gas Development and Conservation	Aims to rehabilitate gas transmission lines and distribution systems to eliminate methane gas emissions to the atmosphere and improve pipeline network performance. As part of the environmental assessment process, studies were carried out to ensure that the project design and implementation will conform with international engineering and safety standards, as well as sound engineering management practices. The proposed project would increase gas supply and reduce coal consumption, thus reducing emissions of sulfur dioxide, carbon dioxide, and particulates. Public consultation has been built into the process of project preparation and implementation, and site selection may be changed according to the preferences of residents.	$945.2/ IBRD $255

Country	Project	EA description	Total project cost/Bank financing (millions of dollars)
China *(continued)*	Xiaolangdi Multipurpose Dam	Aims to introduce flood and siltation control in the Yellow River Basin, provide water for irrigation and for downstream cities and industries, and generate hydropower for the Henan Province and the Central China Power Network. The major environmental impact identified is the resettlement of 171,000 mostly rural residents. A total of 181,000 people will be affected by the dam and its construction; 10,000 of which have already been resettled, 154,000 will be resettled under the Xiaolangdi Resettlement Project, and a final group of 17,000 will move in the years 2010 and 2011, depending on long-term reservoir operation characteristics. Other concerns are dam safety, salvage of archeological relics, and public health and disease control measures. As a result of the environmental assessment, an overall environmental management plan (EMP) has been developed. In relation to dam safety, a wide range of safety features are provided in the project design, including access road systems.	$2,294.7/ IBRD $460.0

Country	Project	EA description	Total project cost/Bank financing (millions of dollars)
China *(continued)*	Xiaolangdi Resettlement	As one of the first large-scale resettlement efforts in China, this project was designed to restore and improve the livelihoods of 154,000 resettlers and 300,000 host people affected by construction and operation of the Xiaolangdi multipurpose dam and to minimize the adverse effects of their adjustment to their new environments. The EA identified impacts related to the social environment, public health, sanitation, and the removal of cultural relics. The EA ensures that relocated and host families will not be disadvantaged by the dam construction, that they will share in the project benefits, and that expenses and losses encountered during the transition will be compensated. A management plan has been developed to ensure that public health issues and treatment of cultural relics are attended to fully under the project.	$571.3/ IDA $110.0

Country	Project	EA description	Total project cost/Bank financing (millions of dollars)
China *(continued)*	Second Shanghai Metropolitan Transport	Aims to enhance economic productivity by improving the operational and economic efficiency of the urban transport system. The project comprises construction of the Inner Ring Road in Puxi. As for the impacts the road caused, the EA identified noise, dust, traffic disruption during construction, and potential increases in pollution levels, vehicle noise, and social impacts after the project opening. The Shanghai municipality will improve site and traffic management on affected streets. Countermeasures—sound barriers, noise absorptive paving, and sound insulation—are proposed against the increased noise levels resulting from the higher traffic speeds made possible by the project. To reduce air pollution, improved vehicle inspection, maintenance procedures, use of fuel additives, and a change to less-polluting fuels are proposed.	$657.1/ IBRD $150
	Fujian Provincial Highway	Aims to develop road infrastructure and an action plan for strengthening the road construction industry. The EA identified measures related to social disruption, air quality, noise control, water management, control of traffic, operation of quarries, and waste disposal during construction and the operation of the Xiamen-Quanzhou highway. In addition, appropriate environmental engineering design and technical specifications for the highway incorporate measures for environmental protection.	$528.8/ IBRD $140

Country	Project	EA description	Total project cost/Bank financing (millions of dollars)
China *(continued)*	Yangzhou Thermal Power	Supports construction of a coal-fired power plant and two transmission lines and reinforcement of the existing power transmission network. Under the EA, the site for the project was selected so as to take up the least amount of land, with the least impact on the natural and human environment. Appropriate technologies such as low-nitrogen-oxides burners will be applied in the power plant design. In addition, the power plant layout provides enough space to enable installation of additional pollution control devices to allow for changes in standards and new technological developments. The mitigation plan ensures that environmental impacts associated with the project are minimized. The institutional capabilities of the Jiangsu Provincial Electric Power Company will be strengthened for environmental management. Public consultations were held by the Yangzhou municipality.	$1,081.4/ IBRD $350 IDA $2.2

Country	Project	EA description	Total project cost/Bank financing (millions of dollars)
Indonesia	Semarang-Surakarta Urban Development	Aims to improve the provision, services, and efficiency of urban infrastructure and investments. Four ANDAL (detailed environmental impact assessment) studies were undertaken for solid waste, sewerage, and drainage in Semarang and for sewerage in Surakarta. The environment impact assessment (EIA)studies led to significant improvements in project design. Intensive public consultation was undertaken, including a multistage consultation on one of the drainage components. An encouraging result of the EIA process was that changes were made in response to the EIAs, such as in the location of the wastewater treatment plant site in Semarang. The proposed flood control works in West Semarang will have an important social impact and will displace people. A detailed resettlement plan was prepared that involved NGO participation, public meetings, and consultations with the affected people.	$320.8/ IBRD $174

Country	Project	EA description	Total project cost/Bank financing (millions of dollars)
Indonesia (continued)	Outer Islands Power, Sumatera and Kalimantan Power	Aims to support the power sector, increase private sector participation, accelerate expansion of generating capacity, and upgrade sector operating standards and practices. The EA proposed land reclamation, terracing, and replanting to minimize soil erosion; dust suppression and noise abatement measures to mitigate air and water pollution; and measures to ensure a healthy construction site. The environmental impact selected several sites for quarrying to minimize clearing vegetation, to avoid deterioration of the water quality, and to avoid scouring of the river bed between the dam and the power station by maintaining a minimum release of water. The internal structure of the State Electricity Corporation (PLN) will be strengthened, and technical assistance will be provided to develop the PLN's capability to formulate environmental policies, evaluate environmental assessments, and monitor environmental impacts. A resettlement plan was developed, and public consultations were held.	$688.9/ IBRD $260.5

Country	Project	EA description	Total project cost/Bank financing (millions of dollars)
Indonesia (continued)	Integrated Swamps Development	Aims to reduce poverty in swamp areas through development of agricultural potential. The EA identified a number of key environmental management issues, the most significant of which related to the potentially deleterious short-term effects of exposure to potential acid sulphate soils (PASS) as a result of poorly planned or executed civil works. This exposure has been reduced significantly following the decision to delete schemes with excessive PASS and to reduce the scope of civil works in the remaining schemes. The construction problems that were identified can be controlled through monitoring and management. Woodlots will be provided for in the three provinces to avoid deforestation. A comprehensive environmental monitoring and management plan has been prepared covering developments in all three provinces. Public consultations were held.	$110.6/ IBRD $61.4

Country	Project	EA description	Total project cost/Bank financing (millions of dollars)
Indonesia *(continued)*	Surabaya Urban Development	Aims to provide urban services such as public transport, water supply, storm drainage, and solid waste disposal systems. The environmental assessment (ANDAL) was prepared for two components: a major drainage and flood alleviation component and the urban roads component. The EA identified resettlement of people and businesses as the main concern. This project, for the first time among the urban sector projects, focused on consultations with affected communities. Local communities were involved and participated in the land acquisition and resettlement processes in the community development programs.	$617.6/ IBRD $175
India	Haryana Water Resource Consolidation	Aims to introduce water resource planning and management and enhance agricultural productivity and diversification. The sectoral EA report delineated a viable and practical program for the Haryana Irrigation Department. The main environmental concerns identified under the project included water quality, waterlogging, and salinity problems; overexploitation of groundwater; drainage; and flood mitigation. The mitigating measures proposed were afforestation along the canal and the bank, notification of construction works to user groups, monitoring and evaluation of water quality impacts, and preparation and implementation of an environmental management plan.	$458.9/ IBRD $211

Country	Project	EA description	Total project cost/Bank financing (millions of dollars)
Philippines	Leyte-Cebu Geothermal	Aims to meet the rapidly increasing demand for power in Cebu and the Visayas region using indigenous and environmentally superior geothermal energy. An EA for transmission lines was conducted. Transmission lines were laid both on land and in the ocean. The EA determined that there was minimal environmental impact on the forests and that the effect on the corals would also be negligible, as it would impinge on areas already damaged by dynamite fishing.	$458.9/ IBRD $211
	Leyte-Luzon Geothermal	Aims to expand geothermal development from 350 megawatts to 700 megawatts. An EA was carried out to determine the effects of transmission lines both on land and on the ocean. The EA concluded that there would be minimal effect on the forests and that the impact on the ocean would also be minimal because the transmission lines rest on the ocean floor, with only minor excavations on sand at the two shorelines for a trench. The mangroves and corals would not be affected. Five hundred and twenty-five households will be relocated a few meters away from the line's right-of-way.	$1,333.6/ IBRD $227

Country	Project	EA description	Total project cost/Bank financing (millions of dollars)

Europe and Central Asia; Middle East and North Africa

| Estonia | District Heating and Rehabilitation | Aims to reduce fuel costs and import requirements, bring about energy efficiency, and strengthen and restructure district heating systems. A sectoral EA was prepared during the early design phases of the project to evaluate the short-, medium-, and long-term environmental impacts of harvesting, processing, and using peat and wood as fuels. A full sectoral EA was prepared for the small program for boiler conversion and replacement. Environmental reviews were prepared consistent with the requirements for a category B project for the district heating rehabilitation program. The EA recommended environmentally sound development of local peat and wood, provided that proper environmental policies and guidelines are used and monitored by the government. Using indigenous peat and wood resources in place of heavy fuel would reduce the level of air pollution and the emissions of sulfur dioxide and nitrogen oxides. Environmental mitigation and monitoring plans have been prepared that will be implemented by the Ministry of Environment and cooperating implementing organizations. | $64.5/ IBRD $38.4 |

Country	Project	EA description	Total project cost/Bank financing (millions of dollars)
Hungary	Energy and Environment	Aims to decrease dependence on energy imports from a single source by increasing efficiency in the production of electricity and heat. The EA identified both air and noise pollution issues. Reductions in sulfur dioxide emissions have been achieved by the phaseout of older, less efficient fossil-fueled boilers and increased use of the Paks nuclear power station. In addition, old and polluting plants will be decommissioned, and some smaller steam plants have been retrofitted with fluidized bed boilers, resulting in reduction of both sulfur dioxide and nitrogen oxide emissions. The chief noise sources are the gas turbine, air intake, and gas exhaust systems. A mitigation plan is included in the project design to ensure acceptable noise levels.	$242.5/ IBRD $100
Russia	Second Oil Rehabilitation	Aims to slow the rate of decline of oil production in Western Siberia and strengthen the Russian Federation's ability to earn foreign exchange. Environmental components of the project will focus on mitigating the effects of implementing the project itself by, for example, improving environmental management, and carrying out pilot cleanup programs, such as bioremediation, to address past damage. The EA proposed that environmental impacts be reduced through rehabilitation and modifications of exiting oil and gas production operations but also through provision of environmental cleanup and spill response equipment, analytical stationary and mobile laboratories, and corrosion-testing facilities.	$678/ IBRD $500

Country	Project	EA description	Total project cost/Bank financing (millions of dollars)
Latin America and the Caribbean			
Ecuador	Mining Development and Environmental Control Technical Assistance	Aims to attract new mining investment and support the development of increased, yet environmentally sustainable, mineral production. EA recommendations were used extensively in project design. Approximately 35 percent of the project is dedicated to environmental improvements through the monitoring of pollution and occupational health issues, the removal of contaminating wastes in the most-sensitive areas, and a technology-upgrading subcomponent (of a pilot nature) that will help introduce and encourage environmentally sound mining and processing methods among artisanal and small-scale miners.	$24.0/ IBRD 14.0
Mexico	Second Solid Waste Management	Aims to improve solid waste services and extend their coverage in participating medium-size cities. The EA has made the following recommendations: containerization and mechanical collection would fulfill requirements of low cost and ease of operation; sanitary landfills would be the most-suitable option for medium to small Mexican cities; high-density landfills would be suitable for cities with high groundwater tables and groundwater pollution. Environmental impacts arising from project siting, construction, and operation will be kept to a minimum through adequate environmental screening and required environmental assessment, including public consultation, of all proposed subloans.	$415.5/ IBRD $200

Country	Project	EA description	Total project cost/Bank financing (millions of dollars)
Mexico (continued)	Northern Border Environment	Aims to improve environmental quality on the U.S.-Mexican border by strengthening environmental planning, management, and enforcement capabilities and carrying out priority investments and action plans that will preserve the environment. A sectoral EA carried out for the Mexico Second Solid Waste Management Project also covered the Northern Border Environment Project, which includes a solid waste manage-ment component. The EA identified gaps and overlaps in the regula- tory and institutional frameworks and proposed institutional strengthening.	$762.4/ IBRD $367.8
Paraguay	Natural Resources Management	Aims to promote environmentally sustainable development and management in the agriculture sector in the Parana watershed. The EA identified the infrastruc-ture subcomponent for rural road improvement as having negative environmental effects and recom-mended that rural roads with the worst erosion hazard should be abandoned where necessary. In these cases they would be reclaimed through proper closure and, where appropriate, reforested. In addi-tion, the following changes were made in the project design: research in agriculture and forestry were combined, and agroforestry and pasture-forestry activities were included; enforcement of environmental provisions defined in law was made separate from the functions of extension and promotion; and the protection of indigenous people was included.	$79.1/ IBRD $50

Country	Project	EA description	Total project cost/Bank financing (millions of dollars)
Uruguay	Natural Resource Management and Irrigation Development	Aims to improve resource management to reduce degradation of soils, enhance productivity and efficiency in agriculture, and preserve biodiversity. In the development and maintenance of irrigation projects, problems such as soil degradation and water contamination from agrochemicals, wasteful use of water, deteriorating quality of irrigation water, some sedimentation of reservoirs, and damage to biodiversity were identified. With the guidance of the EA, steps will be taken to address these issues at each stage of the project cycle: during identification of options to expand agricultural output, initial project selection, feasibility analysis, construction, and monitoring and evaluation of the operational phase. In this process, particular attention will be given to institutional aspects such as dealing with long-run intersectoral conflicts in the management of water resources. Activities will also include strengthening local irrigation organizations and government agencies and promoting beneficiary participation in subproject design and implementation.	$74.0/ IBRD $41.0

Annex F. Global Environment Facility (GEF) and Multilateral Fund for the Implementation of the Montreal Protocol (MFMP) Investments Approved in Fiscal 1994

This annex provides brief descriptions of all GEF and MFMP investment projects managed by the Bank that were approved between July 1, 1993, and June 30, 1994. In the case of GEF projects, dollar figures represent grant financing from the Global Environment Trust Fund, the core fund of the GEF. In most cases, figures represent only a portion of the total project cost. In the case of projects funded by the MFMP, figures represent grant financing from the fund and will pay full eligible incremental costs of phaseout activities for ozone depleting substances (ODS).

Country	Project	Description
Algeria	El Kala National Park ($9.2 million)	Develops and implements a management plan for the national park and wetland complex in the El Tarf Wilaya, including baseline studies, protected area management, natural resource use development, monitoring and adaptive research, environmental education, institutional strengthening of the responsible organizations, and establishment of a conservation fund for use by NGOs and other local groups in relation to preservation of the environment.

Country	Project	Description
China	Sichuan Gas Development and Conservation ($10.0 million)	Supports rehabilitation of gas transmission lines and distribution systems to eliminate methane gas losses and improve pipeline network performance. Main components will focus on safety and operational efficiency of the transmission and distribution system and selection of cost-effective measures to reduce gas leakage through a program of environmental upgrades. The associated Bank project includes a gas pricing reform program that will encourage efficiency and conservation in gas consumption in the future.
Costa Rica	Grid-Integrated Advanced Windpower ($3.3 million)	Supports installation of a sufficient number of wind turbines (40–100 units) to generate 20 megawatts at Tejona, near Lake Arenal. In addition to the wind turbines, the project would add a control center for the wind power plant and a connection to the power grid. Through this project, wind power will displace thermal power plants that would otherwise be needed.
Czech Republic	Biodiversity Protection ($2.0 million)	Promotes protection of ecosystem biodiversity in three representative ecosystem zones: alpine meadows, lowland forests, and wetlands. Includes support for three transnational biodiversity protection networks. Fosters financially sustainable biodiversity protection through the introduction of user fees and related charges for visitors and concessions, in order to respect the areas' carrying capacities.

Country	Project	Description
Ecuador	Biodiversity Protection ($7.2 million)	Supports the restructuring and strengthening of the institutional capacity and regulatory and legal frameworks for adequate management of the National System of Protected Areas. Project activities focus on (a) institutional strengthening of the Ecuadorian Institute of Forestry, Natural Areas and Wildlife in managing the system, (b) creation of an improved legal and regulatory framework, (c) outreach to local communities to involve them in management plan development for protected areas, and (d) investment activities for civil works and infrastructure in seven protected priority areas based on participatory management plans developed with project support.
Indonesia	Biodiversity Collections ($7.2 million)	Strengthens the institutional capacity of the Indonesian Research and Development Center for Biology to support systematic biological collections. Specifically, the project will restore and develop biological collections; design and establish a computerized database; make such information widely available through online networks and publications; develop local scientific, research, and collaboration capacities; and provide project management and coordination.
Iran	Tehran Transportation Emission Reduction ($2.0 million)	Identifies least-cost short- and long-term options for reducing vehicular emissions in Tehran on the basis of an analysis of policy and technology constraints. The study will suggest specific actions that could be taken to overcome those constraints.

Country	Project	Description
Jamaica	Demand-Side Management ($3.8 million)	Strengthens the institutional capacity of the Jamaica Public Service Company and implements an integrated approach to energy conservation developed by the company. The project will acquire the necessary information and data for developing sustainable programs to overcome market barriers to energy conservation. It will test mechanisms to address these barriers, and information acquired through evaluation will be used to design full-scale sustainable long-term energy efficient programs.
Lao PDR	Wildlife and Protected Areas Conservation ($5.0 million)	Supports protection of biological diversity through human resource development and institutional strengthening; the designation, establishment, and management of priority protected areas and protection of associated wildlife; and the planning and implementation of community participatory programs in and around protected areas. Components include the establishment and management of at least four protected areas; technical assistance and conservation training with particular emphasis on recruiting NGOs for community mobilization, environmental monitoring, and evaluation; and the design of a Conservation Trust Fund for long-term financing.
Mexico	High-Efficiency Lighting Pilot ($10.0 million)	Supports reduction of greenhouse gas emissions and simultaneous reduction of local environmental contamination through the replacement of incandescent bulbs with fluorescent light bulbs in two major markets, Guadalajara and Monterey. The project will also work to increase institutional capacity for technological change and energy conservation and strengthen the Federal Electricity Commission and its capacity to practice demand-side management on a sustainable basis.

Country	Project	Description
Philippines	Conservation of Priority Protected Areas ($20.0 million)	Supports government efforts to establish a core National Integrated Protected Areas System for ten sites over a seven-year period, through financing site development and resource management. The project will promote the participation of local communities in site management, as well as strengthen national capacity for coordination and monitoring. The Department of Environmental and Natural Resources will receive a grant to strengthen park infrastructure and services, and a national NGO consortium will receive a grant to provide technical assistance and administer a livelihood fund for local communities.
	Geothermal Energy Development ($30.0 million)	Assists the Philippines in meeting the rapidly increasing demand for electric power using technology that substantially reduces greenhouse gas emissions. The National Power Corporation (NPC) components of the project include the interconnection of the electrical power systems of Leyte and Luzon islands and the strengthening of the environmental and social engineering departments of the NPC. The Philippine National Oil Company components of the project include the development of a geothermal energy field and the construction and operation under a build-own-transfer (BOT) contract of a 440-megawatt geothermal power plant.

Country	Project	Description
Regional (Morocco, Tunisia, and Algeria)	Oil Pollution Management System for the Southwest Mediterranean Sea ($18.3 million)	Promotes the following aims: (a) reducing the input of hydrocarbons into the international waters of the Mediterranean Sea, (b) ensuring commonality of approach, regulatory policies, and methodologies, (c) promoting exchange of information and coordination of implementation, (d) using national data sets to assess long-term regional trends in marine pollution, (f) enhancing national monitoring capacity, and (g) developing a coastal environmental management framework.
Regional (Caribbean)	Wider Caribbean Initiative for Disposal of Ship-Generated Waste ($5.5 million)	Lays the foundation for expanding the ratification and implementation by Caribbean countries of the MARPOL 73/78 Convention, ending discharge of ship-generated wastes into international and territorial waters. Technical assistance will be provided for studies leading to a regional implementation strategy, assessment of existing waste management systems, formulation of criteria of waste reception facilities at ports, development of integrated waste management alternatives, and public awareness programs. Periodic regional consultative meetings will also be supported.

Country	Project	Description
Slovak Republic	Biodiversity Protection ($2.3 million)	Develops management techniques for a biodiversity protection program, a conservation program to develop revenue-generating mechanisms for the protected area system, and a program to provide support for project management coordination at the national level and in the three selected zones (Tatras Forests, Morava Floodplains, and Eastern Carpathians). Includes an environmental NGO small-grants program and the development of a trinational transborder trust to maintain the coordinated management of the international biosphere reserve in the Eastern Carpathians.
Ukraine	Transcarpathian Mountains Biodiversity Protection ($0.5 million)	Supports the Ukrainian part of the tricountry Transcarpathian Network of biodiversity protection through (a) inventories, genetic studies, and GIS critical habitat analyses; (b) a management resources program to enable coordinated management of the discontinuous reserved areas of the Carpathian Biosphere Reserve; and (c) training and institutional-strengthening programs.
	Danube Delta Biodiversity ($1.5 million)	Protects the Ukrainian Delta ecosystem and contributes to biodiversity conservation in the delta by strengthening the capacity of the two main responsible institutions to monitor and manage protected areas effectively, working with local community groups to ensure sustainable resource use and to restore some wetlands to their natural condition. Innovative wetland restoration approaches will be tested and monitored.

Country	Project	Description
MFMP Investments		
Brazil	Ozone Depleting Substances I (Umbrella Grant Agreement) ($10.9 million)	Assists Brazil in implementing its ODS phaseout program by (a) funding the incremental costs of investments resulting in ODS reduction or substitution, (b) supporting subproject identification, preparation, and supervision, (c) supporting training of the Brazilian executing agency and technology dissemination, and (d) supporting preparation of the country's overall program for ODS phaseout.
China	Ozone Depleting Substances I ($6.9 million)	Assists China in implementing its ODS phaseout program by (a) funding the incremental costs for five subprojects based on non-ODS technology in aerosols, foams, and halon substitute applications and (b) strengthening the executing agency, the National Environmental Protection Agency (NEPA).
	Ozone Depleting Substances II ($4.9 million)	Assists China in implementing its ODS phaseout program by (a) funding the incremental costs of ten subprojects based on reduced ODS technology in foams applications and (b) strengthening NEPA (the government executing agency) and the China Investment Bank (the financial agent).
Ecuador	Ozone Depleting Substance Phaseout I ($1.6 million)	Assists Ecuador in phasing out ODS use by establishing an in-country Montreal Protocol project unit to work toward the complete phaseout of CFCs in the aerosol sector and a 50 percent reduction of CFC use in the rigid foams sector by 1996.

Country	Project	Description
Jordan	Ozone Depleting Substance Phaseout I ($1.5 million)	Assists Jordan in phasing out ODS use through the adoption of policies, technological conversions, and monitoring measures. Activities include providing assistance for transfer of ODS-substitution technology to the private sector, emphasizing least-cost and quick phaseout alternatives, and setting up and training a project implementation unit to work with the National Ozone Committee.
Tunisia	Ozone Depleting Substance Phaseout I ($1.8 million)	Assists Tunisia in phasing out ODS use by establishing an in-country Montreal Protocol project unit, introducing CFC substitutes in the refrigeration and foam-blowing sectors, initiating a CFC recycling training program, and completing a study on CFC substitution in the aerosol sector.
Turkey	Ozone Layer Protection ODS I ($6.2 million)	Assists Turkey in phasing out ODS use through the adoption of policies, technological conversions, and monitoring measures. Activities consist of (a) providing assistance for ODS substitution in refrigeration systems, recovery and recycling of ODS around Istanbul, and demonstration projects in ODS recovery and substitution in other areas and (b) establishing and strengthening the public agencies or panels responsible for advising on projects and regulatory frameworks and for monitoring ODS production. A public awareness campaign and a national long-range strategy are also included.

Bibliography

Publications

Under this heading are books, journal articles, reports, and other formal publications issued by the World Bank and other publishers. Titles published by the World Bank may be obtained from the bookstores at the Bank offices in Washington, D.C., and Paris or through the Bank's authorized commercial distributors and depository libraries throughout the world. Abbreviations used are as follows: EDI, Economic Development Institute (of the World Bank); GEF, Global Environment Facility; UMP, Urban Management Programme.

Ahmed, Kulsum. 1994. *Renewable Energy Technologies: A Review of the Status and Costs of Selected Technologies.* World Bank Technical Paper 240. Washington, D.C.

Ahuja, Dilip. 1994. *The Incremental Cost of Climate Change Mitigation Projects.* GEF Working Paper 9. Washington, D.C.

Amuzu, A. T., and Josef Leitmann. 1994. "Environmental Profile of Accra, Ghana." *Cities* 11 (2):5–9.

Anderson, Dennis, and Robert H. Williams. 1994. *The Cost-Effectiveness of GEF Projects.* GEF Working Paper 6. Washington, D.C.

Barnes, Douglas F., Keith Openshaw, Kirk R. Smith, and Robert van der Plas. 1994. *What Makes People Cook with Improved Biogas Stoves? A Comparative International Review of Stove Programs.* World Bank Technical Paper 242. Washington, D.C.

Bartone, Carl, Janis Bernstein, Josef Leitmann, and Jochen Eigen. 1994. *Toward Environmental Strategies for Cities: Policy Considerations for Urban Environmental Management.* UMP Series 18. Washington, D.C.: World Bank.

Bates, Robin, Janusz Cofala, and Michael Toman. 1994. *Alternative Policies for the Control of Air Pollution in Poland.* World Bank Environment Paper 7. Washington, D.C.

Bernstein, Janis D. 1993. *Alternative Approaches to Pollution Control and Waste Management: Regulatory and Economic Instruments.* UMP Series 3. Washington, D.C.: World Bank.

_____. 1994. *Land Use Considerations in Urban Environmental Management.* UMP Series 12. Washington, D.C.: World Bank.

Bradley, Phillip N., and Kathleen McNamara, eds. 1993. *Living with Trees: Policies for Forest Management in Zimbabwe.* World Bank Technical Paper 210. Washington, D.C.

Brandon, Carter, and Ramesh Ramankutty. 1993. *Toward an Environmental Strategy for Asia.* World Bank Discussion Paper 224. Washington, D.C.

Brown, Katrina, David Pearce, Charles Perrings, and Timothy Swanson. 1993. *Economics and the Conservation of Global Biological Diversity.* GEF Working Paper 2. Washington, D.C.

Cernea, Michael. 1993a. "The Sociologist's Approach to Sustainable Development." *Finance and Development* 30(4):11–13.

_____. 1993b. *The Urban Environment and Population Relocation.* World Bank Discussion Paper 152. Washington, D.C.

Cointreau-Levine, Sandra. 1994. *Private Sector Participation in Municipal Solid Waste Services in Developing Countries.* UMP Series 13. Washington, D.C.: World Bank.

Cook, Cynthia, ed. 1994. *Involuntary Resettlement in Africa: Selected Papers from a Conference on Environment and Settlement Issues in Africa.* World Bank Technical Paper 227. Washington, D.C.

Cropper, Maureen L., and Charles Griffiths. 1994. "Interaction of Population Growth and Environmental Quality." *American Economic Review, Papers and Proceedings* 84 (2):250–65.

Dasgupta, Partha, and Karl Goran Mäler. 1994. *Poverty, Institutions, and the Environmental Resource Base.* World Bank Environment Paper 9. Washington, D.C.

Davis, Shelton, Guillermo Castilleja, Peter J. Poole, and Charles C. Geisler, eds. 1993. *The Social Challenge of Biodiversity Conservation.* GEF Working Paper 1. Washington, D.C.

Dewees, Peter A. 1993. *Trees, Land, and Labor.* World Bank Environment Paper 4. Washington, D.C.

D'Silva, Emmanuel, and Simmathiri Appanah. 1993. *Forestry Management for Sustainable Development.* EDI Policy Seminar Report 32. Washington, D.C.: World Bank.

Duda, Alfred M. 1993a. "Addressing Nonpoint Sources of Water Pollution Must Become an International Priority." *Water Science and Technology* 28(3):1–11.

_____. 1993b. "Resolving Conflicts Between Irrigation Development and Environmental Protection in Developing Countries." In D. Manz, ed., *Water and the Wilderness: Development, Stewardship and Management.* Cambridge, Ontario: Canadian Water Resources Association.

English, John C., Mary Tiffen, and Michael Mortimore. 1994. *Land Resource Management in Machakos District, Kenya 1930–1990.* World Bank Environment Paper 5. Washington, D.C.

Fredericksen, Harald D., Jeremy Berkoff, and William Barber. 1993. *Water Resources Management in Asia.* World Bank Technical Paper 212. Washington, D.C.

Fuglesvedt, Jan, Ted Hanisch, Ivar Isaksen, Rolf Selrod, Jon Strand, and Asbjorn Torvanger. 1994. *A Review of Country Case Studies on Climate Change.* GEF Working Paper 7. Washington, D.C.

Goodland, Robert. 1993. "Ethical Priorities in Environmentally Sustainable Energy Systems: The Case of Tropical Hydropower." *International Journal of Sustainable Development* 1(4):3–14.

Goodland, Robert, Herman Daly, and Salah El Serafy. 1993. "The Urgent Need for Rapid Transition to Global Environmental Sustainability." *Environmental Conservation* 20(4):297–309.

Goodland, Robert, Herman Daly, and John Kellenberg. 1994. "Burden Sharing in the Transition to Environmental Sustainability." *Futures* 26(2):146–55.

Hadiwinoto, Suhadi, and Josef Leitmann. 1994. "Environmental Profile of Jakarta, Indonesia." *Cities* 11(3): 153–57.

Howe, Charles W., and John A. Dixon. 1993. "Inefficiencies in Water Project Design and Operation in the Third World: An Economic Perspective." *Water Resources Research* 29(7):1889–94.

Keck, Andrew, Narendra P. Sharma, and Gershon Feder. 1994. *Population Growth, Shifting Cultivation, and Unsustainable Agricultural Development: A Case Study in Madagascar.* World Bank Discussion Paper 234. Washington, D.C.

King, Ken. 1993a. *The Incremental Costs of Global Environmental Benefits.* GEF Working Paper 5. Washington, D.C.

_____. 1993b. *Issues to Be Addressed by the GEF Program for Measuring Incremental Costs for the Environment.* GEF Working Paper 8. Washington, D.C.

Kingsley, G. Thomas, Bruce W. Ferguson, and Blair T. Bower. 1993. *Managing Urban Environmental Quality in Asia.* World Bank Technical Paper 220. Washington, D.C.

Leitmann, Josef. 1993. "Rapid Urban Environmental Assessment: Toward Environmental Management in Cities of the Developing World." *Impact Assessment* 11(3):225–60.

_____. 1994a. "The Brown Agenda and the World Bank." *Third World Planning Review.* May.

_____. 1994b. "Environmental Profile of Katowice, Poland." *Cities* 11(3): 147–52.

Liebenthal, Andres, Subodh Mathur, and Herbert Wade. 1994. *Solar Energy: Lessons from the Pacific Island Experience.* World Bank Technical Paper 244. Washington, D.C.

_____.1994c. *Rapid Urban Environmental Assessment: Lessons from Cities in the Developing World.* Vol. 1, *Methodology and Preliminary Findings.* Vol. 2, *Tools and Outputs.* Washington, D.C.: World Bank.

Lutz, Ernst, Stefano Pagiola, and Carlos Reiche. 1994. *Economic and Institutional Analyses of Soil Conservation Projects in Central America and the Caribbean.* World Bank Environment Paper 8. Washington, D.C.

Meier, Peter, and Mohan Munasinghe. 1994. *Incorporating Environmental Concerns into Power Sector Decisionmaking: A Case Study of Sri Lanka.* World Bank Environment Paper 6. Washington, D.C.

Mintzner, Irving M. 1993. *Implementing the Framework Convention on Climate Change: Incremental Costs and the Role of the GEF.* GEF Working Paper 4. Washington, D.C.: GEF.

Munasinghe, Mohan. 1993a. "The Economist's Approach to Sustainable Development." *Finance and Development* 30(4):16–19.

_____. 1993b. *Environmental Economics and Sustainable Development.* World Bank Environment Paper 3. Washington, D.C.

_____, ed. 1993c. *Environmental Economics and Natural Resource Management in Developing Countries.* Washington, D.C.: World Bank.

Munasinghe, Mohan, Wilfrido Cruz, and Jeremy Warford. 1993. "Are Economy-wide Policies Good for the Environment?" *Finance and Development* 30(3): 40–43.

Narayan, Deepa. 1993. *Participatory Evaluation: Tools for Managing Change in Water and Sanitation.* World Bank Technical Paper 207. Washington, D.C.

Norse, Elliott A., ed. 1993. *Global Marine Biological Diversity: A Strategy for Building Conservation into Decision Making.* Washington, D.C.: Island Press.

OECD (Organization for Economic Cooperation and Development). 1993. *OECD's Core Set of Indicators for Environmental Policy Reviews: A Synthesis Report of the Group on the State of the Environment.* OECD/GD (93) 179. Paris.

Rabinovitch, Jonas, and Josef Leitmann. 1994. *Environmental Innovation and Management in Curitiba, Brazil.* UMP Series 1. Washington, D.C.: World Bank.

Redwood, John, III. 1993. *World Bank Approaches to the Environment in Brazil.* A World Bank Operations Evaluation Study. Washington, D.C.

Rees, Colin. 1993. "The Ecologist's Approach to Sustainable Development." *Finance and Development* 30(4):14–15.

Serageldin, Ismail. "Making Development Sustainable." *Finance and Development* 30(4):6–8.

Srivastava, Jitendra P., and Harold Alderman, eds. 1993. *Agriculture and Environmental Challenges: Proceedings of the Thirteenth Agricultural Sector Symposium.* Washington, D.C.: World Bank.

Srivastava, Jitendra P., Prabhakar Mahedeo Tamboli, John C. English, Rattan Lal, and Bobby Alton Stewart. 1993. *Conserving Soil Moisture and Fertility in the Warm Seasonally Dry Tropics.* World Bank Technical Paper 221. Washington, D.C.

Steer, Andrew, and Ernst Lutz. 1993. "Measuring Environmentally Sustainable Development." *Finance and Development* 30(4):20–23.

Umali, Dina L. 1993. *Irrigation-Induced Salinity: A Growing Problem for Development and the Environment.* World Bank Technical Paper 215. Washington, D.C.

Wheeler, David, and Jeremy Warford. 1993. "Environmental Economics and Development Policies." In Praipol Koomsup, ed., *Economic Development and the Environment in ASEAN Countries.* Bangkok: Economic Society of Thailand.

Wiebers, Uwe-Carsten. 1993. *Integrated Pest Management and Pesticide Regulation in Developing Asia.* World Bank Technical Paper 211. Washington, D.C.

World Bank. 1991a. *The Forest Sector.* A World Bank Policy Paper. Washington, D.C.

_____. 1991b. *Urban Policy and Economic Development: An Agenda for the 1990s.* A World Bank Policy Paper. Washington, D.C.

_____. 1992. *World Development Report 1992: Development and the Environment.* New York: Oxford University Press.

_____. 1993a. *The Environmental Data Book: A Guide to Statistics on the Environment and Development.* Washington, D.C.

_____. 1993b. *Water Resources Management.* A World Bank Policy Paper. Washington, D.C.

_____. 1994a. *Jamaica: Economic Issues for Environmental Management.* A World Bank Country Study. Washington, D.C.

_____. 1994b. *World Development Report: Infrastructure for Development.* New York: Oxford University Press.

_____. 1994c. *The World Bank Policy on Disclosure of Information.* Washington, D.C.

Zilinskas, Raymond A., and Carl Lundin. 1993. *Marine Biotechnology and Developing Countries.* World Bank Discussion Paper 210. Washington, D.C.

Informal Documents

The following titles, produced by various departments within the World Bank during fiscal 1994, may be obtained by writing directly to the department named.

Afsah, Shakeb, Paul Martin, and David Wheeler. 1993. "Promoting Cleaner Industrial Development." Policy Research Department Outreach Note 12. Policy Research Department.

Agostini, Paola, and John Dixon. 1994. "Forestry Values: Much More Than Meets the Eye." Environment Dissemination Note 1. Environment Department.

Anderson, Robert J., Nelson da Franca Ribeiro dos Santos, and Henry F. Diaz. 1993. "An Analysis of Flooding in the Paraná/Paraguay River Basin." LATEN Dissemination Note 5. Latin American and the Caribbean Technical Department.

Asheim, Geir B. 1994. "Sustainability: Ethical Foundations and Economic Properties." Working Paper Series 1302. Policy Research Department.

Bates, Robin, Shreekant Gupta, and Bogulslaw Fiedor. 1994. "Economywide Policies and the Environment: A Case Study of Poland." Environment Working Paper 63. Environment Department.

Bruce, Neil, and Gregory M. Ellis. 1993. "Environmental Taxes and Policies for Developing Countries." Working Paper Series 1177. Policy Research Department.

Christoffersen, Leif, and Lee Talbot. 1994. "Environment in the Africa Region Portfolio." AFTES Working Paper 2. Africa Technical Department.

Cook, Cynthia, and June Taboroff. 1993. "Cultural Property and Environmental Assessment in SSA: A Handbook." AFTES Working Paper 4. Africa Technical Department.

Cook, Cynthia, and Kristine Ivarsdotter. 1994. "Development and Displacement: Resettlement Review for the Africa Region." AFTES Working Paper 5. Africa Technical Department.

Dixon, John A. 1993. "The Urban Environmental Challenge in Latin America." LATEN Dissemination Note 4. Latin American and the Caribbean Technical Department.

_____. 1994. "What are Wetlands Worth?" Environment Dissemination Note 3. Environment Department.

Dixon, John, and Paola Agostini. 1994. "The Economic Toll of Pollution's Effects on Health." Environment Dissemination Note 2. Environment Department.

Dixon, John, Louise Fallon Scura, and Tom Van't Hof. 1993. "Ecology and Microeconomics as 'Joint Products': The Bonaire Marine Park in the Caribbean." LATEN Dissemination Note 6. Latin American and the Caribbean Technical Department.

Fallon Scura, Louise, and Tom Van't Hof. 1993. "The Ecology and Economics of Bonaire Marine Park." ENVPE Divisional Working Paper 44. Environment Department.

Frankhauser, Samuel. 1994. "Global Warming: Measuring the Costs." Environment Dissemination Note 4. Environment Department.

GEF (Global Environment Facility). 1993. "Guidelines for Monitoring and Evaluation of GEF Biodiversity Projects." GEF Coordination Division, Environment Department.

_____. 1994. "GEF World Bank Operations: Pilot Phase Business Review Preliminary Summary." GEF Coordination Division, Environment Department.

Goodland, Robert. 1994. "Ethical Priorities in Environmentally Sustainable Energy Systems: The Case of Tropical Hydro Power." Environment Working Paper 67. Environment Department.

Goodland, Robert, Herman Daly, and Salah El Serafy. 1993. "The Urgent Need for a Rapid Transition to Global Environmental Sustainability." ENVPE Divisional Working Paper 45. Environment Department.

Grepperud, Sverre. 1994. "Population-Environment Links: Testing a Soil Degradation Model for Ethiopia." ENVPE Divisional Working Paper 46. Environment Department.

Guggenheim, Scott. 1994. "Involuntary Resettlement: An Annotated Reference Bibliography for Development Research." Environment Working Paper 64. Environment Department.

Guo, Charles C., and James R. Tybout. 1994. "How Relative Prices Affect Fuel Use Patterns in Manufacturing: Plant-Level Evidence from Chile." Working Paper Series 1297. Policy Research Department.

Gupta, Shreekant, George Van Houtven, and Maureen Cropper. 1994. "The Value of Superfund Cleanups: Evidence from U.S. Environmental Protection Agency Decisions." Working Paper Series 1272. Policy Research Department.

Hamilton, Kirk, with John A. Dixon and Claudia Sadoff. 1994. "Making Natural Resources Count." ESD Vice Presidency Dissemination Note 6. Office of the Vice President for Environmentally Sustainable Development.

Harou, Patrice, Herman Daly, and Robert Goodland. 1994. "Environmental Sustainability and Project Appraisal." ENVPE Divisional Working Paper 48. Environment Department.

IFC (International Finance Corporation)/EU (European Union). 1994. "Papermaking Opportunities Using Recycled Fiber." Environment Department.

Kellenberg, John, and Herman Daly. 1994. "Counting User Cost in Evaluating Projects Involving Depletion of Natural Capital." Environment Working Paper 66. Environment Department.

Kirmse, Robert, Luis Constantino, and George Guess. 1993. "Prospect for Improved Management of Natural Forests in Latin America." LATEN Dissemination Note 9. Latin America and the Caribbean Technical Department.

Kishor, Nalin M., and Luis F. Constantino. 1993. "Pueblos Indígenas y Desarrollo en América Latina." LATEN Dissemination Note 8. Latin American and the Caribbean Technical Department.

Kramer, Randall A., Narendra Sharma, Priya Shyamsundar, and Mohan Munasinghe. 1994. "Cost and Compensation Issues in Protecting Tropical Rainforests: Case Study of Madagascar." Environment Working Paper 62. Environment Department.

Larson, Jeri. 1993. "Financial Mechanisms for Sustainable Conservation." AFTES Working Paper 1. Africa Technical Department.

Lusigi, Walter, and John Buursink. 1994. "Sahelian Operational Review." AFTES Working Paper 11. Africa Technical Department.

Lutz, Ernst, Mario Vedolva W., Hector Martinez, Lorena San Roman, Ricardo Vazquez L., Alfredo Alvarado, Lucia Menno, Rafael Celis, and Jeroen Huisin. 1993. "Interdisciplinary Fact-Finding on Current Deforestation in Costa Rica." Environment Working Paper 61. Environment Department.

Lvovsky, Kseniya, John Pamisano, and Konstantin Gofman. 1994. "Pollution Charges: An Experience in Russia." ENVPE Divisional Working Paper 47. Environment Department.

Munasinghe, Mohan, and Wilfrido Cruz. Forthcoming. "Economywide Policies and the Environment: Emerging Lessons from Experience." Environment Department.

Newcombe, Ken, and Karen Richardson. 1994. "A Profile of the Pilot Phase Biodiversity Investment Portfolio." GEF Coordination Paper. GEF Coordination Division, Environment Department.

OED (Operations Evaluation Department). 1992. "Water Supply and Sanitation Projects: The Bank's Experience 1967–1989." OED Report No. 10789.

_____. 1994. "Twenty Years of Lending for Urban Development 1972–92: An OED Review." OED Review No. 13117.

Olson, David M., and Eric Dinerstein. 1994. "Assessing the Conservation Potential and Degree of Threat among Ecoregions of Latin America and the Caribbean: A Proposed Landscape Ecology Approach." LATEN Dissemination Note 10. Latin America and the Caribbean Technical Department.

Ostro, Bart. 1994. "Estimating the Health Effects of Air Pollutants: A Method with an Application to Jakarta." Working Paper Series 1301. Policy Research Department.

OORG (Ozone Operations Resource Group), Foam Sector Working Group. 1993. "Reducing Ozone Depleting Substance Use in Developing Countries in Domestic Refrigerator/Freezer Insulating Foams." OORG Report 3. Global Environment Coordination Division (Montreal Protocol), Environment Department.

_____, Production Sector Working Group. 1993. "Technical Considerations for Chlorofluorocarbon Alternatives Production in Developing Countries." OORG Report 4. Global Environment Coordination Division (Montreal Protocol), Environment Department.

_____, Refrigeration Sector Working Group. 1993. "The Status of Hydrocarbon and Other Flammable Alternatives Use in Domestic Refrigeration." OORG Report 5. Global Environment Coordination Division (Montreal Protocol), Environment Department.

Sadoff, Claudia W. 1994. "Environmental Indicators: What Can They Tell Us?" Environment Dissemination Note 5. Environment Department.

Someshwar, ShivSharan. 1994. "Capacity-building in World Bank-supported Forestry Projects in Sub-Saharan Africa." AFTES Working Paper 6. Africa Technical Paper.

Sorsa, Piritta. 1994. "Competitiveness and Environmental Standards: Some Exploratory Results." Working Paper Series 1249. Policy Research Department.

Umetsu, Cheiko. 1993. "Wildlife Projects: The World Bank Experience." AFTES Technical Note 1. Africa Technical Department.

Van Houtven, George L., and Maureen L. Cropper. 1994. "When Is a Life Too Costly to Save? Evidence from U.S. Environmental Regulations." Working Paper Series 1260. Policy Research Department.

Van Marrewijk, Charles, Federick van der Ploeg, and Jos Verbeek. 1993. "Is Growth Bad for the Environment? Pollution, Abatement and Endogenous Growth." Working Paper Series 1151. Policy Research Department.

Warford, Jeremy, A. Schwab, W. Cruz, and S. Hansen. 1994. "The Evolution of Environmental Concerns in Adjustment Lending: A Review." Environment Working Paper 65. Environment Department.

World Bank. 1993a. "Environmental Screening." Environmental Assessment Sourcebook Update No. 2. Environment Department.

_____. 1993b. "Final Report on the International Consultation to Advance Women in Ecosystem Management." Washington, D.C., 4–6 October 1993. Office of the Vice President for Environmentally Sustainable Development.

_____. 1993c. "Geographic Information Systems for Environmental Assessment and Review." Environmental Assessment Sourcebook Update No. 3. Environment Department.

_____. 1993d."Public Involvement in Environmental Assessment: Requirements, Opportunities and Issues." Environmental Assessment Sourcebook Update No. 5. Environment Department.

_____. 1993e. "Sectoral Environmental Assessment." Environmental Assessment Sourcebook Update No. 4. Environment Department.

_____. 1993f. "The World Bank and Environmental Assessment: An Overview." Environmental Assessment Sourcebook Update No. 3. Environment Department.

_____. 1994a. "Coastal Zone Management and Environmental Assessment." Environmental Assessment Sourcebook Update No. 7. Environment Department.

_____. 1994b. "Privatization and Environmental Assessment: Issues and Approaches." Environmental Assessment Sourcebook Update No. 6. Environment Department.

_____. 1994c. "Resettlement Review." Environment Department.

World Bank/OECD (Organization for Economic Cooperation and Development). 1993. "Environmental Action Programme for Central and Eastern Europe: Setting Priorities." Report endorsed by the Ministerial Conference, Lucerne, Switzerland. April 1993. Environment Department.